DATE DUE

OCT 1 3 2004	
WATE 3|4|09	

DEMCO, INC. 38-2931

the ride of my life

MAT
hoffman
WITH MARK LEWMAN

the ride of my life

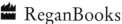
ReganBooks
An Imprint of HarperCollins*Publishers*

MAT hoffman >>>

HARPERCOLLINS BOOKS MAY BE PURCHASED FOR EDUCATIONAL, BUSINESS, OR SALES PROMOTIONAL USE. FOR INFORMATION PLEASE WRITE: SPECIAL MARKETS DEPARTMENT, HARPERCOLLINS PUBLISHERS INC., 10 EAST 53RD STREET, NEW YORK, NY 10022.

FIRST EDITION

Designed by Platinum Design, Inc. NYC

Printed on acid-free paper

Library of Congress Cataloging-in-Publication Data has been applied for.

ISBN 0-06-009415-X

02 03 04 05 06 RRD 10 9 8 7 6 5 4 3 2 1

[FOR JONI HOFFMAN. I MISS YOU, MOM.]

CONTENTS

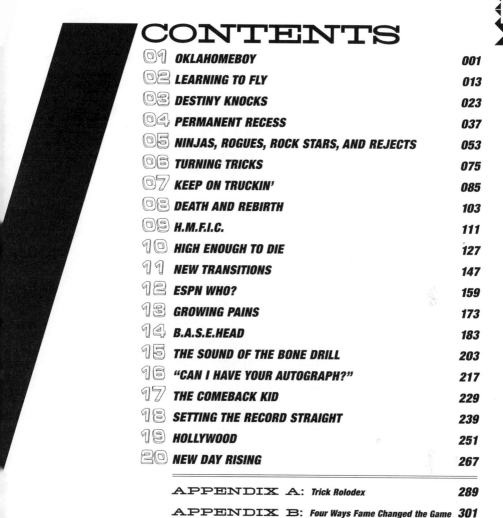

oklahomeboy

OKLAHOMEBOY

My dad, Matthew Hoffman, is the original take charge, do-it-yourself guy. He grew up with nothing. Dad's family were hardworking, salt-of-the-earth midwestern folk, but they were superpoor. The "House of Hoffman" was literally a shack in a field—no plumbing or doors; it was barely a step above camping. My father quickly learned that determination was the way to overcome hardship. As is the case with young people who possess a lot of raw willpower, my dad clashed with authority on occasion. He was not really a juvenile delinquent, but definitely someone with a defiant, reckless streak inside. "Never back down" was his modus operandi. When he was eighteen years old, he'd do stuff like bet his friends a quarter that he could lie across the hood of a car and hold onto the windshield wipers while one of the guys drove it down the street at one hundred miles per hour. Although cashing in on these wagers didn't make him much money, it is how he earned his reputation: wild man.

My mother's family comes from the southern part of Italy. Both her parents' families jumped a boat for America, Land of Opportunity, and wound up in Ridgeway, Pennsylvania, an industrial mining town. My grandmother's family lived on top of the hill on High Street, which was the prosperous section of town. My grandfather's family came from the "other" side of the tracks in Ridgeway. He met my grandmother and the two courted, which started a long tradition in my family of proper, respectable young ladies falling for disreputable young men. My grandfather, Al Papa, began to get restless in Ridgeway, but he had no money to leave town. He hopped a boxcar and rode the rails west, leaping off in Elkhart, Indiana. A small Italian community took him in. It took Al two weeks to get himself settled and then he went to a used car lot to test-drive one of their cars. He cleverly unhooked the odometer and headed back to Ridgeway to give my grandmother a plush ride to their new home. Young, married, and on their own for the first time, they stayed in Elkhart and started a family. My mom, Geovanna Teresa Papa, was the youngest of their three children. She grew up in a house flush with ethnic pride, old country traditions, and heritage.

Dad met my mom when he was a cook in an Elkhart restaurant—he was seventeen, she was sixteen. He loaned his car to a buddy in exchange for getting set up on a date with her. Almost immediately their relationship aroused the suspicion of Mom's father. Her dad did everything possible to discourage the two teenage lovebirds from seeing each other. My grandfather tried intimidation, Italian style, to convince my dad to back off: "If you don't stay away from my daughter, I'll have your legs broken." But my mom and dad were in love, and that's a hard force to disrupt. When their love was forbidden, that was the proverbial gasoline on the fire.

My parents got married in a secret ceremony in 1962 and hit the road in a beat-up Oldsmobile. My dad's instructions to the minister were to wait three days before submitting their marriage license, so their names wouldn't show up in the newspaper until after they had made a clean getaway.

The newly wed Mr. and Mrs. Hoffman left Indiana and made brief detours through Minnesota, then Nebraska, finally stopping at the outskirts of Oklahoma City. Oklahoma is the dead center of the United States. It's where the original "forty acres and a mule" concept of post–Civil War American freedom started, and it seemed like the perfect nesting ground. My dad figured that nine hundred miles was enough distance from their past to allow them to start their life together. When my parents settled here, they had nothing but a car, some clothes, and their dreams. There was no turning back; their only option was to make it.

Equipped with an outgoing personality and a drive to succeed, my dad was a natural salesman. He got his break selling hospital supplies for Zimmer, a big distributor of everything from ankle braces to artificial hips. He rolled over whatever stood in his path like a tank, closing sales, earning customers, and reaping plenty of commissions. He became the number one salesman in the country. He had found his true calling, and before long he struck a deal with Zimmer to run a distribution hub in Oklahoma and West Texas. Things were looking up.

When my mom found out she was pregnant with their first child, Dad bought her a diamond ring to celebrate. After Todd was born, they made amends with my mom's parents. Having proved his good intentions and ability to provide for his family, my dad even smoothed things over with Grandfather. In the next five years my dad and mom had two more children: my sister, Gina, followed by my brother Travis. The Hoffman kids were spaced two years apart . . . boy, girl, boy . . . like a beautiful flower arrangement.

Then I showed up. I was an accident, right from the get-go. This time, when my mother announced she was pregnant, there was no diamond ring. She sent my dad out to get a vasectomy. I arrived kicking and screaming on January 9, 1972. My parents wanted to call me Matthew, but rather than make me a "Jr." they left out a T: Mathew. Easy enough, but they also needed a middle name. Both my brothers' middle names are Matthew, so each brother thought it was only fair that their first name be my middle name. My mother, being the great mediator, came up with an idea. Instead of calling me Mathew Todd Travis Hoffman, they shortened my middle name to the letter T and told my brothers that it stood for "Travis and Todd." It sounds a little odd, but I was a product of their environment. My parents were freethinkers, and it was the seventies.

When Todd was born baby bottles were sterilized. He drank out of a cup at six months, walked at ten months, and was potty trained by eighteen months.

But with me, things were a little different. As my father tells it, "When Mathew came along, I was traveling for my business a lot and was gone a lot of nights. I always called home to check on my wife and kids. One night, I asked Joni, Mathew's mother, what he was doing. Mathew was about eighteen months old. She said, 'He's eating dog food in the pantry.' I started to laugh—we'd gone from trying to be perfect parents with the first child, to a free spirit approach with the fourth child. Joni said, 'Look, if he likes dog food, let him eat dog food.' "

As I was growing up, to make it easier, I spelled my name the traditional way, M-A-T-T. Then at age twenty-five, I realized if "Mathew" was only spelled with one T, I'd been spelling "Mat" wrong my whole life. So I dropped the extra T. That's one thing I think my siblings and I picked up from my parents: Life is yours to design and change at will. So M-A-T it is.

Floppy, Moppy, and Me

My dad's skills in the medical business had afforded our family a home on twenty acres, populated with farm animals. My father grew up in the middle of nowhere, which he equated as more space to do whatever you pleased, so he wanted his kids to have the same. The combination of fresh air, sunshine, hard work, and gentle creatures were supposed to do us kids some good.

There is a distinctive smell to a barn that's in use. Part of my job as a kid was to monitor the smell and fix it by cleaning out the stalls when it became unbearable. This was the shittiest job, literally. Travis and I were the barn boys, and we fed the animals. The horses were fed mixed oats, sweet feed, grain, and hay. (In the process of serving them breakfast, I would sneak some of the corn out of the sweet feed and feed myself.)

I made up bottles for the baby goats, Floppy and Moppy, and fed those to them until they could join the oats and hay family. I threw out bird feed for the chickens, rooster, peacock, and our three ducks, Huey, Dewey, and Louie.

When the animals were hungry, it was a circus. If I fed the smaller animals first, the horses chased me to get their food. If I tried to avoid the horses, the rooster would chase me. I used to throw chicken eggs to keep the rooster away from me. I danced around like a boxer in a ring to avoid his razor-tipped beak and claws made of nightmares. (I think this is where I started developing survival techniques.)

When I was five, our family was really into horses. Todd and Gina both got into rodeo-style racing, riding fast and slaloming barrels and poles. Gina was great at it and was the resident animal queen. She wouldn've slept in the barn if my parents had allowed it. I entered a few of these rodeo events, in the "Peanuts" category. I was a reckless rider, but I had my moments when control came easy. Once, one of our horses, Little Britches, told me he was thirsty. (I couldn't pronounce my R's yet, so I called him Little Bitches.) So I took him out of the barn and led him into our house to the kitchen sink. My mom, thinking fast, grabbed a Super 8 camera and didn't intervene, she just documented. I got Little Bitches a drink and led him out the back door.

We all had our list of daily chores, and if we got those finished, my parents would pay us four dollars an hour to do additional chores. They then encouraged us to buy livestock and pets with our Saturday paychecks. In a way, it was genius: We learned to work hard because we got paid well (for kids), and the animals provided us a perpetual supply of entertainment. The more animals we took in meant we had a steady stream of chores just keeping up after them. It instilled a work ethic in us.

Dealing with Disaster

However, life on the farm wasn't all petting the ponies; some rough stuff went down occasionally. My poor mom. Between my brothers, our friends, and me, there was almost always a carpool going to the hospital with various moaning, bleeding, and damaged juveniles in the backseat.

When I was six, I broke my leg playing Frisbee. I was trying to get the disc before the dog, and I stepped in a random hole in the yard. Snap. My first broken bone. Two days after the Frisbee incident I was climbing our fifteen-foot-tall slide with a cast on my leg and fell off, breaking my wrist when I hit the ground.

When I was seven, I was banned from the go-cart after I drove it into Travis (who was on the motorcycle) while playing chicken. I had to get stitches in my wrist, and Travis's hand went through the motorcycle chain. His palm got gouged up, and I still have the scar to this day. I also got in trouble for trying to jump the work truck over a barrel in our horse arena. I took the keys to the truck and leaned some two by eights up against a barrel with the intention of jumping, but when I hit the ramp it pitched the vehicle sideways. I landed on a barrel, smashing the side of the truck. I had to work random jobs around the house until I paid it off.

There was a trailer park nearby our place, the KOA campgrounds, with lots of transient residents and some permanent ones, too. We'd hang out with the campground kids, and sometimes they would come to our house and start trouble with my brothers or me. Since I was small and naive, I was an easy target to be exploited. One afternoon some of the crew from the trailer park came by and described a new game to me. At first, the object of the game was to stand up and drop a knife into the ground between your feet, getting it as close to your foot as possible, with the closest winning. Then it evolved into, "Let's see how close to Mathew's foot we can stick a knife into the ground, closest wins." They would throw the knife like Vegas magicians, and it was heavy enough to *thunk* into the dirt and stand up. I closed my eyes and clenched my fists tight, waiting for the next toss, and sure enough felt an incredible pain on the top of my bare foot. I looked down, saw the knife handle sticking up, blade buried in my flesh. My eyes welled up with tears. My "friends" tried to hush me and offered to take me over to our swimming pool to flush out the germs. After dunking my raw laceration into the highly chlorinated pool water, I let out a yell that could have shattered a wineglass. My mother materialized instantly. They weren't invited over too often after that.

For as long as I can remember, I have been a crisis magnet. Things just seem to go

to hell when I'm around. My family used to draw straws to see who had to sit next to me, because meals usually involved a lap full of water, milk, or the always-devastating Hawaiian Punch.

There were more serious close calls, too, which made me realize how life can end at any moment—so each day should be lived to the fullest. My dad's passion was flying, and he had his own plane, a Beachcraft Dutchess. He used it for business travel, but also for joyrides and long-distance family vacations. When I was eight, we had a full load in the cockpit, so Dad put me in back with the luggage. After he landed and went to get me out, he noticed the compartment door latch was broken. If I'd have leaned against it in flight, it would have given way and I'd have had my first and last skydiving experience.

We also had guns around our house, and while target practice was always adult supervised, one time Travis and I found the gun case had been left unlocked. Travis pointed a twelve gauge at me, not knowing it was loaded. It went off. The spray of steel missed me by a foot and blew a hole in the wall the size of a Big Mac. Travis got very grounded for that one, and my dad never left the gun case unlocked again.

Disciplinary action was occasionally administered to me for the typical kid violations: I had a mean sweet tooth and would hunt down and eat entire caches of candybars. Whatchamacallits were my favorite, and I could find them wherever they were stashed. I also recall sliding down the laundry chute into the basement a few times, causing my parents to get pretty upset. And streaking. I definitely had a problem with streaking.

When I enrolled in grade school, it wasn't long before I got into a fracas with my teacher. One day during class I was either spazzing out or talking out of turn and my teacher asked me to go outside and bring her a stick. I did as I was told, not knowing her intent was to beat me with it in front of the class. After the first lash of the switch, I took off my moccasin and gave her a dose. We exchanged blows, and an uproar ensued. It ended with my mom going down to the school and the teacher being fired. For the rest of my years in the educational system, things were never the same. I got Bs and Cs in most subjects but never really trusted teachers again.

When Travis and I were younger, my dad didn't let us join any teams until we were in the sixth and seventh grade. He thought wrestling would teach us discipline, so he signed both of us up at the local YMCA.

His favorite story is from a meet in El Reno, Oklahoma. He told me the correct way to have good sportsmanship was to pray for my opponent before the match. According to my dad, I looked at him and said, "Dad, could I pray for him *after* the match?"

When I was twelve, I came home after basketball practice and our house was in flames. There was an electrical short in the stove, and the kitchen caught on fire. The whole structure went up fast. My brother Travis was in the shower and escaped with nothing but a towel. My mom and I pulled into the driveway just as the dog ran out of the house, fur on fire. The rescue squad aimed their high-pressure water hose at the dog to put him out, and it blew him in two. This was on a Saturday. Our homeowners' insurance policy had run out on Friday, and the new policy didn't take effect until Monday morning. Nearly all of our possessions were gone. The only thing I had was the basketball uniform I was wearing at the time. My mom, who was crazy about photos, lost almost all the family photo albums, negatives, everything.

We moved into a trailer with my cousins until we bought another house. The new place was by a creek, which flooded twice, wrecking the ground floor of the house each time, taking any remaining family photos and mementos we had with it. Having everything and then practically nothing was rough, but we stuck together as a family.

I learned that even the nicest material things in life are temporary.

LEARNING TO FLY

Thirty-five years before I was born, inventor and former circus worker George Nissen envisioned the first trampoline. He was inspired by flying carpets. George's preliminary designs provided about the same amount of bounce you'd get from, say, leaping up and down on a hotel room bed. Nissen used rubber bicycle inner tubes as the next techno-logical step, honing his design until he felt it was time to give his invention the ultimate field test: get some kids on it. The trampoline made its public debut at a YMCA camp, and the reaction among the first test pilots was so overwhelming that George was convinced he was onto something big. It would take a few years to attract a mass audi-ence to try this new kind of fun, but George stuck to his guns and kept on bouncing. During the feel-good 1950s, the trampoline became an American phenomenon.

Wherever you are, George: Thank you.

I was raised on trampolines. I started jumping when I was two years old. To me, it was a big stretchy thing that made you go bouncy-bounce. By the time I was six I had backflips wired. From there I learned to do thirty backflips consecutively, with only one jump between each flip. Travis, Todd, Gina, and I would come up with different combinations and string our tricks together into runs. One of my favorite runs was a backflip and a half, landing on my back and launching into a front-flip to my feet, then following through into another flip. I had one trick I called a suicide. I would jump as high as I could and do a front-flip and arch as hard as I could, coming down staring straight at the canvas, then turn my head and land on my back right before I hit. This one never failed to frighten bystanders.

There are two disciplines in trampolines: the backyard style and the more formal gymnasium style. At one point when I was a kid, I enrolled in a gymnastics class, ready to demonstrate my skills for the instructors. They insisted I start out on the balance beam. After a week balancing on a narrow beam, I decided gymnastics wasn't for me and reverted to backyard style. I owe a lot to the hours we spent experimenting on trampolines. Before I discovered bike riding, the canvas catapult was my halfpipe. It increased my equilibrium and taught me how to spot. It also developed my craving for individual sports, things that combined physical and creative abilities.

I think it was Todd's idea to move the trampoline next to the slide. We worked our way up the steps on the ladder, until we were jumping off the top of the slide. This was a hoot, and we soon got a new tramp. We put scaffolding in between the two trampolines and learned to do flips over the scaffolding from tramp to tramp. We'd raise the bar on the scaffolding to see how high we could go as we flipped back and forth. Soon we built up the confidence to begin moving the trampolines apart, creating a gap: four feet, six feet, eight feet. Anything farther than eight feet across and over the scaffolding got pretty intense.

We also tried doubles routines on the trampoline. There's a technique called double bouncing, where two people jump together to harness their momentum, using the canvas like a teeter-totter. If you do it right, you can really sky doing double bounces. Attaining maximum height was a conquest we never grew tired of. We would also hose the canvas down to make double bounce marathons and scaffolding sessions more challenging.

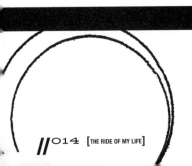

I was trying a double front-flip when things went crooked. I overrotated and ended up doing an extra half flip, and all my momentum was channeled into my head. I came down and whacked my face on the steel springs, punching through them and connecting with the metal support bars of the trampoline. It made a sound like a bell in a boxing ring, and the springs peeled my eyebrow back, putting a bone-deep gash just above my left eye. My dad took me to the emergency room, my head wrapped in a bloody turban. The ER doctor undid the bandages to reveal a slab of skin dangling from my hamburgered forehead. As the doctor prepared his suture tray he said to us, "I don't know if this is going to ever heal properly. There's going to be extensive scarring, and . . ." At that moment my dad did something that made a dramatic impression on me and came in handy many times later in life. He told the doctor if he didn't have the confidence to do the job to keep his hands off my head. We left the doctor standing there holding the needle and thread. Dad used his connections in the medical field to find the best plastic surgeon he could find, and my eye healed up fine—there's barely a hint of scar today.

Thanks, Dad.

MEDICAL TIP FROM MAT

New doctors are often assigned to the emergency room shifts to give them plenty of experience dealing with a variety of traumas. Sometimes you get a great doctor; other times you get a green one. Trust me, it sucks to be somebody's learning curve. Any time you find yourself in a situation where you need a doctor, remember that you have a choice in the matter. Insist on a doctor who has 100 percent confidence in the outcome of the procedure, and don't be afraid to get a second opinion.

Like Father, Like Son

When I was growing up, my dad was in his heyday. His go-for-broke approach to life hadn't faded with age, but it had become more refined. He was enjoying success as a business-man, and his leisure activities reflected his freewheeling, high horsepower persona. I don't think my dad paid attention to how much money he made, or spent. He was good at spend-ing it, sometimes too good.

He had a penchant for Porsches. Once he made a bet with one of his salesmen that he could leave their meeting and make it in time for my brother Todd's football game, which started in ten minutes—and it was a twenty-minute crosstown drive to the game. He hit the road doing 110 miles per hour in his Porsche Targa, and took a short-cut. He didn't see the ravine in the road built for the drainage of a lake. It was a twelve-foot drop and fifty feet across the ditch. With a slight pitch on the takeoff, it was a scene right out of a Burt Reynolds movie. Dad's foot never left the gas pedal. He later said he was so high in the air he could see a little old lady in a white Chevrolet as he flew over her. He landed hard and blew out the motor mounts in the car, wasted the engine, lost the bet, and missed Todd's game.

Dad loved to race his cars. He was in Dallas with my mom when some knucklehead in a hot rod goaded him into a street sprint. Despite the fact that my mom was his pas-senger, Dad accepted the challenge and the two cars tore through town. Dad drove like a nut until he was confident he'd tromped his opponent, then realized they were rapidly approaching a stoplight. He locked up the car sideways, screeching the tires and leav-ing melted Goodyear imprints smoldering in the intersection. Dad was stoked he beat the guy, but my mom was steamed. Her philosophy was to give you as much freedom as you wanted, but if you screwed up she held you responsible for your actions. She was definitely the voice of reason in our family. She helped balance out my dad's stubborn side.

My dad went through a phase where he kept two Maseratis—one to drive and the other as a backup vehicle. He was in the habit of rocketing down lonesome highways at 150 miles per hour with one finger on the wheel while en route to his next sales call, or just to clear his head. Even with the two Maseratis, one was constantly wrecked and in the shop. He'd swap them back and forth between crashes, and eventually his hazardous driving in these cars is what made him find religion.

My dad didn't need a motorized vehicle to test himself. Once, when he was away on business in Texas, he went out for some cocktails and found a guy with a bull. Dad expressed his desire to be a matador and seized the opportunity by the horns. Before the night was through, he was in the bullring waving a red cape. The fifteen-hundred-pound steer charged, and my dad quickly came to his senses. He ran for cover. Unfortunately, he made his move clutching the cape right in front of his chest. The bull zeroed in and rammed him dead center in the torso and almost blew out Pop's lungs.

During another midnight rodeo escapade, Dad made a bet he could rope a calf while riding a bucking bronco. He got flipped off the horse a few times but climbed back on and rode him out, eventually winning the bet. Later he found out he'd split his sternum.

Even during activities as innocent as going out to eat, my dad usually managed to take control of a situation. One day we were in a hurry and stopped at a Waffle House for a quick breakfast. As fate would have it, the food was taking forever. Finally my dad said, "We gotta get this food going." We all watched, shocked and sort of psyched as Dad marched into the kitchen and shooed the cooks away from the griddle. He wasn't aggressive about it, but he definitely exhibited, how shall we say, extreme confidence. The bewildered chefs didn't know what to do, so they got out of the way and let my dad make the waffles.

Bring the Pain

If I inherited my dad's "no compromise" genes, the characteristic my brothers helped bring out in me is a tolerance for pain. I wasn't a Kevlar-coated superchild. I bruised, bled, and cried like a typical seven-year-old. But I did begin to toughen up under the influence of Travis and Todd.

Todd has always had a natural ability to do everything and make it look easy, and he could talk anybody into anything—even climbing into a clothes dryer. We were playing hide-and-seek, and I was looking for a good spot. Todd suggested I hide in the dryer. "Perfect!" I thought. I'd never be found in there. I climbed in and the next thing I knew I was tumbling on high. I clonked and bonked around inside until I figured out how to kick the door open. When the hatch popped and the dryer shut down, I could hear Todd in the laundry room, cracking up at his own cleverness and my gullibility. I put my feet and head out, and my brother offered to help me. He pulled on my feet and my hands and at the same time wedged my back and ass in the dryer. I was stuck. This got him laughing again, until finally he took pity on me. Todd gave a good yank on my arms and jerked me free. The top of the doorway scraped the length of my back and took off some skin. My back hurt like second-degree sunburn for the rest of the day.

Travis, he liked to kick ass. That was his thing. He had a reputation as a macho, hair-trigger, borderline lunatic. He became a local legend when a schoolyard bully began picking on some of our friends. My brother cornered the guy and fought him, only Travis won using his mind, not his fists. He kept his hands in his pockets and let the bully take as many shots as he wanted. The kid kept beating on Travis, who would comment on his weak punches with a cocky, "Is that all you got?" Eventually the bully got so freaked out by this psychotic behavior that he was scared away, and he stopped picking on people.

Travis studied Ninjitsu and he would demand that I spar with him. If I balked, he'd make me an offer I couldn't refuse: fight or bleed. As the little apprentice, I had to take what Travis dished out during his "training" sessions. Occasionally I would emerge victorious. Once we were fighting in the living room and I got him down. He couldn't escape my patented vice grip sleeper hold headlock; he was turning purple, trying to muster up a burst of Incredible Hulk-style rage strength. I was in total control, but I knew if I let him go I was toast. We got stuck in that position, and I began screaming, so the whole family could come in and see that I'd won the fight. I also called them for backup: I knew I'd need protection until he calmed down.

Boot Camp for Bikers

With twenty acres of territory to roam outside the realm of adult supervision, my brothers and I found many ways to entertain ourselves. Sometimes our fun was dangerous, but more danger meant a faster learning curve on new activities.

We were war freaks. We played a hybrid form of hide-and-seek combat. In addition to the previously mentioned farm animal purchases, our allowances were also funneled into a never-ending need for army surplus. Todd, Travis, and I took pride in our status as surplus store locals. We sported fatigues, army shovels, combat caps, and helmets. We drank exclusively from canteens, which we wore on our olive drab utility belts. Out in the field, the only food we'd consume was survival rations: dehydrated beans, tinned fruit, dried meat products, and potted meat. Yes, I used to eat Spam recreationally. Basically if it had a ten-year shelf life, we were down to chow it. We started out staging our wars with plastic M16 replicas, but there were too many arguments about who shot whom and discrepancies over flesh wounds versus kill shots. The Travis and Todd war tribunal voted to allow BB guns into the game.

Since I was the youngest, my brothers told me that I was too little to use the "real" weaponry. I turned into a human target. To avoid getting nailed in the forehead, groin, or shoulder blades with a well-aimed brotherly bullet, I had to adapt. Fast. I learned to scramble through the underbrush. Hiding. Running. Climbing. Burrowing. My brothers originally promised to only pump their pneumatic air rifles once, giving them a limited range. Before long, the single-pump rule was abandoned. After all, there are no rules in battle. Travis and Todd would pump their guns as many times as they could until they had a good shot at me. With copper BB's zipping past at six hundred feet per second, I honed my evasion techniques. Still, I sort of sucked at it and was wounded in action countless times. These battles motivated me to start building fuselages out of wood and get everyone to play out air battles instead, which was safer for me.

Learning to Fly

Building airplanes also helped fuel my dreams of flying. We used plywood, two by fours, bar-rels, and other barnyard debris to create our planes. My cousins, brothers, and I would sit in these splintery contraptions for hours, pretending we were airborne. Eventually this wore thin. Travis and I tried building a side-by-side hang glider out of two by fours and bedsheets and called out the whole family to watch our maiden voyage. We launched off our slide and hit the ground in a hurry. I was unscathed, but Travis broke his finger.

I became increasingly obsessed with flight and could usually be found in the yard or barn area conducting gravitational experiments. After seeing *Zorro* on TV, I *had* to try jumping off the barn onto the back of a horse. The horse moved as I jumped, and I landed on the ground heels first. I had bruised feet for weeks. Another TV influence was the Sally Fields sitcom *The Flying Nun*. Deeply affected after viewing an episode, I leaped off the roof of our house holding an umbrella—which didn't work either.

Eventually my brothers and I discovered a new attraction that involved flying: jumping bikes off the roof of the house into the pool. Todd came up with the idea, and soon Travis was copying him. Then I got in on it. At first I jumped without my bike, but the gap was at least eight or ten feet and there were some close calls. I didn't have the bike skills to pull any tricks, but I knew how to pedal full speed, hold on, and scream. And that's all it took. Roof to pool became our version of *Fight Club*. (The first rule is: Don't. Talk. About. Fight Club.) During the summer this clandestine pastime became a daily rit-ual. As soon as our parents were gone for the day, we were on the roof. It charged me up so much. My parents uncovered our extracurricular aquatic activities and shut us down, but not before I'd felt a few brief moments of how much fun one could have with a bicycle and some air.

DESTINY KNOCKS

destiny knocks

DESTINY KNOCKS

Mr. T has a saying: *Those who fail to plan are planning to fail.* In theory, I like that motto. But when applied to life, I have discovered an opposite, equally powerful cosmic truth: You can't plan shit.

Sometimes the path appears as you walk blindly down it, with no idea of what fate has in store for you.

There were always motorcycles around when we were growing up. My brother Todd was the family's resident gifted athlete, the do-everything, fix-anything superman. By the time I was seven or eight, Todd was a full-blown motorcycle hellion. He'd roop through the horse pastures or down our long dirt driveway, roosting ruts in the sod and cranking wheelies forever. The trickle-down theory was in effect: Watching Todd make it look like cake inspired Travis and me to take up the throttle.

My first motorcycle was a Kawasaki KDX 80. I paid for half of the bike by mowing lawns and doing extra chores around our property, and my dad sponsored me for the other half. At first I had no strategy, no style, and no clue. My riding was purely a matter of twisting the throttle and white-knuckling the grips. I'd keep it pegged wide open through the trails, building speed until I hit a solid object or lost control, going down in a cloud of rubble. Then I'd get up, kick-start, and do it again. By riding over my head I mastered the art of crashing, which is kind of the same principle as learning how to take a punch in boxing or how to fall in martial arts. It was so hard for me to learn to relax and flow through my environment like the wind; being stiff is usually at the root of any crash. I'd get especially nervous when another rider was right on my tail, trying to pass me. But Travis and I picked up a few tips from Todd, and our skills began to improve, ignited by brother-to-brother competitiveness. By the time I was ten, I knew I wanted more motocross power. I mowed more grass and upgraded to a Yamaha YZ 80, then traded that in for Honda CR 80, which was fast as hell.

The turning point in my micro-motocross days began as I spent more time with my cousin, Tom Rhude. Tom was ten years older than I was, and he was a dirt bike disciple. After a few sessions together, he gradually slipped into the Yoda role, and I was his pupil. Tom's tutelage was exactly what I needed to take my riding to the next level. Every weekend he'd take me out with his buddies, and we'd ride some of the best spots in Oklahoma. The Draper Lake trails were about two hundred miles of track, trail, sagebrush, and sandpits where we'd go riding. We'd gas our bikes up, grab an extra tank, and then take off full speed down a dirt path into the wilds. We'd ride until we ran dry, then top off our tanks and head back. These trips opened up a new world, full of independence and adventure, the fuel that all kids crave.

It was Tom who introduced me to the organized motocross-racing scene. He taught me MX assault tactics like how to start in second gear and get the holeshot, leading the pack into the critical first turn. I also learned how to wail through the berms and position myself to swoop and pass high or low out of corners, and I converted Tom's advice into a few trophies. Near Oklahoma City we had the Interstate Motocross track, and the 59th and Douglas motocross track. We occasionally made the long drive to Ponca City, Oklahoma, to try our luck at the track there. The different tracks each offered a distinctive layout over winding, serpentine sections that threaded through several acres, full of jumps and mud bogs.

My riding skills were improving, but part of the equation in racing is getting the most out of your equipment. I learned about bike maintenance the hard way at the 59th and Douglas track. I got the holeshot and led the pack for two laps before my bike bogged down and sputtered to a standstill. I couldn't figure out how to revive it and later found out the gas tank was fouled with water. I got last that day. Tom hipped me to the concept of maintenance for maximum mechanical performance. He taught me everything from fast flat tire changes, to how to swap out the rods and pistons and bore out the engine to increase horsepower. My bike got more dialed, and my riding got faster.

Tom also taught me how to merge technical knowledge with the practical. One afternoon it came in handy. I'd ridden my cycle down the road to a gas station near our neighborhood trailer park. As I bent over the bike to fill the tires with air, shadows fell across me. Then came the "hey, nice motorcycle" jeers, followed by several requests to hop on and take my bike for a ride. I knew where it was heading; these were the kind of comments that can only lead to a bike jacking. I flipped the cap to the spark plug off to discreetly disable the engine and turned around. I told the wolf pack of local toughs the

motor wouldn't run, offering to let them try kick-starting it. After some unsuccessful attempts, I got on and said there might be a way to get it to turn over. I put the cap back on the plug, kick-started, and gunned it, roaring away to freedom.

My parents were always incredibly supportive of anything their children wanted to do, but I could tell they weren't that into my motorcycle phase. Dirt bikes are obnoxiously loud, make you smell of oily two-stroke smoke, and it's a lifestyle synonymous with mud. When they did come to watch me race, Mom and Dad usually scoped from the safety of the car. I think they were also starting to worry about my odds for getting injured. I was consumed. I raced Friday night, Saturday afternoon, and Sunday afternoon, plus during the week, I rode after school. I began developing an appreciation for jumping and was always trying to go higher, land farther. If I took a weekend off from my bike, my throttle wrist would get so sore and feel broken my first race back. My body was a revolving landscape of scraped shins, bruised elbows, and pepperoni-scabbed knees.

It was a knee injury that raised my parents' eyebrows toward my fixation with speed and jumping. I was out by myself, ripping around the fields in our backyard without a lot of safety gear on. As I powered through a turn, my front tire spit a splintered tree branch into my exposed kneecap and tore open a deep gash. I plastered on the biggest Band-Aid I could find, concealed the limp, and didn't tell anyone what had happened. I hoped I could hide the injury and still go on a family trip to Whitewater, a nearby water park. That much blood and swelling is tough to keep secret, and Whitewater made the cut even worse. When my mom found out, there was a scolding, followed by stitches. Just after I got the knee sewn up I went out riding again and slipped off my foot pegs over a jump. I put another puncture wound in my knee, prompting another trip to the doctor. This time I got additional stitches and a knee immobilizer. This injury was the beginning of the end of my motocross days. My attention was being stretched in several other directions.

Crazy Legs

Let's face it; eleven-year-old kids are flaky. I was at a point in my life when my interests were all over the map. In school, I was a shape-shifting social chameleon, transforming from a glasses-wearing superpreppy nerd one year, to a curly-mohawked (frohawked?) loner the next. I got into wrestling for a spell and won a few matches. I was drawn toward the sport by the incredible mental focus and individualist aspect; if you got beat, there was no team to blame it on, just yourself. I also experimented with basketball and football; I was okay shooting rock, but on the gridiron I was the kind of kid who ran the wrong way and scored touchdowns for the opposing team.

My first true BMX bike was a red Mongoose that I picked up during my chameleon phase. The bike's main purpose was entertainment and to get me around Edmond. There were a few different trails in town where kids congregated to dirt jump, tell lies, and throw down breakdancing challenges.

I was known to partake in the art of electric boogaloo on occasion, and after learning the basic robo-style popping and locking moves, I graduated to the gyroscopic stuff. Since backspins in dirt are pretty rugged, we'd leave the trails and seek out smooth surfaces to polish our skills. Battles were organized at the local Wal-Mart and other random places that had good floors. In these spontaneous spin sessions I learned to do backspins, which progressed into the crotch-grabbing shoulder-blade-torquing windmills.

I got a chance to show off my Straight Outta Wal-Mart style when my school had a cotillion. Like most of the unlucky bastards I knew there, my parents had dressed and signed me up against my will. It was rough. Everything I didn't like under one roof. A posse gathered, and we took over the floor, converting the most sanitary sanctuary into a breakdancing battlefield. My friends and I were part of the younger crowd, but there were older kids ring leading it, rocking the moves to the cheesiest eighties Top 40 music. It was a defining moment, and a lightbulb flipped on over my head that helped shape my attitude of, "if you don't like something, do your own thing."

Waking Up at the Bottom

I also followed Todd's lead and dabbled in BMX racing, but instead of staying low and going fast, my goal was to go slow and get passed, then sky off all the jumps. It was a sign of things to come.

My life changed the day I went with my mom to the Edmond Bike Shop to pick up Travis's birthday present. It was a Skyway TA frame and fork. To some it was "just" a bike, but the TA's chrome-plated teardrop tubing and TIG-welded seams were practically glowing with possibility. It screamed pure performance, a brand-new ride for brand-new times. Freestyle was an upstart hybrid sport that was spreading like wildfire from the West Coast. An extension of BMX racing, it was an activity that revolved around individuality, freedom, and style. And it was about to hit Edmond, Oklahoma.

When I told my dad I wanted to give up all sports and only concentrate on bicycle riding—it nearly killed him. He wanted to be in the stands watching me play basketball or football and say, "That's my boy out there."

But he and my mother were supportive. They built the first ramp for Travis and me. Mom was so worried that we would get hurt that my dad said, "Don't look out the window for two weeks." That helped—but it was a rough two weeks.

My brothers and I had seen ramp plans in a copy of *BMX Action* magazine and set about acquiring the plans, permission, and materials to make a quarterpipe. Tom's dad, my uncle Larry, had the carpentry skills needed to create our first driveway ramp. The early ramps were deadly compared with what we have today. They were typically about six feet tall, five feet wide, and the transitions had more kinks than the Amsterdam red-light district. Our driveway was made of dirt, so we got used to riding a lumpy, rock-pocked runway up to the wooden ramp. It's a wonder anybody who rode those things survived.

The first time I rode a ramp is the day it all clicked for me. I was eleven years old, and it freaked me out just standing on the deck looking down the barrel of our mighty six-foot quarter. The thought of pulling aerials or dropping into the thing seemed impossible. Todd talked me into letting him hold me on my bike over the edge of the ramp. I wanted to be held in a bomb drop position, to see what the perspective would look like. "Don't let go," I warned him. He promised he would hold me steady. I peered over my bars at the ground below, pretending, and without warning, Todd let go. I dropped to the transition and rolled away, barely in control. As I whisked down the runway I realized I'd just pulled what I didn't think I had the balls to do. In a split second my mental outlook had been changed by a burst of accidental action, erasing the limitations that existed in my mind. I wanted to try it again, without second-guessing myself on what I could or couldn't do.

I dropped in on that ramp for the rest of the afternoon, over and over. Todd and Travis went inside the house, leaving me to ride alone. Eventually, I got caught behind my seat while dropping in and went straight to my head. I woke up on the bottom of the ramp, with no idea how long I'd been unconscious. All I remember is my sister's boyfriend waking me up, asking me if I was okay. That was my first experience with tunnel vision. But there was a glimmer of something good at the end of that tunnel.

Vert is an intense discipline. It takes years of dedication to get to the point where you can go off and blast big, and along the way you don't get many instant payoffs. But that first spark early on was enough to kindle my curiosity. I imagined what else I could do with my bike, and I was hooked.

New Kids in the Shop

For a new life-form to thrive, the organism needs the proper environmental conditions. Our sterile atmosphere was Edmond, a vacuum of culture. BMX exploded nationwide in the early 1980s, but in our town, riders were outsiders. Freestyle had a rebellious vibe to it, because it was often the dividing moment, separating the kids who liked racing from the kids who liked showing off. Riders in the early eighties caught the rush of being swept up in something new, and the activity wasn't restricted to the confines of a dirt track. Riders were free to experiment with tricks on flat ground, in the streets, and on ramps. We'd camp out in the magazine aisle of the local grocery store and read BMX Action, BMX Plus!, *and* Freestylin'. *Every issue seemed to cover a new stunt, breakthrough trick technology, and fresh faces and places. There were barely any boundaries or rules—as a sport, the paint wasn't even dry. It was up to the participants to shape it.*

Our petri dish was the Edmond Bike Shop. Aside from the trails, the shop was where local riders gravitated. Ron Dutton was the good-natured owner of the Edmond Bike Shop. He was tolerant enough to allow a pack of spastic eleven- twelve- and thirteen-year-olds to cluster around the shop for days on end, ogling the inventory and steaming up his sticker counter with our sweaty faces. Sometimes Travis and I would ask to get dropped off there for a couple of hours, like we were going to the movies. To us, it *was* a form of entertainment. Dutton kept the shop stocked with the cream of the crop in BMX technology. Product hung from the ceiling, covered the walls, and crowded the showroom floor: Hutch, Torker, SE, JMC, Redline, and more. Whenever we'd notice a new part or accessory had arrived, my friends and I would descend on it and begin babbling with plans to purchase that new set of Skyway wheels or the Vector stem/handlebar combo, or we'd debate what brand of foam donuts to get for our Oakley grips. I'd walk in the door and be rendered powerless, the wad of lawn mowing money melting a hole in my pocket. The interior of the shop had an energizing effect on us. After being thoroughly charged up, we'd get on our bikes and ride.

I was so into freestyle that I wore Dyno BMX pants to school, regardless of any fashion laws I was violating with my dangerously bold color themes. I treated my bike like a priceless artifact, polishing my seat, grips, and the surface of my Tuff Wheels with Armor-All liquid silicone sealant—a substance that kept my bike shiny, but incredibly greasy. Taking my cousin Tom's engine performance tips even further, I began experimenting on my bike with power tools. I ended up accidentally boring a hole into my forearm when I attempted to drill through the length of the handlebar stem bolt, to run a brake cable through it. This one hurts to admit, but I used to put my bike in bed, under the covers, and fall asleep next to it.

Over a couple of golden summers, Travis and I made the transition from grommets to bona fide bike shop rats. I forged a few of my lifelong friendships inside that building—guys who I still work with nineteen years later, like Page Hussey and Steve Swope. The crew also tended to congregate at my house, and I'm certain I wouldn't be where I am today if it weren't for the incredible support of my parents. We needed to rebuild our six-foot quarterpipe to eight feet? The construction site was at our place. And later, when it was crucial we get a halfpipe? Mom and Dad had no problem letting us build it in the backyard, or with allowing all the locals to session it. Our freestyle fever was matched by Mom's enthusiasm—whether it was making us custom riding shorts or helping us figure out how we could put on a trick team show—my mom was at the heart of it. When our small band of friends formed the Edmond Bike Shop Trick Team, my mom was so proud.

Just Dew It

The team consisted of Ron Dutton's son, Chad, and Jeff Worth, Josh Weller, Eric Gefeller, Travis, and me. Our first public performance was at a nearby park, after a parade. We put a fancy paint job on our six-foot BMX Action *quarterpipe and wrestled it into a truck; then it was hauled via parents to the demo site. It was the first time I'd ever ridden a ramp on cement. It was a show filled with mistakes and nervousness, but we really got into riding in front of a crowd. It only took one show for us to realize we needed a bigger, more transportable ramp.*

A carpenter was hired to make an eight-foot quarterpipe. He convinced us there was no way to make an eight-foot radius (there is), so we got a nine-foot-tall ramp instead. We called it "The Wall." It was massive, way bigger than standard ramps of the day. We didn't know any better so we rode it, eager to do more shows. My parents kept watch over the community calendar, and if a festival or public gathering was approaching, they'd make some phone calls and get us a gig. The Edmond Bike Shop Trick Team posse shifted members when Chad Dutton and Jeff Worth dropped out and were replaced by Steve Swope and Keith Hopkis. We'd travel out of town, performing wherever we could. It wasn't a moneymaking endeavor; we just did it because that's what freestylers were supposed to do.

My habit was starting to pay off in other ways—my airs were getting higher, shooting out of the ramp and into the seven-foot range. I invented my first variation, a switch-handed aerial. Another arrow in my quiver was the frame stand air. I'd do an air, jump up from the pedals to the top tube, and ride out doing a frame stand. The no-footed can-can had become the trick of the era when California pro Mike Dominguez unveiled it during the King of the Skateparks contest—*Freestylin'* magazine ran a full-page photo of the trick. No-footed can-cans were pro level and rumored to be incredibly hard to pull. During a show, I accidentally did one when I tried my frame stand air and missed the top tube, flinging both feet out sideways. It was a mistake that inspired me to start practicing them, and before long I could extend both legs in photo-perfect form.

In 1985 a Mountain Dew commercial started popping up on TV, which featured freestyle greats like Ron Wilkerson, Eddie Fiola, and RL Osborn. Its flight lasted all summer, and Travis, Steve, and I would surf around channels trying to avoid the shows but find the advertisement. My mom saw how psyched we'd get and called the local Pepsi bottling and distribution center to talk about creating a local form of promotion in sync with the commercial. A few days later we set up our ramp in the Pepsi distributorship parking lot and did a show in full uniform for a couple of executives from the plant. They were stoked, and we were in. We painted a big Mountain Dew logo on our ramp, got jerseys and stickers, and they set us up with a sponsorship through Edmond Bike Shop to keep us flush with parts and inner tubes. In exchange for the Mountain Dew support, we'd do shows at random supermarkets that sold the soda.

The Best Bet I Ever Lost

Competition was another aspect of the freestyle scene. The American Freestyle Association (AFA) was starting to take root, and we got word of sporadic, organized local competitions happening around Oklahoma. I entered my first contest as a novice. It was in the days when we still rode the six-foot quarterpipe, before we built "The Wall." The contest had an eight-foot-tall ramp, and I wasn't used to the height. I'd hit the ramp really fast and crashed every time. On one of the slams I held onto my bars and my brake lever pinched my fingernail like a pair of pliers and tore the nail clean off. That one sucked.

By the spring of 1986, freestyle gatherings were becoming an extension of the sport that we read about in magazines. The biggest contests and tours were often covered by the bike magazines, but that seemed like a fantasy world compared with the scene in my state. On a lark, I sent a photo of me on "The Wall" to *Freestylin'* magazine and they printed it in their letters section. It was a shot some lady took at a local show; I was clocking a one-footed air about seven feet out. I was psyched.

A couple months later the Haro team came through Oklahoma, and Steve Swope's mom drove us to the show, to check out Tony Murray and Dennis McCoy. They let us ride their ramp with them before the demo, and I unleashed everything I had to impress the famous factory superstars. They paid me the ultimate honor, asking me to ride with them during their demo. This was the equivalent of an aspiring local guitarist being asked by Metallica to come onstage and jam. Afterward, Dennis took Steve and me to dinner and announced that he wanted to bring me on the road for the rest of their tour. I was so blown away I could barely stammer out "sure," and during dinner I was already mentally packing my gear bag for the tour. Dennis made a phone call to tell the guys at Haro the good news. He came back with a weird look on his face that said the call hadn't gone well. Today, I understand how silly it must have sounded when he phoned in his request: "Hey, I found some random fourteen-year-old kid in Oklahoma who rules. Can we pick him up and take him on tour around the rest of the United States?"

In August of that year, I got another chance to mingle with the elite, factory-sponsored riders at the AFA Masters Series contest in Tulsa, Oklahoma. Any local notoriety I had because of my riding had been doubled after the Haro show incident and getting my picture printed in the letters section of *Freestylin'*. Suddenly my peers dubbed me a local hotshot, and it was time to compete against riders from all over the country. I was expected to show these guys what Oklahoma City kids were made of. I was so nervous I spent the contest morning barfing up breakfast. During my run, my jittery hands could barely flutter back to my grips. When they announced the results, I couldn't believe it: I'd won my age class, 14–15 Expert Ramps.

I missed the next few contests after taking myself out of commission. I was practicing 360 drop-ins at a local show and was just getting the trick down when I slammed so hard I suffered a fourth-degree AC joint separation on my shoulder. I shattered my left collarbone so badly they had to remove a large chunk of it—at least it happened right next door to a hospital.

On June 29, 1987, there was a massive AFA contest scheduled in New York's Madison Square Garden. I'd been riding every day from sunup to sundown, and my friends told me this would be the comp where I'd earn a factory sponsorship. I bet my friend Page five dollars that he was wrong. Then, just days before the event I crashed and broke my toe. I taped my foot up so I could ride in the contest and flew to New York with my dad, mom, and sister. I was nervous to be entering but stoked to be present around all the other riders. I hit it off with Skyway rider Eddie Roman after meeting him in the stands, and we passed the time heckling bystanders and cracking corny jokes. When it was time for my run, I put the butterflies out of my stomach, bowed my head down, and cranked toward the quarterpipe. A slew of can-can lookbacks, switch-handers, no-footers, no-footed can-cans, and everything else in my arsenal poured out of me. Out of nowhere, the arena burst to life with applause and camera flashes. I won 14–15 Expert Ramps and lost the five dollars to Page.

Before I'd caught my breath after my run, the team managers from Skyway and Haro had approached with sponsorship offers. Haro wanted to try me out on their B Team, and let me work my way up. Skyway didn't operate like that—I would be part of their factory squad and get to go on tour, get flown to contests, and draw a salary.

I signed on the line with Skyway and was soon flown to their headquarters in Redland, California. The team manager had been hyping my skills, and the owners wanted to witness their new kid in action. During the show I slammed so hard I snapped my other collarbone and wound up in the hospital again.

Luckily, they decided to keep me on the team.

TESTIMONIAL

LIFESTYLE SUPPORT

I didn't actually meet Mat until he was signed up on Skyway and came out to do a show at Skyway's local bike shop. He arrived with his mom, dad, and sister. I thought it was cool that they all came out just for this little bike shop show we were doing.

When Mat was warming up, he looked a little sketchy on the new bike. He landed an eight-foot air too far over the nose and got ejected from the transition onto his shoulder and head. He was down for the count with a broken collarbone and concussion. He sat dazed in the Skyway van, not really recognizing any of us for quite a while. His family was remarkably calm—I guessed they'd seen it before.

I was really surprised at how strong Mat's family support was. They never tried to steer Mat away from what he loved. Not many parents could watch their kid break himself up and believe that it would lead somewhere. They saw it in Mat, even way back then.

—MAURICE "DROB" MEYER / SKYWAY TEAM PRO, BIKE RIDERS ORGANIZATION COFOUNDER

PERMANENT RECESS

Hooking up with the Skyway team put me one step closer to the lifestyle I lusted for: touring, hitting all the contests, and spending as many hours a day as possible on my bicycle. From the time I was twelve years old, I'd dreamed of riding for a living, and at age fifteen I found myself in a fairy tale that had come true. Sort of.

A shady-looking Ford conversion van tooled slowly down our winding gravel driveway, kicking up clouds of dust. The van was painted metallic blue, and stickers adhered to various surfaces. From a distance, it resembled something a band of retired people might drive on a fishing trip. But the vehicle was towing a Skyway-logoed quarterpipe and a launch ramp, on a trailer stacked with bikes. I'd been anxiously awaiting their arrival and when they pulled up, I got a lump in my throat. This was it—welcome to the big time, kiddo. The first day of my first tour.

Doors opened and everybody stumbled out, fatigued and goggle-eyed after pulling a twenty-hour long haul from California to Oklahoma City. This rig would be my home for the next couple of months, and, well…it smelled like feet. The same way a seasoned homicide detective knows the stench of death, any biker who has ever gone on the road can identify "Tour Smell." It's the gamy, fungal funk of humans trapped in a sweaty metal box, living on fast food and truck stop beef jerky. My compatriots for the next several thousand miles greeted me with wolf howls, jive handshakes, and high fives.

There was Maurice "Drob" Meyer, a twenty-year-old power rider who'd honed his pro class skills on the streets of San Francisco. Eddie Roman, the sixteen expert ramp/flatland/joke-cracker extraordinaire from San Diego, followed Drob. And finally, there was Skyway's golden boy, Scotty Freeman, a top-ranked fifteen expert flatlander with the flashy smile and polished style of a child actor. The man in charge of our traveling circus was Ron Haro, the twenty-one-year-old team manager and younger brother of the legendary inventor of freestyle, Bob Haro. Ron was the driver, responsible guy, and show announcer. He was also a mischievous party starter who went by the

nickname Rhino. Rhino traveled with an extensive collection of wacky hats and considered himself "a professional idiot." It was his job to get the crowds riled up and cheering, even if it meant looking stupid so his team could look cool.

These guys were my posse, and we were in for a tour that would take us through twenty-five states with fifty show dates. My family stepped out onto the lawn to see the grand entrance, and my mom was at the ready with provisions for the gladiators—an industrial-sized box of snacks and goodies. The Skyway team caught a swim and some rest, and then we crammed my stuff into the van. It was time. I gave my family hugs, and they waved us off.

As the van drove down the driveway toward our first stop, I looked out the window as my house got smaller and smaller. My family was still waving on the front lawn, and my mom and dad looked a bit teary-eyed to see me shipping off for uncharted waters. They were also really stoked for me. They'd had such a big hand in my career, and this was a turning point. I was about to start doing what the guys in the magazines did—take my show on the road.

The modus operandi was the same for each performance: pull up to a bike shop parking lot and get greeted by hundreds of sunburned superfans who'd been standing on hot blacktop for hours. We'd set up the ramps and PA system—the Skyway ramps featured a simple one-piece flip-up design and were good to go in ten minutes. Then for the next hour, sometimes hour and a half, the crowd was wowed with every stunt we could bust, on the ground and in the air. Rhino would slap on a propeller beanie or a foam shark fin and scream himself hoarse. The crowd reciprocated. Afterward, the team would sign some stuff, toss some stickers, and be off—to a budget hotel, or, if it was a tight schedule, toward another town with another bike shop and another sea of kids, sometimes two thousand people deep. It was, in a word, awesome—if you like being surrounded by strangers asking you all sorts of questions.

Me, I was painfully shy. I don't think I had full-blown agoraphobia, but it definitely freaked me out being the focal point for hundreds of people I didn't know. Growing up, I was seldom around anyone besides my family and a tight circle of friends. As I began traveling around the country, I was exposed to a lot of new experiences, and it was tough for me. I liked hanging out with the guys on my team, and I met some cool people . . . but it would take years before I learned to relax in public (I still prefer being withdrawn in social situations). I think one of the reasons I spent so much time on my bike—besides the fact that I loved riding—was because I didn't have to talk much. I could remain anonymous beneath my full-face helmet, do some airs, and let my actions speak on my behalf. Ironically, the more I rode, the louder I was communicating, and the more people paid attention to what I had to say.

Paranoia would overwhelm me whenever I had to travel solo. I would go to great lengths to avoid having to hang out among strangers, like pretending to sleep in my hotel room and not answer the phone or the door. It was stupid.

All these feelings of bashfulness came to a boil on a trip to England for the International BMX Freestyle Organization World Championships. It was my first time overseas; I was alone, didn't know anybody, and was hating it. The event was sponsored by Tizer, some weird British beverage, and it took place over the course of a week in seven places around England, climaxing with made-for-TV finals held in Carlisle. There were TV cameras everywhere, and each day I had to psych myself up to make it to the contests, knowing I would have to mingle, chitchat, and explain my actions for European television. I felt really timid around my fans, and as soon as the riding was over, I bolted straight to my tiny six-by-ten-foot dorm room. As I sat in my room staring at the wall, bored out of my skull, I realized something had to change. If I didn't learn to be a little more outgoing, my life was going to be pretty dry. During the week, I forced myself to

interact with the promoters, fans, and other riders. Gradually, I began to shed my fear of being in the limelight. I'd also been crowned the Supreme Amateur Ramp Champion of the World (whatever that meant). They also held a contest between all the winners of the week's events, and I won that, too. I was declared the Champion of the Champions.

That summer I also got the opportunity to tour in a series of shows featuring a special all-stars team. Dannon Yogurt was launching a new product called Dan-Up and was promoting the goop using flying bike riders. The shows were cosponsored by the "Just Say No" antidrug foundation. I flew in to amphitheaters, schools, and parks around the country and hooked up with Eddie Fiola, Rick Moliterno, Gary Pollak, and Dennis McCoy. We'd click airs, gulp yougurt, and just say no for the local TV news crews. It was weird, but fun. The Dan-Up demos were where I got my first taste of meeting famous people. At the Los Angeles show, I got to hang out with Soliel Moon-Fry, the girl who played Punky Brewster on the eighties TV sitcom. The same day we rode for the Queen of Just Say No, Nancy Reagan. I think I must have been riding a little out of control that afternoon, because as soon as I started my runs, the secret service agents plucked Mrs. Reagan out of the crowd and far away from the runway. Just say whoa.

KOV versus AFA

Skyway wanted the maximum number of kids exposed to their new marketing tool (me), so I was sent to just about every major freestyle contest from Alabama to western Canada. Usually my mom and dad, my friend, Steve Swope, and a sibling or three accompanied me. I rode hard at each comp and began picking off wins, building a reputation. Victory was kind of cool, but not my main focus. As I started getting media coverage, I was irked by details that came out in the press. Like when the magazines critiqued the way I really went off in practice—skying as high as I could and throwing in stretched variations—but then noted that when I was being scored, my runs were raw, especially when compared with the tightly choreographed routines of some competitors. I was also fairly notorious for the music I rode to at AFA contests—typically some vintage Dr. Demento–style novelty rock, like "Flyin' Purple People Eater." To me, riding was riding, and it didn't matter when and where it went down, whether it was "practice" or "real." As long as I tried my hardest and went the highest, I was content. Usually that alone was enough to win the 14–15 Expert Ramps category. After I landed my first magazine cover, the coveted front page of Freestylin' *magazine, there was no turning back. Everybody in the sport knew who I was, and I had become public property. People wanted to see me ride, to see if the hype was true. Media coverage put the zap on my head; I'd read a caption or description of my riding abilities, and they'd paint a picture of this figure that I could never live up to—but I felt like I was expected to anyway. I didn't yet understand the difference between reality and hype. It wasn't until later that I learned to deal with it when Public Enemy let me know, "Don't. Don't believe the hype."*

My favorite part about the contest scene was the feeling of being immersed in bike riding, bonding with my friends one epic weekend at a time. Contests were about seeing the new tricks, kicking a little ass on the ramp, heckling my teammates, and at the end of the day, getting goofy at the Denny's dinner tables. All that began to change midway through 1987, at an AFA event in Columbus, Ohio. It was the biggest AFA contest to date, about 260 riders strong. Eddie Roman and I were amusing ourselves (and no one else) using a home-brewed geographic joke: With a cheerful expression, we'd approach other riders and exclaim, "Oh. Hi! *Oh . . .*"

The sport was booming, and the influx of new riders meant the manufacturers were pumping a lot of cash into freestyle bikes, tours, and teams. Each month the number of kids seemed to multiply and companies added to the sport, defining it with a contagious energy. T-shirts and 'zines were being created, forming the bike subculture that surged up from the underground. At the Ohio comp, it was evident how popular riding had become in a short time. There were thousands of spectators, and hundreds of bikers who swarmed like lemmings to the contest—some didn't even compete, they just came to ride.

Ohio was one of the first contests where the extracurricular activities surrounding the competition overshadowed the event itself. Rebellion was in the air. Big parking lot flatland jam circles and all-night street riding were becoming the norm. Despite the best efforts of AFA president Bob Morales and his affiliates

around the country, the riders at AFA events wanted more than just a contest. They wanted a scene.

A lot of guys had traveled to Ohio on their own, unsupervised by parents, for what seemed like the first time. The host hotel was a Holiday Inn. It was inundated with riders who found power in the pack mentality—sometimes it was five or eight guys, plus bikes, to a room. Mayhem ensued. The telltale signs were all around—skid marks on the carpet, tire scuffs in the elevators, stickers on lampshades. And there was noise, constantly. High-speed, ride-by pillow jousts left the hallways littered with shredded feathers and giggling idiots. Room service trays were sent flying out of hotel room windows, clattering onto the sidewalk below. Patio furniture found its way into the swimming pool, Coke machines toppled over, trashcans were sent tumbling down stairwells, and fire alarms rang at least once a night throughout the weekend. The hotel managers were beyond irate and called in the cavalry. The flicker of red and blue police lights sent riders scattering like roaches—seeking cover in their rooms or taking off for the streets. This was repeated a couple times over the course of the weekend.

Most people had arrived at the contest Friday night, and by Sunday morning, rumors were flying about bikers-versus-helicopter street chases with twenty or fifty guys trying to elude the searchlights. Many had been threatened by the hotel management with eviction from their rooms or had been forced out by the chaos. Legend was born when Large Ray, a

freestyle cult figure, hatched a fist-sized turd on a napkin, then placed it in the continental breakfast kitchen microwave, set to "high." Ten minutes later, the odor swept through the hotel ventilation system and penetrated the entire building with a suffocating, sulfuric stench.

Everybody needs to rebel against something, but that contest was an all-time low. I was satisfied just being annoying with my Oh-Hi-Oh joke.

The other major contest series of the era were the King of Vert (KOV) events. The KOV was a rider-conceived and rider-run vert series put together by Haro team pro Ron Wilkerson and his all-volunteer crew. Ron's comps went down on halfpipes and were the first contests of their kind. (He later pioneered the sport's first street contest series, called Meet the Street.) Often the KOV ramps would be assembled on-site the night before the contest, with harrowing tales of trailer trouble and a thirty-hour drive just to get there. Sometimes the halfpipes were incredibly solid and fast; other times

the ramps flat out sucked. (One comp was held on a floating barge, which bobbed and caused the ramp to absorb your entire pump.) But one thing that was a given at any KOV was a great vibe—the atmosphere was loose, fun, and the whole thing operated from a rider's perspective. Ron would casually ask everyone on deck, "Hey, um . . . should we start yet?" before the event officially began. A mix tape of the latest hip-hop, hard-core, or vintage new wave would be jacked into the tape deck, and Ron's right-hand man, Kevin Martin, would hop on the mic and start barking at the crowd to get loud. The contests felt more like a demo or a backyard session, but with the top guys and the most innovative riding. The pros who followed Ron Wilkerson on his KOV series—Mike Dominguez, Josh White, Brian Blyther, Dennis McCoy, and handful of others—were the effortless rulers of their domain. The contests operated in a jam format, so riders had as much time as needed to finish their runs in the finals. Most people could go for about two minutes, tops, but at a KOV in Colorado Springs, Bob Kohl (inventor of the super-man air) took a lung-busting, eight-minute run.

A guy named Craig Grasso took the casual atmosphere of the KOV to new heights. He introduced a different kind of riding—the naked kind. Desperate for cash to get his broken-down car running again, Grasso dropped in at the KOV finals and did a run wearing nothing but shoes, a helmet, and a wild grin. It was pretty funny; however, my dad and mom had flown out with my aunt, uncle, and cousins to watch me compete. My father was furious that Grasso had tarnished the sport and scarred the innocent children (myself included) for life by subjecting the crowd to blazing no-footed airs and scrotum-dangling can-cans. Grasso's performance got him $250 in deviant spectator donations to revive his ailing Honda Civic. His sponsor dropped him like a hot potato the following day. Craig never rode another KOV again but went on to help pioneer street riding.

Despite the fun and folly, sometimes even the KOV series turned into a pressure cooker situation for me. A big difference between KOV and AFA events were the classifications: at Ron's comps, there were no age-based classes. You were either an am or a pro. This meant on halfpipes I rode against Joe Johnson, an older am with a Bostonian accent and a devastating array of tricks. Johnson was from Stoughton, Massachusetts, and sponsored by Haro. He was so rad it was ridiculous—he stretched his aerial variations, had smooth style, and seemed to soak up new moves without trying. Joe could spin 540s five feet out or pull equally high fakies while twisting off a totally sideways lookback in the middle of the trick, and these were contest-winning moves at the time. The two of us typically traded off wins at KOV events, and sometimes my team manager, Rhino, would get a betting pool going with Bill Hawkins, the Haro team manager. Rhino and Big Bill were old friends, and the two of them instigated a friendly, make-believe rivalry between Joe and me. I don't know about Joe, but that was a little nerve-racking for me.

School's Out, Forever

One aspect of my life that seemed to clash with that fantasy world of bike stardom was school. And after the magic of riding all summer, reality came crashing down around me. Like any public educational environment, my high school offered a limited number of social categories. There were jocks, there were stoners, and there was the clique that I fell into: other. The outcast minority consisted of the brains, the dorks, the punkers, and the bikers. Including myself, there were three kids in my whole school who knew the difference between Woody Itson (flatland pro) and Woody Woodpecker (cartoon bird). Being naturally shy compounded the fact that I didn't fit in with 99.8 percent of the student body. I spent my institutional time lying low, and academic excellence never came easy. I brought home the best grades in my mathematics and art classes and found most of the other subjects pretty dull. Once, I was able to get a little use out of my French 101 class—I brought in a copy of Bicross magazine, a bike publication from France, and had an interview they'd done with me translated so I could read it. However, the more time I spent in the confines of school, the less comfortable I was with the rigid learning and social structure. It didn't help that I got picked on a lot for my choice in recreation.

Being a bike rider back in the mideighties made me a natural target for ridicule. Basically, the jocks loved to torment me, and a couple times these taunts boiled over into fights. Once it was in phys ed—the teacher's pet was a powerful jock who bullied everybody in class, but he seemed to gravitate toward me more than anybody. The instructor really liked the guy, and during our "introduction to wrestling" segment of the class, the teacher told his star pupil he could demonstrate the brutal art of gymnasium wrestling by challenging any student to a match. The bully called me out, the coach blew the whistle, and it was on. I had a much smaller build than my opponent, but I had a secret weapon—years of YMCA wrestling meets when I was younger, not to mention constant "training" with my bro Travis. The jock and I grappled for ten seconds and my reflexes kicked in—I pinned the guy to the floor on his back and had him bound in a knot. It sent a little ripple of respect through the class—but best of all, the bully cut me a wide berth after that day, which was a relief.

I had another gym class incident at the start of ninth grade that would change my life. Another bully—bigger and meaner, and with a backup posse of football team friends—challenged me to a fight that I couldn't avoid. It was more like a psychotic scuffle, but before it was broken up I'd made a mortal enemy. A few weeks later, he stole money out of my wallet in the locker room. When I called him on it, his reaction was to accuse *me* of accusing *him*—*Them's fightin' words, bike boy.* Later that day I got a note passed to me in class that said the battle would take place after school. The clock ticked off the minutes toward three in the afternoon, and I worried my way through every class. A one-on-one fight would be fair, but this guy was bringing an ass-pounding team to grind me into the dirt. The odds were definitely stacked against me. Then, around fifth period, the clouds opened up and it started pouring rain. I received another note written in shaky, devious handwriting: *"Fight postponed until tomorrow, by the bike racks after school. You're dead meat."*

I left school that day with a heavy heart and a head full of anxiety. When I got home, I bolted over to my dad's medical supply distribution warehouse to work on another project I had going—an indoor halfpipe. The ramp already had a name—The Secret Ninja Ramp—and it was getting close to completion. This was going to be my new training facility. I was tired of having to dust snow off our backyard halfpipe and blast frigid airs in the winter months. With cold days right around the corner, I couldn't wait to complete the construction so I could ride my gourmet indoor halfpipe every day after school. My dad donated the space, and my Skyway salary bought the wood.

Construction was coming along nicely, thanks to the help of Steve, Travis, and a few of his skater friends. These guys were older than me but had endured through similar tough times at school—being part of the outcasts was a right of passage, and it was never easy. They quickly noticed I was acting tense and glum and asked me what was wrong. I told them about the unfair odds of tomorrow's fight, and they began to get riled up. Even though my brother and his friends liked to pick on me, they were not down with some group of jocks trying to rough me up. They also knew it was the second time I'd had trouble with the same jackass. A few phone calls were made, and word quickly spread through the tight-knit punk rock community of Oklahoma City.

The next day—doomsday—was also the day I'd be leaving town for a long weekend. I was scheduled to ride in the AFA Masters finals in Los Angeles, California. As the afternoon crawled by in slow motion, school rumors swirled. The word in the halls was that the fight was going to be fast and hard. I was favored to lose, big time. My mind was split between trying to concentrate on my studies, worrying about what my vert routine was going to consist of, what crazy music I'd ride to, and of course, the fight. I hoped I wouldn't have to go to California with a black eye.

My last period was English class. About a half-hour before school let out, I perked up my ears to the sound of an approaching rumble. Down the hallway came the tromping of Doc Martens—lots of them. Suddenly the door burst open and a dozen older punk rockers barged into the classroom. The teacher was flabbergasted by the scene, which was right out of a movie. "Mat needs to be dismissed a little early today," one of the punkers told the teacher. She gave me a "what the hell is this about?" look and then surveyed the determined tribe of weirdos decked out in flight jackets, studded leather, combat boots, and bright hair done in Mohawks and liberty spikes—she clucked and waved me out the door. It was surreal. I picked up my books, and on the way out I half grinned, half ducked past the teacher, and my stunned classmates. With a punk rock escort to the fight, the odds were suddenly in my favor. The punkers had brought clippers and planned to crop the long blond locks off the lead knucklehead who was instigating all the trouble. After the haircut, the game plan involved holding him down, stealing his wallet, and then letting me fight him one-on-one. However, the melee never happened quite like it was supposed to. My adversary showed up at the bike racks with his jock backups, freaked out, and called everything off as a "simple misunderstanding." The punks were pissed, but I was relieved that it hadn't come to blows and thanked my circle-A backup squad.

The AFA contest that weekend was at the Olympic Velodrome in Carson, a city on the south side of LA. I won the contest with a run that was sprinkled with tricks like no-handers into can-cans, and nice, big fakie variations floated over the canyon between two quarterpipes. I also took home the year-end title for 14–15 Expert Ramps class. Afterward my dad, who'd flown our family to the contest in his plane, let me pilot the aircraft home (he handled takeoff and landing detail). It was a good weekend.

We arrived back in Oklahoma on Monday and found an official-looking letter from the school board in the mailbox. It was my fate, sealed in an envelope: In bureaucratic jargon the letter informed my parents there was a school policy rigidly stipulating the number of acceptable absences per student, yadda, yadda, yadda. Because my contest schedule had taken me out of town a few school days too many, I was asked to "pursue other means of education." It took me a second to figure out what it meant.

I was fifteen years old and kicked out of school. Permanently.

Career Day

Ironically, years after they had kicked me to the curb, the same school asked me to come back and speak to a class for "Career Day." At first I was going to decline and remind them that they had asked me to leave school because of my career. But, instead, I put the past behind me and decided to tell the class all about my occupation.

The day I returned to school it felt weird. I hadn't been in the building for ten years and the look and smell brought back a few memories of my days inside the institution. Using autopilot, I found the class I was supposed to be in and stepped to the front of the room.

I started by telling the students that they could choose a traditional career like a doctor or a lawyer, and if that was what they were into, then great. More than likely, they would have a lot of support. But I also noted the great thing about life is the freedom—that it's possible to build a career around just about anything you're passionate about, no matter how abstract it may seem. The trade-off is the less mainstream your path, the fewer acceptances you may receive along the way. The important thing is to let your heart lead you, because every field has hard times, and even going "the traditional route" isn't worth it unless it's what you truly want to do.

I told them my career was a good example of a line of work that didn't receive a lot of support. My choice of riding bikes took me out of school for tours and competitions so much that even though I made up my work, I was asked to "pursue other means of education." Even though my career had caused the absences that led to me being kicked out, I didn't lose my thirst for learning and growing. I'd followed my passion, and that provided me all the purpose I needed, regardless of whether it was an accepted occupation by society's standards. "By breaking convention, I was able to make a career worthy enough to be invited to speak in front of you here today on Career Day." I concluded with a sly smile.

The teacher who invited me had no idea I'd been kicked out, and her wide-eyed expression and the awkward pause that followed said it all.

"Why don't we watch a video?" I suggested and popped the tape of my career highlights I'd brought with me into the classroom VCR. As the action unreeled on the TV monitor, the students got stoked, and I was glad I'd made it back to class to deliver a dose of subversion. Mission accomplished.

NINJAS, ROGUES, ROCK STARS, AND REJECTS

I was booted from school, but Mom and Dad took it in stride. Since my dad had been kicked out of *his* high school and *he'd* turned out okay, I joked with him that I was following in his footsteps (he didn't find this quip nearly as comical as I did). My mom, an educator, helped me create a self-learning curriculum so that I could maintain my riding career and learn what I needed to know.

My first act of self-education was to get a Ph.D. in Nintendo. For about two months solid, I stayed in my room playing Mario Brothers until my thumbs cramped up and my eyes twitched from watching a TV screen all day. Rumors of my recently completed Secret Ninja Ramp reached Dennis McCoy, prompting him to come down for a session. He glanced at my bike, covered in cobwebs, and asked what tricks I'd been working on. "I can get the hidden mushrooms and power up to beat the last boss!" I told him happily. Dennis looked at me like I was insane. I probably was. He brought me to my senses by doing what he's so good at: merciless ridicule. He pointed out the obvious facts—I had an incredible new indoor ramp, some upcoming contests, all the free time I wanted, and an obligation to myself to use my gifts. Dennis was right, of course. I said good-bye to Mario and Yoshi, stowed the Nintendo console under my bed, and proceeded to get back the proverbial eye of the tiger. If it was my job to ride my bike, then I was going to be Employee of the Month, every month.

I drew a modest paycheck from Skyway, but it was still more than I could spend. I hadn't ever considered the politics of being paid to promote a product while retaining amateur status. I always thought the definition of a pro was a rider who kicked ass. I knew there were amateurs who made a lot of cash, just as there were pros who didn't make any. The rules of the bike industry seemed to clash with the way conventional sports worked, which I thought was pretty cool. Plus, I didn't question things that were working in my favor. My understanding of money was that my ATM card was a magic thing. I carried it in my wallet. I could stick it into a machine, punch a few numbers, and the machine spat out twenty-dollar bills. It was in*credible*.

I stimulated the local economy by making regular purchases at record stores (I'd taken a liking to hip-hop and punk rock) and stayed on top of what was playing in movie theaters (although I still considered sneaking in a sport). And of course, I bought a ton of food. With my natural craving for sugar fueled by a river of cash, I went into sweet tooth overdrive. Braum's, the local ice cream emporium, got so used to seeing me order the same thing that they named the dish after me. A Mat Mix is a scoop of chocolate peanut butter ice cream, a second scoop of chocolate chip cookie dough, with hot fudge and caramel spread over both, then peppered with pecans and topped with a glob of whipped cream and a cherry.

Ticket to Ride

The first AFA contest of 1988 was in Palmetto, Florida. There was more mayhem, Ohio-style, but the new wave of scuffing and rolling flatland trick combinations had many riders focused on keeping up with the Joneses rather than raging in the streets. I blew out the candles on my birthday cake just before my run. My wish was to ride forever. A lot of guys stopped riding after turning sixteen, lured away by the power of operating a car, growing up, adopting a lifestyle that was normal, by society's standards. I vowed to be different.

But I still wanted a car.

A week after I turned sixteen, I converted a majority of my bank account into a shiny, new white Toyota Supra. It was slick and lightning-quick. I found out I had inherited my dad's speed genes. The second time I got behind the wheel of my new Supra, I got clocked going God knows how fast in a forty-mile-per-hour zone. I was slapped with the maximum allowable fine for a reckless driving ticket, with a side order of extra points—my license was revoked. Suddenly, I had an expensive car I couldn't use, and I had to endure many more driving classes and promise to be good before the state of Oklahoma trusted me on her streets again.

I was on the accelerated learning plan. Life was teaching me basic, but important principles, such as, "Don't drive like a jackass," and "Riding progress and Nintendo addiction don't mix." I could clearly see it was up to me to figure out my direction in life and then make it happen. A massive challenge, but also pure opportunity. The person who best understood what I truly wanted was *me*—not a teacher, guidance counselor, or a predetermined class schedule. I was enrolled in the school of hard knocks, in which the only way to learn was to jump in and figure things out as they came. Every morning I woke up and designed my day. Sometimes I knew the steps I had to take to reach whatever goal I had set for myself, and other instances I didn't have a clue. I just knew where I wanted to go and what I wanted to do. Being kicked out of the public school system taught me the most valuable lesson I'd ever learned: I didn't have to subscribe to another system. I could create my own culture, travel down my own path, and define my own meaning of success. I never received a frown or a happy face on my paper, but I knew when I'd done it right, and when I screwed up.

Switching Sponsors

Skyway wanted me to turn pro. At first they just dropped the hint, but then they dropped a couple of their longtime squad members, including Drob and first-generation vert vet Hugo Gonzales. I was asked to fill the top slot on the team, but I wasn't so sure I wanted to reclassify as a pro. I was starting to hit my stride as an amateur. I was still contemplating Skyway's proposal when I broke my leg practicing 540s on my ramp. My first question to the doctor in the ER was, "How soon before I'm riding again?" He chuckled and said I would be lucky if I ever walked again without complications. I walked all right—straight out of the hospital and into the office of the best sports medicine practitioner in Oklahoma City, Dr. Carlan Yates. It would be the start of a long and bloody partnership. I got a titanium plate and ten screws bolted into my broken leg, and I was riding again in six weeks. While I was out of commission I had missed a couple of AFA and KOV contests, including a trip to France for an invitational. As I was healing, there were some interesting developments swirling about in the freestyle industry.

Rhino had resigned as the Skyway team manager and was going back to work for Haro, his brother Bob's company. For years, I'd wanted to ride for Haro—the first company to create a freestyle bike, run by the guy who *invented* the sport. It was a pure respect thing. Adding to the appeal, Haro's roster of sponsored riders was the coolest in the world: Ron Wilkerson, Brian Blyther, Dave Nourie, Joe Johnson, Dennis McCoy . . . it was the dream team.

Around this time, a shady lady had entered the bike scene with high hopes of turning bike riders into Michael-Jordan-level megabrands. Despite having little clue as to what bike riding was even about, she began handling the careers of a few riders—including Joe Johnson and Dennis McCoy. Whispers of big-buck sponsorships convinced McCoy and Johnson to quit the Haro team, which left gaps in Haro's am and pro ranks and loosened up quite a bit of cash in their team rider budget. It took months for the drama to unfold, but their manager almost "managed" to torpedo their careers. It was unsettling to see two of the best riders in the sport paying their own way to contests, wearing Adidas track suits and doing demos at Chrysler dealerships, just to make a little extra money until that bazillion dollar Pepsi/Huffy deal kicked in (which, of course, never did).

But Dennis and Joe's lapse in judgment was my gain—I made a phone call to Rhino and secured a spot on the Haro team. I would remain classified as an am

for at least the rest of the year, but I got a pay increase and was making about $50,000 in annual salary—approximately ten times what I earned with Skyway. A day after I signed my Haro contract, I flew out to an American Bicycle Association (ABA) contest held in California, at the Velodrome. The stands were eerily empty, with only about two hundred spectators (chalk that one up to the ABA, a BMX racing organization, attempting to get into the freestyle game). But people freaked out when I debuted in Haro gear riding alloys instead of Skyway's trademark mags. My bike felt light as a feather, and I took home my first win for my new team, jamming my run full of my best stunts. I nailed bar hop airs, one-handed cross-legged can-cans (also known as the Indian Air Classic), nothing fakies, decade drop-ins, and a slew of tricks spanning across an eight-foot-wide gap that was between a pair of quarterpipes. As long as I live, I'll never forget Mike Dominguez's pro run. He'd given up everything he had—the high 540s over the channel, a couple fakies in the seven-foot range—everybody knew he'd won. With a few seconds left ticking on the clock, Mike charged across the arena and whipped off a 900 from about five feet out. He spun past the 720 mark but slammed on the way back around. It was unbelievably close, and totally inspiring. Mike had attempted 900s before at KOV contests, but now he was getting real close. Just by trying it, Mike got every serious vert rider's brain working overtime.

The Secret Ninja Ramp

Eddie Roman, my old Skyway teammate, had a home video camera, some nunchakus, and a vision. He wanted to make a movie, an epic riding adventure, filmed on location in the Secret Ninja Ramp and in areas around Edmond. It was a no-budget underground production, and the plot changed from corny comedy, to random riding drama, to flubbed-overdub laden kung fu action several times in the span of forty minutes. Probably the best part of making Aggro Riding and Kung Fu Fighting was that it quickly led to a sequel, Aggroman, in which I played a golden-suited superhero who battled ninjas. I love ninjas. Hence, the name of my indoor ramp.

The Secret Ninja Ramp was a curved slab of nirvana. The joists were solid, and I even sanded the transitions to make it smooth as glass. The thing was twenty feet wide, which sometimes wasn't wide enough. When coming down off a thirteen-foot air into the ramp, you were going fast. We quickly learned (the hard way) that the roof's support posts at the edges of the ramp needed foam padding.

The ramp was ten feet tall, and we were hitting the ceiling with our airs, so the roof had to be raised to thirty-six feet. This turned the room into a big metal cave that stayed ice cold in the winter and hot in the summer.

The warehouse became our clubhouse. We added a few custom touches to give it a little homeboy charm. The sanitary white walls were begging for creative expression, so with a few cans of Krylon and some ladders we threw up aerosol slogans, creatures, skulls, and slang words on the interior walls. We built a catwalk from one deck to the opposite side, for photographers, deck monkeys, and coping loafers. Beneath one transition I kept a graveyard of broken bike parts—the price of progress was extracted in smashed rims, fractured Haro frames, or exploded forks, at least once a week. I kept a stockpile of brand-new replacement gear on hand as well.

There was a thrift store couch under one of the transitions that had miraculous properties. We dubbed it the Healing Couch, and after a bad slam, a fifteen-minute rest on H.C.'s nappy tweed cushions could mend aching flesh better than any pain reliever. A megawatt sound system was needed to bring the noise, so we lugged huge Peavey speaker cabinets right up onto the decks for maximum sonic enjoyment. Steve, Travis, our riding friends, and I rode the Secret Ninja Ramp day and night. A steady rotation of out-of-town guests stopped in to session, too. Dennis McCoy and Joe Johnson were frequent flyers.

A lot of history went down on that ramp. I stood on the deck and watched Joe pull the first tailwhip airs. Another casual session between Joe, Dennis, and I yielded a whole new style of lip tricks. We were just dorking around and I came up with icepicks (rear peg coping stalls), while Joe invented toothpicks (front peg coping stalls). Serendipity was flowing that day.

The Secret Ninja Ramp began to get pretty famous, so I don't know how long the "Secret" part lasted. In the beginning, on Friday and Saturday nights, five or eight people was about as crowded as it got. Then word got out. Skaters skated, riders rode, and hangers-on hung out. When I was out of town it was Steve's job to keep the peace; there would be twenty or thirty people we vaguely knew, wandering around the warehouse.

Eventually, we had to make up some rules. Rule number one: No Earlin'. Earl was a dude we knew from the wrong side of the tracks, and when I met him he seemed cool. He rode. As it turns out, Earl was also hanging around so he could pull an inside job. One evening, he and a small crew of local dirtballs broke in and made off with ten complete bikes, helmets, the sound system, and our entire CD collection—the grand total was $18,000. I found out through the grapevine who'd ripped us off and drove over to pay Earl a visit, blaring my N.W.A. CD. My blood was pounding in my temples in sync with the drumbeats. I had a broken wrist, but I was pissed enough to use my cast as a blunt instrument should the need arise. We pulled up and caught Earl rolling my bike out his front door. Busted. Earl ratted out his accomplices, and we stopped at two more houses and caught the conspirators with other bikes. Cops were called, and in the end, insurance paid for most of the gear. I'd always been raised to trust people and believe in friends. Getting Earled made me a little more cynical, a little wiser, and brought about a new era of tighter security at the Ninja Ramp compound.

Chasing Fun with the BMX Brigade

The first time I hung out with Rick Thorne, he'd just gotten his ass kicked. The beatdown was courtesy of a group of skinhead U. S. Marines who'd taken an instant disliking to Rick's smart mouth, his passion for hardcore music, and riding bikes. Rick bore his welts and bruises like a badge of honor. He was from Kansas City, and a charter member of the BMX Brigade. The BMX Brigade was a salty assortment of riders who ripped. They sometimes referred to themselves as "rogues" because they cut a path of destruction through whatever environment they chose to session. Dennis McCoy was the lead rogue, and Rick was his sidekick.

Steve Swope and I took a trip up to Kansas City to go riding with Dennis and Rick. We hit some local ramps but quickly found out they were way into street riding. The reason was chases. They lived for getting chased—by the cops, security guards, gangsters, or irate hicks. Sometimes, if it was a slow night, they would call the cops on *themselves*. The BMX Brigade guys were different from Steve and me—we were innocent, naïve, very *Leave It to Beaver* compared with the rogues. The guys from Kansas City were all tight friends, but they expressed it by constantly cracking on one another, trying to cause as much havoc as possible. This was epitomized when Steve and I got introduced to "Swap Rock," a Brigade-created hybrid sport that's like hockey, or war, on bikes. Using the front wheel as the hockey stick, the puck is anything found in the street—a rock, a hunk of asphalt, an old champagne bottle, a dirty diaper, and so forth. The object was to "swap" the "rock" toward your opponents and try to take them out with a kill shot. If you get hit hard enough to fall over, you're out. If your foot touches the ground, you're out. Swap Rock was a fast-paced game, and the rogues were ruthless at it. "Doof the innocent!" was their battle cry, the *doof* being the sound of a rock connecting with a target. Steve and I foolishly let these sharks talk us into a game, and within seconds Dennis had masterfully sent a rock into the spokes of Steve's brand-new, high-dollar, hard-to-come-by, graphite Tuff Wheels. Steve was aghast at the outcome—a ruined front wheel. Dennis just shrugged his shoulders and suggested to Steve he get a little faster on the defense. The more we rode with those guys, the more Rick and Dennis opened our eyes up to a slightly more evil, deviant style of friendship. We began making regular trips up to ride with the Kansas City crew.

If there's a major negative of the current popularity of the sport of bike riding, it's that we're accepted by society. Now you ride down the street, and people want to see you do a trick. They want to see something like on the X Games. But back in 1988, the most common response when people saw bike riders out after eleven at night was, "Isn't it past your bedtime?"

This was the magic question for McCoy. He'd perk up and begin to expertly provoke the situation until it had evolved into a chase. It was after midnight and we'd gone to the corner convenience store to hook up with some sodas. We were chilling on the curb when the attendant came out and made a stink about the "No Loitering" sign posted to the wall. A few yards away at the gas pumps, a drunk was filling up with petrol and overheard the attendant. He took this as his cue to chime in. "Yeah, son, you need to get home," he slurred aloud to our group. Dennis stepped to the guy—he approached him and piped up, "Okay, Dad, I'll get right home. But first I got to ask a big favor. I know it's a lot to ask, but I was wondering if I could *borrow* those really tight corduroy pants that you're wearing, just one night. I'd be a *hit* with the girls . . ."

The drunk wasn't quite aware of how he'd been burned, but we were all laughing at that point, so he grunted and lurched over to challenge McCoy to a fight with his fists raised and thumbs pointed straight up in the air. Dennis loped around him, mocking his unorthodox boxing stance, prancing and dancing like a dork. Dennis maneuvered his opponent into position while Thorne had crept up from behind, down on his hands and knees. Dennis shoved the drunk backward over Rick and he hit the ground. We mounted up on our bikes and could barely ride straight; we were laughing so hard. The drunk hopped in his car, a thrashed old Cutlass, and chirped his tires after our crew. We crossed the street into a huge parking lot, where we clustered in the lot of an empty business park. The guy charged across the lot and spent a few minutes trying to mow down targets with his Cutlass. Finally he got frustrated enough to stop with a screech and hopped out of his car to continue the chase on foot. Bikers were shooting around him, just out of his reach, and he'd run a few steps at one target before somebody would attract his attention by throwing pebbles or making noise. It was like being trapped in a pen with a mad bull. While this was going on, Rick snuck over, leaned in through the guy's open door, and shifted the idling car into drive. The car slowly began rolling forward, and we started cracking up again. The drunk abandoned chasing us and had to chase down his runaway car. Then he got inside and revved the engine. We scattered, Dennis leading the way. He used a tried-and-true BMX Brigade emergency exit, which they'd been using for years to elude pursuers. All you had to do was bunny-hop over a planter box, and drop down off a three-foot-high wall into the parking lot below. Anybody following in a car would have to stop. However, the emergency exit had never been tested with a determined drunk guy in a jacked-up Cutlass.

We were already in the parking lot below and taunting the drunk. He stuck his head out the window and hollered at us. Then he floored it, slammed over the curb, and jumped his car down the drop-off—sparks flew and the guy momentarily lost control. So did we. We had tears in our eyes by the time we realized the drunk had recovered from his gravity slam and was steering his wrecked, barely functioning car at us. I was the last guy in the pack, and the drunk chose to take out his frustration on me. I had to ride as fast as I could and barely got out of his way. I ended up losing him by throwing my bike over a fence and cutting through a backyard. After the BMX Brigade met back up at Dennis's house, we had a good laugh and stayed high on adrenaline for the rest of the night.

The outcome of any chase depended on a lot of factors—what city you were in; how many people you had with you; how well they could ride; and what the ramifications were if you got caught. Cities began putting police on mountain bikes. They were new at it and didn't really have the skills built up yet to ride down stairs or bunny hop up tall ledges. But the cops would see a "little kid" on a BMX bike jump down a six-foot drop-off and assume there was nothing to it. We evaded some big tickets before the cops learned the art of urban riding.

Sometimes citizens tried to take the law into their own hands and clean up the streets. For Dennis's bachelor party a group of us all dressed up wearing impromptu thrift store costumes and went on an all-night street ride. Dennis, a true pioneer of street riding, was dressed as an old woman wearing a gray wig. He freaked out a ton of people that night on the Kansas City cruising strips. Bystanders would see an old lady blur by on a bike, crank off a 360 down a huge flight of stairs, then drop into a nose wheelie hauling ass down a hill, followed by a pack of badly dressed bike-mounted mutants. The night ended with some vigilante chasing us into a gas station parking lot and trying to fight us because we were disturbing his peace. He pulled a crowbar out of his trunk and figured he had us "cornered." Dennis rounded up the only weapons available—squeegees. Our costumed gang of freaks started swinging squeegees and screaming like howler monkeys at Mr. Crowbar, who found us confusing and threatening when he realized he was outnumbered and totally out of his element.

Of the countless Kansas City chases, there was only one that had a bad outcome. I'd just smashed two eggs on a bearded hotel manager's face (he accosted me for cutting across a lawn), thinking the eggs would completely discombobulate him and allow me time to escape. But the egg raid seemed to sharpen his focus and fury. He grabbed my coat and tried to get a grip on me long enough to land a punch. In the struggle I slipped out of the sleeves and left him standing there, holding my coat with egg on his face as I fled. More chasing followed, culminating with a Three-Stooges-style standoff involving Rick Thorne, the angry egged man, and a large pole. The guy attempted to tackle Rick, who was darting around a concrete parking garage pillar like a leprechaun, taunting him with a steady stream of gibberish, saying "Gary Gnu, you got to catch me." They must have circled the pole for five minutes, the whole time Rick providing "Gary" with a running commentary on his poor strategic thinking, lack of speed, and excessive facial hair. Eventually we all got away. As the rush wore off, I realized I'd just sacrificed my brand-new Life's A Beach coat. Better to wind up with a lost jacket than a jacked loser.

Growing Up at
Seventy-five Miles Per Hour

Haro was a team with a reputation that preceded them wherever they went. They were the hard-living, high-flying, free-spirited, rental-car-wasting, nightclub-scouring commandos of the freestyle world. I looked forward to my first summer tour as a Haro-sponsored rider. Two Haro teams were going out on the road in the summer of 1988: the seasoned squad of Ron Wilkerson/Brian Blyther/Dave Nourie, with an Australian named Nick announcing. Then there was us: Rhino on the mic, and Rick Moliterno, Joe Gruttola, and me handling the riding. Joe was a new-breed East Coast flatland wiz. Rick was from Moline, Illinois, and was good on ground and quarterpipes. He was a former BMX racing pro who'd turned to tricks.

We worked really hard at making our show a state-of-the-art display of everything that was great about bikes—and what was possible if you applied yourself. The demos were like a rolling classroom for kids who didn't get to see riding of that caliber, and those who came to see us ride witnessed a jam-packed hour of the newest stunts and a handful of oldies thrown in to show we had soul.

I was at the helm of the Haro van (license still suspended, by the way), plowing through Utah. As traffic slowed, I looked for a Beastie Boys tape. I heard my name called from the back of the van, but I ignored it. I knew it would only take me a second to find that tape. They said my name again, with more urgency. *Where did that tape go?* Then I heard "*MAT!*" a third time, with a tinge of terror behind it. I looked up just in time to see an Oldsmobile stopped dead in front of me. The vehicle received an enema with the full force of the Haro van, trailer, and quarterpipe. There was screeching and swerving behind me, and a split second later the Dyno freestyle team's tour rig flashed by, threading the needle between our wreck and a roadside telephone pole. Dyno's driver, Hadji, pulled off an incredible feat of surgical control, saving us all a lot of extra grief. There was a fierce corporate rivalry between Haro and Dyno, and we weren't supposed to be seen near them. But out on the road, away from the bosses, the riders were friends and when our paths crossed in the Midwest we paired up for about two weeks.

Everybody jumped out of the vans to check out the damage, while I bolted into the backseats and began chanting, "I'm an idiot! I'm an idiot!" I was beyond bummed. The old lady we'd hit saw the large logos on the rig and immediately began complaining of neck and back pains. Later, her $300,000 lawsuit against Haro and me was dropped because I was only sixteen at the time of the incident. In fact, despite not having a license, I avoided all legal repercussions. For the rest of the tour, I was banned from the driver's seat, and my teammates gave me hell for my sloppy steering skills.

Touring is a life of extended stretches of boredom between show dates. We made the best of the situation by keeping ourselves entertained, or distracted. We had a van policy to pull over and session wherever we found a good bank, ditch, or transition. Ditto for fireworks stands, which are found dotted throughout the southern half of the United States. And, there were a lot of girl-related delays. Some of the guys on tour would spend hours on the phone with their homesick chicks, and others on the tour...well, there was a stack of Polaroid photos on the dashboard of topless "friends" we met on the road. And somewhere in the van was a box of underpants that had been donated by other "friends." You'd be surprised, and perhaps disturbed, to know how many girls out there were willing to climb into the back of a musty old trailer full of greasy bicycles and donate their undergarments after hearing the sales pitch as to why a vanload of expert bike riders needed their thongs.

In the city of Rockville, Maryland, there was a freestyle mecca, a store called Rockville BMX. They put on shows that regularly drew two to three thousand kids. One year, disaster was narrowly averted when my mom and dad showed up in the crowd to see their son shine. Before the show my dad and Rhino were chatting in the front seats of the van, and Rhino was telling him what a great kid I was and how smooth the tour had been so far. My dad noticed a stack of Polaroids on the console—THE pictures—and idly picked them up. There were a few riding shots and goofy mug shots on the top of the stack, but somewhere in the middle the content shifted from rated PG to rated R. Rhino diverted Dad's attention and hustled him out of the van without Dad seeing our extracurricular snapshots. How Rhino managed that, I don't know.

This was also the tour in which Rhino introduced me to beer. I can remember slurring to Rhino, "Hey, theesh things are pretty good," as I held aloft a frosty forty-ounce bottle of Colt 45. I can't remember much after that. There was another incident involving beverages, Joe, and me. We'd been left alone at an apartment shared by two girls we'd met on tour. They were gone, we were bored, and so we freestyled our interior decorating skills and rearranged their entire apartment—couch in the bathroom, bed in the kitchen, houseplants in the fridge. Upon the tenants' return, they were pretty steamed.

The temperatures that summer during some shows were insane, topping 105 degrees at a few stops on the East Coast. Between the pads, helmet, and safety gear, sweat was a constant. Meeting a couple thousand kids a day exposed me to a lot of germs that wreaked havoc on my body. I spent about a week of the tour lying down, panting like a sick dog in the back of the van while Rick and Joe rode. When I heard my name, I'd pop up and grab my bike, do a couple of airs, and then return to the sick bay. One show, I was so fevered and delirious that I passed out in the middle of a lookdown air and woke up in that position, on the ground.

Swapping Swatches

It was the brainchild of West Coast concert promoter Bill Silva, who was a friend of Ron Wilkerson's. The idea was to assemble a fistful of the best skaters and bikers, put them on a killer ramp in front of ten thousand people a night, and export that energy all over the country. It was called the Impact tour, and Swatch pumped in sponsorship dollars to make it happen. I looked forward to checking it out, but then I lucked out. Days before the tour embarked, Wilkerson broke his ankle, and they needed a replacement. I was all over it and hopped a flight to Southern California. The team had been practicing their complicated choreography for three weeks, but I missed all that and arrived just in time for the opening show. "Tell me when to ride," I asked. The debut was a success, and I picked up my cues with the help of the other riders. Apparently I hadn't missed much during practice—the ramp had been set up inside a hot warehouse in San Diego, without ventilation or air conditioning. Next door there was a crematorium, and it was close enough to cough on the smoke that puffed out of the chimney—yuck.

Impact was the first large-scale production in action sports, and the first time that many bikers and skaters shared a ramp on tour. The ramp was thirty-six feet wide and ten feet tall and constructed of metal. Blyther, Wilkerson (from the sidelines), and I were the two-wheeled contingent. The skaters included Chris Miller, Jeff Phillips, Mark "Gator" Rogowski, (who in the nineties changed his last name to Anthony) Kevin Staab, and rollerskater Jimi Scott. We got treated like stars—decent hotels, custom leather jackets for "the talent," catered food, after parties, and plenty of interviews from local radio, TV, and newspapers. A semi truck pulled the ramp and equipment, and a crew set everything up at each sports arena we played. We traveled in style via a posh tour bus—

and at first everybody was stoked to find out it had just been used by a popular metal band on tour. A few days into the tour, however, some of the guys noticed their crotches were on fire—leftover presents from the band: crabs in the beds. Sheets were tossed, mattresses were sanitized, and underwear was jettisoned.

Each show was choreographed and went like this: A short film played on a jumbo monitor above the stage and individually introduced the athletes. We'd roll out onto the ramp for an introductory run, one at a time, and once we were all assembled on the decks, the music kicked in, the house lights were triggered, and all hell let loose. We dropped in and rode—doubles, triples, and even a suicide run with everybody in the production on the ramps at once. The show peaked with a heart-stopping run: The lights were off and black lights on the coping barely illuminated the ramp, and our clothing, bikes, and boards had just enough bright highlights to makes us visible. It was freaky. Then the lights came on, and we did a five-minute-long doubles and triples run linked with all talent dropping in on different walls and keeping the airs flowing over, under, and around each other. It was super techy and burly.

The Impact tour was a moment of total enlightenment for me as a rider and changed my style forever. I had a philosophy that freestyle was all about control. Part of this mentality came from the early days of the sport, when riders would meticulously plan out their routines and even write a trick list down in the order each trick was to happen. After years of riding, one trick would flow into the next on autopilot. Then I saw Jeff Phillips skate. He blew me away because he was completely unpredictable—I never knew what trick he would set up until he hit the wall of the ramp. Even Jeff didn't know what he was going to do until he was in the moment. He was totally in control, but he was equally unpredictable. It was an organic approach to vert that I loved—so much, that I threw out every preplanned run I'd programmed myself with over the years and learned to flow vert, riding it one wall at a time.

My mom and dad flew down to see the show in Dallas. They were glowing with pride when they saw the slick presentation, the pure spectacle of the event, and the riding. It was a far cry from the days of the Mountain Dew Trick Team shows from just three years prior. That was probably my favorite Impact show.

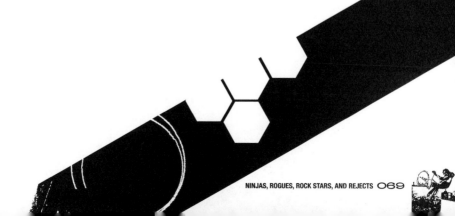

French Fried

Shortly after the Impact tour ended, I got another chance to do some biker-skater demos. It was the last trip of the year. Wilkerson's KOV contests had an annual invitational each year in Paris, and the top four pro and am bikers got to go. This time there was the added bonus of riding with vert skaters Tony Hawk, Mark Gonzales, Danny Way, Adrian Demain, Joe Johnson (there was a skateboarder and bike rider who shared the same name—both Joes were on this trip), and Jimi Scott. I was extramotivated to make the trip. I'd missed the previous Paris KOV, because I was out with a broken leg. All year I heard tall tales about how insane it had been.

Counting down to the departure date, I got my tickets, did my laundry, and dug my passport out. I tried to remember some of the elementary French phrases from my eighth-grade class. I couldn't wait. Then, the day before I hopped on the plane, I couldn't remember who I *was*.

I'd been riding the Ninja Ramp and came in off an air when my forks broke. I got hurled into the flat bottom headfirst and was knocked out cold for seven hours. This was probably the worst head injury I'd ever suffered riding bikes—and I was beginning to realize how burly vert riding could be. A month beforehand, Ron Wilkerson had slammed on his trademark nothing air (no-hander no-footer) on an AFA quarterpipe and was laid up in a Wichita hospital with a bad head injury for two weeks. After Ron's condition stabilized my dad converted his plane into an air ambulance, hired a paramedic, and flew to get Ron and bring him home to San Diego. The whole time, plenty of people in the sport were holding their breath, hoping against hope that Ron would recover. He did. But it underlined the severe consequences of ramp riding, and most of the sport switched to full-face helmets just after that terrible crash.

I came down so hard on the Ninja Ramp that even though I was wearing a full-face helmet, I had amnesia for three days. Bits and pieces of my memory floated back to me, in random order. When I saw my bags packed and my plane tickets to France, I remembered I really, really wanted to go. But I couldn't exactly remember why. I faked like I was fine and boarded my flight.

Standing on the decks of the halfpipe in Bercy stadium in the middle of Paris, I realized I was in over my head. My bell was still ringing, and I had no idea how to ride. I wasn't even one hundred percent sure I *had* riding experience—watching Lee Reynolds, Chris Potts, and Joe Johnson (the biker) doing airs, I couldn't believe anybody would be stupid enough to drop in and actually do airs that high. I was wearing all my gear, sitting on my bike, and shaking my head. "No *way* would I ever do that," I told them. "You guys are going *ten feet* high." They told me I could do thirteen. I laughed at the silliness of what they were saying. After much convincing on their part, I psyched myself up and figured I could maybe drop in, ride across the bottom, and pop out on the opposite deck. That didn't look too hard. As soon as I entered the first tranny, my body's muscle memory took over—my first wall I did a five-foot air, and a six-foot air on the next. Within an hour or two I got a few tricks back (my friends convinced me that I could not only do them, but that I'd invented them). It's weird not being yourself. Very, very weird.

The best part about the Paris invitationals was that the promoters from *Bicross* magazine put the events together as goodwill ambassadors. They were trying to get American pros psyched on Europe. It worked. Our crew stayed in a medieval castle. We were treated to helicopter rides over the city and trips to the catacombs under the streets as well as carted up to the top of the Eiffel Tower and out to plenty of nice dinners and nightclub excursions. The trip lasted a week, and our big demo/contest was only a one-day event. The rest of the days were reserved for practice, and the nights were for playtime. We went to the Crazy Horse, the original French burlesque club that cost four hundred dollars a table and required ties to get past the doorman. Nobody in our group had ties, but Mark Gonzales emerged from the bathroom wearing a tie he made from toilet paper and quickly origamied another half-dozen to get us past the rude bouncer. Another night, breakdancing bravado was called into play. *Freestylin'* magazine's staff photographer and fire-starter, Spike Jonze, instigated our entire posse into dance floor combat against some French B-boys, and we pulled out all the moves. It was a matter of pride, and I'm proud to say we left that Eurodisco in awe, I think. Since nobody spoke French very well, it was hard to tell if they were yelling at us in joy or anger.

The big riding day started off with the KOV contest and blended into a demo. The stadium was at capacity, with about nine thousand spectators, but the French are masters of hype. They'd miced the stands and amplified the applause through the stadium sound system, making nine thousand people sound like thirty thousand. It was nuts.

In France, they knew everything there was to know about wine. Flavors were said to taste even better if the glass of grapes you were enjoying had been fermented during a particularly great year. When I returned to Oklahoma after that trip, I reflected on my collective life experiences of 1988. If I could've bottled everything I'd done that year . . . I think it would've made a damn fine vintage.

TURNING TRICKS

The subject of history has always left me a little disengaged. I never wanted to read about it, I wanted to make it. I turned seventeen years old in January of 1989 and decided to usher the new year in by turning pro. It was at the biggest King of Vert contest to date, held in an arena in Irvine, California. There were commercials on the radio leading up to the comp, and ads on MTV. It was sponsored by Vision Street Wear, a powerhouse force in freestyle at the time. The Vision skateboard company was the first action sports brand in the eighties to really break into the mainstream, and they wanted to own a piece of bike riding. Blaring STREET WEAR logos were wrapped around the trunks and backs of half the riders in the sport like a giant rash.

The event resembled a rock concert, complete with Intellibeam lighting system, fog machines, jumbo TV screens, a monster ramp, and about five thousand superfans foaming at the mouth in the stands. I started the evening by entering in the amateur class.

I won. The hardest part was saving some of myself for what was still to come. Immediately after the amateur competition they ran the pros. The rules didn't prohibit it, so I resigned my amateur status and signed up for both the pro class and the highest-air contest.

Feeling anxious, energized, and high on my decision to leave the am ranks behind, I rolled in for my first run as a pro. Nothing had changed, but then again, everything was different. This was the big boys class, and from now on at contests I would be riding with (and technically, against) heroes I had grown up watching: Brian Blyther, Ron Wilkerson, Josh White, Mike Dominguez, Craig Campbell. These guys weren't just peers, they were people I'd had postered to my bedroom walls as a kid. I remembered having my mind blown seeing old photos of Blyther and Dominguez riding cement skateparks. Now it was time to test myself against the standards my idols had set with their style, smoothness, and sick riding.

My first run as a pro, I unleashed everything I had: supermans to barhops, big 540s, a barhop fakie; and I busted out with a new trick I'd just invented. I blasted about five feet out of the halfpipe, removed all my limbs from bike contact, then grabbed back ahold in time to reenter the ramp backward; I called it a nothing fakie. It updated the famous nothing air that Wilkerson had practically patented when he'd invented them a year earlier. For the finale, I tried (and missed) a double tailwhip. At the end of the contest there was brief break while the judges tallied their scores. The crowd had seemed to be on my side, and I waited for them announce the results, wondering who would come out on top.

They results of the pro finals were announced in reverse order, starting with eighth place. By the time they got to third place (snagged by Joe Johnson), I still hadn't heard my name called. Then they called Brian Blyther's name as the second place winner—his run had been in his typical high-altitude soul storm style, looking effortless as he carved up the ramp like a Thanksgiving bird. Brian had capped off his last run trying a 900, but he didn't have enough spin and came down sideways, which sent him limping off the plywood with a fresh crack in his tibia. Suddenly, my brain did the math; I hadn't heard my name in the pro finals results yet, and if Blyther got *second* that meant . . .

That night at the Irvine KOV I made history. I won the amateur contest, won the pro contest, won the highest-air contest (a little over ten and half feet), and won the 1988 Amateur of the Year series title. My first hour as a professional, I'd made $2,200 and won two snowboards. Happy birthday to me.

Spin to Win

The first KOV contest of the 1989 season went down in Waterloo, Ontario, in Canada. I had a broken thumb from trying varials on my bike (never have learned 'em) but was feeling good enough to enter the comp. I had my hand cast molded in the shape of my grip so I could ride. It felt solid during my early runs, and the crowd was pretty loud. I got a wild hair and decided to try a 900 in my final run.

To pull a 9 would be a pretty big deal, as it had never been done in snowboarding, skateboarding, or bike riding. It was a mythical "Wish List" trick among the top contenders in all three sports. The trick had been a biker crusade for years; Mike Dominguez had been trying them since 1987 but never landed one in public, and he wouldn't deny or confirm that he'd actually pulled it off in his backyard ramp. Brian Blyther had also twirled a few but had missed the mark, and British upstart Lee Reynolds came close and lost teeth in the process.

I saved the 9 for the last trick of my final run in Ontario. I felt it in me. The first one I ever tried, I didn't get all the way around on my last rotation, and I went down in flames. It felt close, though. I rolled in for another go, pumped a few feeler airs around five feet out while I psyched myself up. Then I fired off the coping spinning furiously. This time I committed all the way, leading with my shoulders and head. The thing about 900s is the horizontal rotations happen in a flash, because you have to spin so fast: 180 degrees, 360, 540, 720 . . . 800 . . . 850 . . . 900. I was airborne for two seconds, then *Boom!* I landed low on the tranny but rode out of it. The stadium of Canadians went ballistic. I was still rolling across the flat bottom when I got tackled by fellow pro Dino Deluca, who led a stampede of about a hundred and fifty very excited people onto the ramp. I was raised onto shoulders in a mosh pit of glory. I'd put my stamp in the history books, the contest was over, and I won. It was a cool moment.

For a while thereafter, the 900 became a cross I had to bear. It was the miracle that everybody wanted to witness firsthand, and I was the only person who had proved it was possible. The expectations were high every time I rode at a contest, and the fans didn't so much request the 900, they demanded it. One of the next contests I went to was billed as the Freestyle War of the Stars—hyped as the biggest bike event ever, with $20,000 in cash up for grabs. Before I could even start my run, the crowd was chanting for a 900, breaking up my concentration. I figured I might as well get it out of the way, so I dropped in and ripped off a 9 as my opening trick. My next run I did six back-to-back 540s. I also tried a run with a bouquet of helium balloons strapped to my back (Spike Jonze's bad, bad idea); I spun a 540 and the balloons tangled around me like a spiderweb, nearly taking me down. I ended up winning the event. Within a few days I realized, like every other pro who entered, that my rubber paycheck had bounced sky high. Yes, welcome to the bike recession.

Life Turned Upside Down

There was another trick I'd wanted to learn for years, so Steve and I brought a launch ramp down to a nearby lake, like scientists setting up lab equipment. The first guy in the sport to pull a backflip was a cat named Jose Yanez. He used toe clips to keep his feet attached to the pedals, and then did the trick ramp to ramp. For his skill, Jose scored a steady gig with the circus. I was on a mission to bring flips to vert, but it was a risky riddle trying to figure out how to do it without breaking my neck. Hence, I started doing backflips off the dock, into the water. After a few soggy trial runs off the dock, Steve and I returned to the Ninja Ramp and built a platform extending out of the transition. The new section of deck stretched away from the coping and out over the middle of the ramp, so it would catch me as I carved my flips off the vertical wall. I scoured the Dumpsters outside Goodwill and found a few old mattresses and couch cushions, and those became my low-tech landing pads. I practiced pulling flips off the coping, hoping to land on the platform. The first few attempts were ugly, and painful. A couple times I missed the platform, landing upside down from fourteen feet up. I woke up puking.

Slowly, I learned the mechanics of the motion and began to lower the platform to simulate the feel of landing a flip on a solid surface, until finally I just took it down—I had to make the trick or trash my body. My goal was to pull a complete flip, coming into the transition backward and riding it out as a fakie. To make it, I needed at least six feet of air so my head would clear the coping. It was the kind of stunt that required 100 percent conviction each time. I practiced them every day until I had the flip fakie pretty wired, landing high on the transition rather than jarring into the flat bottom. Then, I got invited to France.

Every year there was an annual spectacular race in Bercy stadium in Paris. The French magazine *Bicross* put on these events, and they were the same folks who'd arranged the KOV invitational contests and demos. The French promoters loved to make a spectacle, regardless of the sport. They had been known to fill the Bercy stadium floor with six feet of water and hold indoor jet ski races, or bring in huge fans and create an artificial windsurfing ocean. The Bercy BMX races were always quite the production, and the trips were legendary. The previous year I'd gone out to do demos with Brian Blyther, and we were lowered into the stadium from the ceiling in a boxing ring to the "Theme from Rocky." Nine thousand screaming French lunatics greeted us, and we put on a good show. On the last trick, though, I did a no-hander over Brian, who was doing a 540, and something went wrong. Brian slammed, breaking his ankle.

My demo partner this time around was the best flatland rider in the world, Kevin Jones. The fact that every ground wizard had copied most of his moves didn't seem to affect Kevin in either a positive or a negative way—his true focus was just riding his bike, regardless of who took note of him.

Since the Bercy event was a race, Kevin and I were outnumbered by a lot of pro BMX racers on the trip, including Mike King, Todd Corbitt, and Matt Hadan. Spike Jonze was there shooting for *Go* magazine (with advertising dollars dwindling, *Freestylin'* and *BMX Action* had morphed into a single title covering both sports, called *Go*). On the Paris trip, Jonze, Jones, and I spent a lot of time hanging out together. The trip contained the usual trappings of a luxury vacation custom-tailored for a biker. We rode the insane brick-banked lunar surfaces and planters in front of Les Gulleiottes in Paris—basically a building façade with perfectly shaped craters and ridable pillars, turning it into a pub-

lic skatepark that nobody planned. We all got in a few food fights with the rock-hard bread of France, which our hosts kept telling us was "breakfast." There were numerous bewildering attempts to use tactical French on random people, introducing ourselves as "helpful monkeys," "moody jugglers," "crazy eggs," and whatever other phrases we could piece together in our translating dictionaries.

After the last stadium race was run, it was demo time. Just before we started, Kevin and I were handed silver space suits and helmets. We thought it was a joke, but, the promoters actually wanted us to put them on. We would be lowered in a smoking space shuttle and emerge from the ship wearing the suits (which made us each look like Q-Bert, the video game character). There were French girls dressed as cheerleaders on the spacecraft. And the theme song, as I recall, was "2001: A Space Odyssey." When we touched down in the stadium I was supposed to get on the mic and greet our fans with a "Je m'appelle Mat Hoffman." All I wanted was to ditch the fruity silver suit and get on my bike.

The show went well; Kevin ripped up the ground with his trademark swirling flatland boogie, and I pulled all tricks out of my bag, saving the best for last. While I caught my breath I called Spike over. "Put in a fresh roll and shoot a sequence of this next one," I said to him, trying to sound casual. "I'm going to try a flip." Spike found his angle just as I was ready, and I hit the Coca-Cola quarterpipe at full speed. I pulled off the coping, leaning back as hard as I could, and got about six or seven feet out as I peaked. I remember being upside down, seeing flashbulbs popping. I don't think the French spectators were ready for what they saw, but the reaction was thunderous. I landed hard and slid out, but I guess that didn't matter. History was made. People freaked, and the promoters wouldn't let me ride anymore because things were rapidly getting out of control. The floor was rushed by fans and riders, and some kid grabbed the laminate around my neck, strangling me until he got his souvenir. The flip fakie made the cover of five bike magazines, including *Go,* with a headline that read: "Sickest Trick Ever."

The cover photo from *Go* was also the cover of a video. After France, Eddie Roman came out to visit and we filmed *Head First,* another home-brewed Roman production. The action opened with Eddie posing as a kitchen appliance and basically eating garbage, regurgitating it, and then feeding the mixture to his friend. This was the first video to feature excessive coverage of street and mini-ramp riding, which were becoming all the rage in the sport. I also rode a lot of dirt jumps. I was riding for Haro but was going through a bike a day while we compiled footage. My bikes change color every other scene, and after some tricks, parts can be seen literally breaking off my bike. While making *Head First,* I adapted the art of big handrails from skateboarding to bikes. I pulled a burly twenty-two stepper while filming with Eddie in downtown Oklahoma City.

Flying Solo

It was fun documenting and progressing my riding, but even as I reached new highs, some dark clouds were blowing into the freestyle scene as the 1980s drew to a close. Most riders didn't seem to question it, or didn't want to acknowledge what was coming. But if you read the writing on the wall, it was apparent things were going to get worse before they got better. A lot of manufacturers who had jumped on the bandwagon in the early 1980s to cash in on the sport were filing for bankruptcy or focusing their business efforts elsewhere. Green grips, turquoise tires, pink pegs, and other novelty colored bolt-on components began to collect dust in bike shops. Sales also flatlined for cheap line extension freestyle bicycles pumped out by corporate giants like Murray, General, and Schwinn. Some attributed this to the fact that riders were just getting smarter and knew what worked and what didn't. Of course, there were other signs, too. At one point in the mideighties, six different monthly freestyle magazines were on newsstands in the United States; these too began to fall like leaves from a tree.

As the bike industry recession began to take root, there were plenty of theories about why freestyle was ailing. It was reasoned that the kids who, a few years prior, got freestyle bikes when they were fourteen or fifteen years old had grown up, gone to college, or joined the workforce, leaving trick riding behind. A new crop would need to grow and take their place. In the meantime, the bike industry was shifting gears, riding the momentum as mountain bikes got hot. Companies responded by diverting dollars and energy into the new savior/flavor of the month, which resulted in budgets slashed from their hemorrhaging freestyle programs. In some cases, entire freestyle teams disappeared from the contest and touring circuit.

The riders themselves were also partially responsible for bringing about change. As bikers, we had evolved out of our BMX ancestry and were creating our own culture and identity. Street riding came up fast and dirty; it was jarring, often illegal, and you looked totally stupid doing it wearing stuffy nylon BMX-style pants and a long-sleeved jersey. Street fever brought with it new attitude, and it made the bike industry conservatives nervous. What was once a well-behaved golden child had become a sweaty, bloody, public-property-destroying rebellious teenager wearing a new uniform of ripped shorts and a T-shirt with a giant anarchy symbol emblazoned on the front.

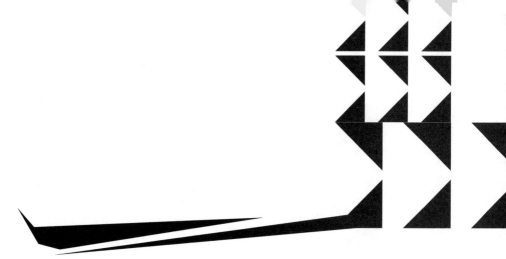

As the reins were tightened and income potential evaporated, those who were in it for the money left bikes to pursue other dreams. I quit Haro and began to pay my own expenses to get to contests. Pretty quickly I realized I needed to figure out where I wanted to go with my career. Nobody was going to hold my hand and lead the way. My first concern was to make sure my riding was pro caliber.

Being my own sponsor meant I had to pay for everything myself, and sometimes it was tight. I won $950 at the next KOV contest, held in New York City. My victory check was the only money I had to finance my trip and to live on. Dennis McCoy and I couldn't find a hotel in our price range, so we did a little urban camping in the streets of Manhattan. While I slept, Dennis stole the check from my hip sack. I was rousted in the early morning hours by a belligerent wino, who was pissed off that I was occupying his special spot. After wiping the sleep from my eyes, I realized my wallet was about a grand lighter. I looked all over for my check, asking everyone I knew if they'd seen it. No one had, so I accepted the money was gone. Dennis savored my distress for another five hours, until we got to the airport, where he finally broke down and started laughing. He handed me my check, and I thanked him with a good sock in the arm. *You're a real kidder, McCoy.* The worst part about the New York KOV contest: It was the last one Mike Dominguez ever entered. He slammed hard on a 900 and bloodied his face and jacked up his wrist. It was a definite downer to see him go.

KEEP ON TRUCKIN'

Even with my contest winnings, it was tough supporting myself. The louder the bike industry blowhards declared freestyle was dying, the more I vowed to be the cure. I wanted to help turn on new kids to riding. The key to finding a new generation of riders was to seek out places where there were lots of people and show them what was possible on a bike. To make it happen, I became four different people: business owner, trucker, athlete, and carnival attraction.

TRY
Porky's

RIBS
TEXAS BBQ BEEF
PORK
CHICKEN
Smoked TurkeyLegs
JUMBO PorkChops

I went into business with my dad, my old tour manager Ron Haro, and Dennis McCoy. We formed a company called VIP Concepts, and our goal was to shoot for the big time, doing bike demos at major events. Dennis and I would be traveling performers, like a rock band. The first order of business was to get together a rig. The age of the quarterpipe was over. And frankly, quarterpipes were getting dangerous to ride, because the level of tricks was getting so out of hand. It was time to evolve. We wanted to have the first halfpipe freestyle show. Halfpipes kept the action flowing smoothly and were perfect for a demo, but nobody had ever tried making a portable one. We commissioned a custom-built, portable halfpipe from a local welding wizard. After the ramp and trailer were done, we needed a truck to haul it, and bought a C-60 class truck, a big commercial-grade vehicle that runs on gasoline instead of diesel fuel.

We landed a few gigs doing demos at fairs, festivals, and amusement parks. It was a rocky start, but slowly we began breaking into the business. My dad and Ron Haro had helped get VIP started with their business wisdom, but they didn't have the connections to get us into the glamorous world of rock-concert-level production and promotion. Our operation was losing money. I bought out the equipment from my partners with the last of the cash in my bank account, and we shut down VIP. The way I look at it: If you're going to fail, the best thing you can do is fail fast and learn from your mistakes. I prepared for my next business venture with the help

of my accomplice, Steve Swope. But first we needed to make few adjustments.

A posse of us were out street riding in downtown Oklahoma City one night when we met a babbling genius. From behind his crusty shopping cart he called us a pack of "Sprocket Jockeys." The name was perfect. We thanked him for his concept and treated him to some free entertainment. Then I enlisted the aid of another consultant, a bike rider named Brian Scura, who I thought could help us break further into the state fair demo circuit.

Scura was from a different school of freestyle. He'd been around the bike industry forever and had a ton of success as the inventor of the Gyro, a device that kept brake cables from tangling while allowing the handlebars to spin freely. Scura was also, to his credit, over the age of thirty and still riding. Or I should say, still performing. His forte was doing demos: elementary schools, fairs, petting zoos, the grand opening of a donut shop—you name it, he'd ride it for crowds. I wanted to get the booking and promotional knowledge out of his head and into mine. This would be a test of patience, however.

We both had our own ideas about what a freestyle show should consist of. Scura was fond of wearing BMX pants with a nylon jersey that was printed up like a fake tuxedo. A white tuxedo, with custom tails. It was rumored he even wore a top hat. For a good portion of his shows he rode around on a special one-trick-bicycle dubbed the wheelie machine. He did choreographed performances that included lots of ground tricks, dancing, audience participation, blatant hand-clapping, lip synching to pop music tunes, and air guitar. He even wrote new lyrics and overdubbed them to songs like "Johnny B. Goode" or "The Devil Went Down to Georgia," to make the songs reflect his deeds on a bike. Granted, his young audiences ate it up. But that showmanship-centric approach to demos just wasn't me.

Scura wanted to, in his own words, "manage the H-E-double-toothpicks out of the Sprocket Jockeys." He invited me to join him at a trade show dedicated to the carnival, state fair, and amusement park industry, to show me the ropes and discuss a rider/manager business arrangement. I flew to California for the trade show. Scura took one look at my style of worn-out jeans, Club Homeboy T-shirt, and long hair and said we couldn't go in the convention center until I had a makeover. He took me to a Chess King store in a local mall and bought me a crew-knit golf shirt and some other fancy duds. He also got me a hat, alluding to the fact that I'd need to cover my hair, which I was growing out.

While we shopped, he painted for me in broad strokes his vision of what would need to be fixed before the Sprocket Jockeys were ready for the big leagues of state fair demos. First, he went into a tirade about firing Dennis for his cocky attitude. "That McCoy kid is trouble," he insisted, not really going into details. Then Scura suggested I issue Steve the ultimatum to chop off his hair or hit the road. At that point I knew his ideas and mine were going to clash, but I finished the trade show and we shook a few hands, then I returned to Oklahoma. A few days later Scura called me.

I listened as he laid out his plans for reworking the Sprocket Jockeys show routine to include more choreography, a whimsical cops-and-robbers-style chase scene, and a part of the show where I'd purposely crash so I could rise up and lip-synch to the hit tune, "Broken Wings."

Give me Fugazi, Dag Nasty, or a little Public Enemy. But I could not merge my riding with Mr. Mister music.

"Let me get this straight, Brian," I said. "You want me to *crash* my bike on purpose, in a show?"

"Trust me," he said. "They'll love it."

There was no way.

"This is *show*manship," Scura started to get defensive about it. I explained to him the only show I was interested in creating would revolve around the talent I'd developed riding my bike. No gimmicks, no singing, no cops and robbers. I'd go big, build up to my hardest tricks, and ride my best. Period. That's the business I wanted to be in.

There was a long pause and I could sense the gears whirling in his head. Finally, in a cold tone, he told me, "You're never goin' *any*where with that attitude, Hoffman," and hung up on me.

I cracked up.

Rigging It Together

We needed a semi. The C-60 truck just didn't have the horsepower to pull the portable half-pipe. At sixty miles per hour, the ramp created considerable drag and was essentially a giant parachute. The C-60 would dog out and wheeze up the slightest hill or headwind, unable to cut the mustard. Steve and I found a diesel truck headhunter, who tracked down rigs for sale around the country. Since nobody would sell a semi truck to a seventeen-year-old in the state of Oklahoma, we had to go out of state. After some searching, we got a line on a flat-nosed Peterbilt cab over a 350 Cummins diesel engine, out in the boondocks of Kansas. Steve and I hopped a flight, then took a taxi down a dirt road to a farmer/trucker's house. I knocked on the door with a $12,500 cashier's check in my hand, a smile on my face, and no idea how to start the thing. Much less a license to drive it.

"Son, you *do* know how to drive a semi, don't you?" was the first thing the owner of the truck asked, skeptically. The inside of the cab was a wall of buttons, knobs, and levers. My eyes glazed over. I assured the guy I was a quick learner. We started the truck up, and it rumbled like thunder. Steve and I drove off in first gear, waving to him out the window. We kept driving down the dirt road and most of the way to the highway in first—first gear tops out at five miles an hour.

It takes a certain rhythm, and an ear for the right rpm whine, to know when to shift a truck through her sixteen gears. After the low gears, you don't use the hydrostatic clutch, you just throw the stickshift and let off the gas pedal for second. Your body gets in tune with the road speed, engine vibrations of the truck and you just sense when it's time to upshift or downshift. It's almost like playing chords on a giant instrument—when you don't get it into gear right away the music turns into the most incredible, unsettling, jolting metal-grinding sound. It's the ultimate penalty buzzer. Steve and I had shifting figured out by the time we arrived home a few hours later. Unfortunately, we smoked the clutch to a crisp during our training session.

The first order of business was to get the rig outfitted with a booming stereo. It got a fresh paint job next, which we did ourselves with the help of our friend Davin "Psycho" Hallford, an expert at art and fire. Soon there were lacquered flames curling down the side of the truck and trailer. And of course, we got us a CB. My handle: Condor. Steve's: Bull. The cab had a sleeper section, but it was pretty grim, like a metal prison cell on wheels. The bunk stank like a public toilet and featured the comfort of a thin mattress.

However, nothing was more punishing than having to ride in the Mephistopheles Mortuary. The Mortuary was a small room at the front of the trailer, which I originally envisioned as a rider's lounge or a recreation room. I wanted the Sprocket Jockeys to have a plush air-conditioned oasis with a little TV set, a couch, a shag carpet, and a minifridge stocked with snacks. I envisioned it as the cushiest place on the road. Unfortunately, I never got around to making it highway-friendly. It was pitch dark inside, and hot as hell in the day and freezing at night. It was unprotected from the engine sounds, the road vibrations, and the constant howling of wind. The springs and shocks on the truck were heavy duty enough to haul a hundred thou-sand pounds of iron, but not designed for the pleasure of soft humans. It rattled so badly inside the Mortuary that if you were lying down on the couch, you would often catch two or three feet of air at random and get slammed to the floor in total darkness. Any time there were more than four guys on the road, it meant somebody had to ride in the Mortuary. If you drew the short straw and had to ride in back, you would be on your own for a few hours because there was no way to communicate with the people in the cab of the truck. The Mortuary smelled like diesel fumes and other fluids the truck would periodically leak, and, technically, it was illegal to ride back there.

The legalities of operating a big rig were a bit of a grey area for the Sprocket Jockeys. I honestly tried to get a semi driver's license, the legal route, and passed the state's written exam but failed the driving part. I never quite got around to retaking the test. Besides, it was illegal for me to drive the semi outside of Oklahoma under the age of eighteen anyway. Steve eventually got his CDL license, and when he turned twenty-one he could take us anywhere in the country. Being up to code was *on* our list of concerns, it was just never that high a priority. Our mantra became "Avoid Authority." We learned to switch drivers at sixty-five miles per hour. We bought the special trucker maps with the interstate weigh stations clearly marked, so we could take alternate routes. We couldn't afford to pay fines.

The weigh station inspectors seemed to take pleasure in giving us a hard time. The rig looked like a carnival ride, which had bad reputations for causing highway accidents. We didn't have four seat belts in the cab, and the truck typically had at least one mechanical violation. The inspectors always hassled us for narcotics. Searches could take hours. At a weigh station in the Bible Belt, after being detained for a while and repeatedly asked where we kept our weapons or drugs, the inspector asked Dennis McCoy, "Do you have any weapons in your possession?" Keeping a straight face, Dennis held up his fists and said, "Just these." The inspector's mood shifted from grumpy to irate, and we ended up spending about three hours getting searched for nonexistent contraband.

If there was no other way around the weigh station, I'd pull in and they'd shut me down and tell me I had to get a licensed driver to move my rig. I'd hang out until they closed down their booth for the day and then sneak out. Once, we came up fast on a checkpoint in Mississippi and there was no way around it, no way we would pass inspection, and we were in a hurry. I blazed past the station and kept the semi pointed straight down the highway. Minutes later a wildy gesturing man in a white truck with an orange light and Department of Transportation insignia on his doors had pulled up alongside us, yelling, and pointing, and carrying on. Steve and I pretended not to see him, which made the guy even madder. We debated pulling over and just decided the guy didn't look like enough of an authority figure to get us in *real* trouble. So I put the pedal to the metal and drove on. He gave chase for another few miles, and finally we crossed the state line and left our pursuer in his own jurisdiction. The weigh stations were a pain in the ass, but these were actually the least of our concerns with the semi.

We would roll into remote truck stops in the dead of the night in a rig with flames and names painted down the sides, and a pack of freaky, longhaired, tattooed, shit-talking joke-cracking kids would stumble out and proceed to act goofy. It attracted the stares and glares from the seasoned road veterans we encountered. I started to work on my Oklahoma accent, letting it thicken up nice and hicklike. I peppered my convo with plenty of hellfire and swear words and grew sideburns and shaved them in the shape of lightning bolts. I got an "American by Birth, Trucker by Choice" solid pewter belt buckle

and had the word "Condor" branded into the leather across the back of the belt. I also practiced the lost art of spitting, and even though I didn't dip tobacco, I could fake it so real nobody knew the difference. I also figured out the best way around trouble was total denial.

"Are you the crazies who jump them bikes on the U-Track?" fellow truckers would ask with an ominous tone, confused about what to call the halfpipe.

"Hell, no. We just drive the damn rig around for the crazies," became the standard reply. I could talk the talk, and after visiting a few hundred truck stops, I was gradually accepted into the trucker family.

At first it was the coolest feeling to settle down in the Naugahyde booth of a truck stop diner, macking in the elite "Professional Drivers Only" section. Then we realized how many truckers are also chain smokers and got a peek at the menu: chicken-fried this, country-fried that, deep battered with a side of butter covered in homemade savory gravy. Truckers are not the healthiest group of guys on the planet. Sometimes we'd pull into a truck stop at four in the morning, blind tired, and find truckers packed in the video game room, bleary-eyed and hands vibrating with two cigarettes going at once, a supertanker-sized jug of coffee at their side, pumping quarters into a *driving* video game. I couldn't figure if they were warming up, or coming down. Steve's vice was chewing ice cubes to stay awake, and I discovered the black magic of coffee. I'd talk rapid-fire and he'd have a numbed mushmouth effect going as we cranked Operation Ivy and Minor Threat, and rum-

bled down the interstate. It was like a punk rock, trucker buddy movie.

The Sprocket Jockeys started landing shows in states as far away as Texas, Virginia, Florida, Washington, and Michigan, and close calls became more frequent. One time we were driving to a show and the trailer got a flat, then another flat, then all three wheels on one side had blown out. I couldn't tell the difference behind the wheel, the 350 Cummins was unstoppable and would go seventy miles per hour, no matter what. We dragged the trailer like a giant steel sled, metal melting onto concrete for who knows how long. Finally some frantic motorist got my attention and I casually glanced in the side mirror to see a twenty-foot-tall rooster tail of sparks showering behind the truck, causing cars to swerve and traffic to hold back behind our Peterbilt powder keg. I started laughing hysterically as I pulled over to the side to sort out the mess.

Keeping the semi running was a constant game of duct tape fixes and shoestring budgets. The first priority was always putting money into paying the Sprocket Jockeys and making sure the riders were taken care of. Rarely was there leftover cash. The truck seemed to know exactly how much money I had on me and would break down and need exactly that amount for repairs. People would sometimes ram their cars into the truck to collect on insurance. There was one situation involving high speed and a low bridge—I hit an overpass and knocked the ramp off the trailer into the highway. Steve and I had to retrieve ramp hunks from the fast lane of the freeway, like

Frogger only while dragging giant sheets of metal and plywood. We got the ramp almost entirely out of the road and some guy in a station wagon hit the last piece and got a flat. The police made us pay for his tires on the spot, and then two months later we got an invoice from his insurance company for a $3,000 transmission.

Even the daily operating expenses of being a trucker were steep: It took $350 just to fill the gas tank. The truck would leak a gallon of oil every ten hours of driving. It also lost a quart of power steering fluid every eight hours, and since power steering fluid is expensive we'd use transmission fluid, which is cheaper but thinner, so it bled faster. There was no heat and no air conditioning in the cab, and if we got stuck in traffic, it would overheat and take three hours to cool down.

Once, I hired a disreputable chop shop in Oklahoma City to do an air ride axle conversion, which would smooth out the trailer and maybe make my dreams of a Sprocket Jockeys lounge a reality. Our first trip on the new axle, Steve, Rick, Dennis, and I drove to a demo in Michigan and made decent money. Driving home I was happy because I had enough to pay for a project I'd been cooking up—building a twenty-one-foot-tall plywood ramp and going for the highest airs possible. As I let my mind wander, we hit a small bump in the freeway, and there was a snap. Suddenly the view out my windshield changed from the two-lane blacktop of I-94 to pure blue sky. We were skidding down the highway at sixty-five miles per hour with a broken axle, sparking and grinding holes through the bottom of our dual fuel tanks. The nose of the truck was pointing straight up. I wrestled the steering wheel for control, unable to see as we plowed to a halt at the side of the highway overlooking a steep ravine, which led to a drainage ditch. A hissing haze of smoke and steam sputtered from the truck carcass as we climbed out and surveyed the damage. The whole truck had snapped in half. To make matters worse, there was a gurgling sound of rushing liquid, as the fuel tanks let go. Several hundred dollars worth of diesel fuel ran down the hillside and collected in the ravine below. Just then the state police showed up and informed us we were not allowed to leave the scene, or the state, until the Environmental Protection Agency had surveyed the situation and provided a cleanup estimate—which, of course, I would be responsible for. Damn.

After a few hours, the guys in white rubber Haz-Mat suits finally arrived and told me it was going to cost two grand and that I had to help clean up. None of us were too stoked to be mopping up stinky diesel fuel from the bottom of a ditch in the sweltering heat, after a long trip. Dennis, Rick, and Steve pitched in, and we got the job done. The whole fiasco, including tow truck and rig fixing, ended up costing seven grand, the exact amount I'd cleared at the demos.

Fair Game

I didn't let anything alter my plans to bring a portable halfpipe show to the people: Not the fact that I was "only" seventeen, or that I had to become a trucker, or that I had no sponsor to pay for the equipment. I approached every obstacle as a mere detail that stood in the way of riding my bike. I didn't really have a choice.

The Sprocket Jockeys were a band of brothers who came together during tough times and rode it out. We lived off Taco Bell value menu items and usually packed into one hotel room. The core of the group was Steve, Dennis, Rick, Jay Miron, Dave Mirra, and I. Over the years, many different people rode in Sprocket Jockeys demos, and looking at the talent roster today is pretty amazing. In the world of state fairs, we earned a reputation as a decent act and became known as "rebookable" entertainment. This is a term reserved for attractions that consistently drew a good crowd, and fair organizers would often rehire the Sprocket Jockeys for the following summer. Not a lot of acts were bestowed that honor. Our contemporaries on the circuit included the Shark Tank Thrill Show, a vaudeville-style Donny and Marie tribute, and a damn fine mobile puppet show called Grandpa Cratchet and His Puppet Ice Cream Truck.

The Sprocket Jockeys were hired every year to do the Texas State Fair, four shows a day for twenty-four days straight. The fair drew up to two hundred thousand people a day during boom weekends, and there were sometimes eight thousand people amassed around our ramp watching us ride. This was the kind of exposure I was hoping for, and when wide-eyed kids and freaked-out parents made their way over to our autograph table after a show, I felt a glow inside. There's nothing like the look on somebody's face after they've witnessed bike stunts for the first time. Kids would always ask what kind of bike they needed, how we learned, where we rode. Operation "Next Generation" was taking shape.

Admittedly, some of the folks occupying seats during our sold-out shows were senior citizens who'd merely wandered over so they could rest their bones while they tore into a deep-fried turkey leg and some Tornado Taters. But we'd also be surprised by some of the random people we converted into fans. The same squad of United States Marines came to see the show every year. They'd sit in the front row, and even though they didn't ride, over time they had developed an eye for good tricks. They would bellow their approval when we were going off but also scream like drill sergeants if they caught us slacking: "You call that a no-hander? Get those arms stretched!"

At the fairs, we had two priorities: Ride hard, and amuse ourselves. We sometimes had shows where there were less than ten people in the audience. We'd start these backward and announce "We're going to warm up with the easy stuff, and we'll work our way up the ladder to the big tricks." I'd roll in and spin a no-handed 540 as high as I could, or a barhop tailwhip, maybe a 900 if I was feeling perky. For the "hard trick" section of the show, we'd make the crowd scream themselves hoarse for an elementary stunt, like a peg stall on the coping.

The way the shift rotation worked was a Sprocket Jockey had to ride for three days and on the fourth day, he'd get a break and be on announcing duty (Dave Mirra and I both sucked at announcing, so we never got days off). It became a tradition for the announcer to try disrupt the show by doing something stupid to make us laugh so hard that we couldn't ride properly. There was a point in the demo where we'd circle around behind the semi trailer to build up speed as we pedaled toward a box jump. It was a blind spot, hidden from the crowd's view. One day as I sprinted around the truck, Dennis dropped out of a tree wearing a ninja mask on his head and landed on my back. I didn't make the box jump. When it was Steve's turn, he upped the ante by placing a mysterious paper bag right in our path labeled "bag of kittens." He also moved random barricades to completely block the runway. Rick got us by dressing up as one of the fairgrounds maintenance men, complete with an orange jumpsuit and a pushbroom that he tried to club us with. The audiences never had a clue about what went down behind the curtain, which made it even funnier.

Our ramp was sixteen feet wide, ten feet tall, and made of metal. It would get hot enough to fry meat on it in the midday sun and slick when it was dusty or wet. My attitude is that the show must go on, rain or shine. I've stood atop the wet decks during demos and sprayed the ramp with lighter fluid, then set it on fire to burn off the moisture. People assumed I was trying to add a dimension of danger to the show, but it was actually to make it safer, so our wet feet wouldn't slip off the pedals.

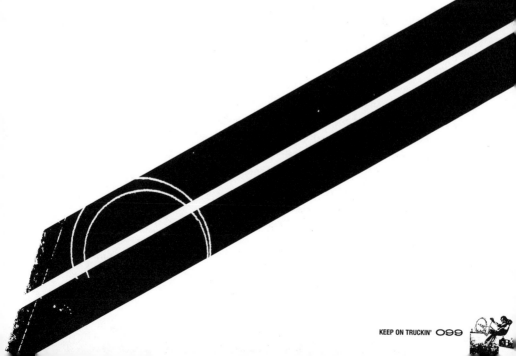

Evening shows were the ones that drew the biggest crowds, and I would be extra motivated to go off. Seeing Jay, Dennis, or Dave blasting big would help get me psyched. Anybody who's ever been to a freestyle demo knows the announcer's favorite phrase to pump up the crowd: "Come on (insert name of state here), the louder you get, the higher they'll go!" The Sprocket Jockeys fed off one another's energy, and the crowd's reaction put us over the top. I'd do a 900 on my first big wall, into a 540 on the next, into a tailwhip on the next wall, linking them together in the gnarliest run I could think up. I would also uncork double tailwhips pretty consistently, and I was working on barhop tailwhips for a time but kept crashing them. This was a ramp that sucked to crash on, too. The flat bottom of the thing was elevated four feet off the ground, and there were crank handles sticking up along the edges that raised and lowered the transition. It required pinpoint accuracy and was a pretty hairy ramp to ride or skate. Tony Hawk did a demo with us once and got gored by a crank handle, which sent him to the hospital. I also took my share of bad slams during shows and often had to run behind the trailer and vomit, then hop back on my bike and complete the demo.

We spent up to 220 days a year on the road and became immersed in the surreal subculture of carnival workers. A lot of carnies are honest, nice people, but living in a trailer full-time and making an income on the midway is a rough life and has the potential to attract some shady characters. We encountered the entire spectrum. Carnies thought we were insane in the membrane after seeing us take devastating crashes on our bikes and keep getting back up to ride again. In turn, we'd see them socializing at a local bar, wearing big knives on their belts and getting rowdy, and thought they were pretty tweaked. It never crossed my mind that I was in a vulnerable situation being around these guys. If a carnie approached me like a pal, pointed to another fair worker, and said, "See that bastard over there? Stay away from him . . . he's nothing but trouble," I knew the real guy to watch out for was probably the one giving the advice. The only carnie recommendation I ever truly trusted was something I learned after seeing how the rides were put together: Don't ride the rides.

We were also exposed to plenty of music on the fair circuit. For some reason the fair organizers would schedule attractions that were right next to each other at the same time. We'd be forced to battle the Donny and Marie tribute act—they would turn up their PA system to try and drown out our music, and we'd turn our Bad Brains CD up a few notches. Then they would break out with some fancy two-step shuffle dancing to get their crowd cheering, so we would respond. Jay would fling a no-footed 540, or Dennis would throw some technical deck tricks, or I'd link together some combos, and our crowd would roar louder. It was back and forth.

Once we were doing shows at the Deer Creek Fair in Indianapolis. There was a concert pavilion connected to the fairgrounds, and REO Speedwagon was playing a midday show. A severe thunderstorm blew in fast, and the fair had to be shut down. As the sky turned black, the wind kicked up and the radio was full of talk about tornadoes. We closed down our rig, which was essentially a giant lightning rod, and took off in search of shelter. As the posse of Sprocket Jockeys rode full gallop across the fairgrounds parking lot, we could hear REO Speedwagon still on stage, playing "Riding the Storm Out." I was cranking my hardest into a gale-force headwind as newspapers and trash flew past like tumbleweeds. I felt like I was trapped in a music video.

Another time, the Deer Creek Fair featured the Monsters of Metal tour: Slayer, Megadeth, and Anthrax. During our afternoon Sprocket Jockeys show, Scott Ian and a couple of the Anthrax crew were in the crowd. It turned out they were bike fans and got stoked on our stunts. Backstage passes and front row tickets were flowed and gladly accepted by Steve, Dennis, Rick, videographer Ed Roman, and me. I happened to have some wigs with me (because you never know when they'll come in handy), and we decided it would be a good idea to break them out and attend the metal concert. After a quick thrift store shopping spree, we had a barrage of new disguises. We looked like idiots.

We hit the concert a bit late and had to boot some leather-clad heavy metal cretins out of our seats. Everybody around us was pretty bewildered by our ensembles, and when we started mutant redneck moshing in our seats, they were annoyed. Anthrax noticed the flurry of activity coming from the front row and leaned over the edge of the stage to see what the hell was going on. My wig fell off while I was headbanging, and the guys in the band realized the jackasses in the front row were their special guests. They started laughing and had to stop the song until they regained their composure. During Slayer's evil set, Dennis, who was dressed like an elderly transvestite, stood on a chair and danced explosively. The security guards who'd been giving us the eye all night had an excuse to yank him down. Dennis was escorted off to the sidelines, and his wisecracking retorts to their questions didn't help matters. Just as he was about to get his ass kicked by two well-built security guards, we surrounded them and began doing our interpretation of a Native American rain ceremony dance—whooping, shuffling, and waving wigs in the air like we just didn't care. The guards thought we were dorks, but it saved Dennis from a beating.

During the era of Sprocket Jockeys shows, there were many times when we acted foolish, but we never fooled ourselves that fair demos were glamorous events. It was often a pain in the ass, sometimes it was superboring, and other times it was *"How did I get here?"* weird. But it was a good recruiting system, and I was in it for the long haul. I saw what happened when kids who stumbled onto the Sprocket Jockeys realized how much fun you could have on two wheels and aspired to get a bike. Each kid I rode for was another brick in the new foundation.

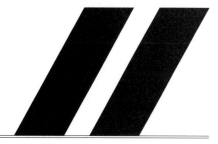

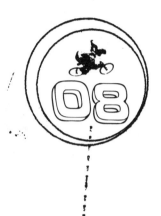

death and rebirth

DEATH
AND REBIRTH

Just about everybody in Edmond loved Joni Hoffman. Her passion was to help people, and she was great at what she did; she worked with disabled children and was involved in our community. My mom was the peacekeeper, the encourager, the brains, the organizer, and the binding force that made our whole family work together. She was the absolute center of our household. Her own upbringing was kind of difficult, but she didn't let whatever struggles she overcame in her childhood affect the way she carried herself as an adult and a parent. That was her inner strength. She and my dad were the ideal pair. Mom balanced out his stubborn, uncontrolled side. She had so much love to give, which was exactly the thing my dad needed.

As a mother, she was the best. She supported all her kids in anything, regardless of how unconventional the idea, and looked at our successes as her own. I was the youngest and last child, so I got a lot of extra attention from her, which really made me shine.

By the time the tumor was found in one of her lungs, it was serious. She had an operation the same week and immediately began an aggressive chemotherapy campaign. The medicine made her sick for nearly a year, but after the months of treatment it looked like she was getting better. Throughout the ordeal, my mom never lost hope or let any of us feel sorry for her. To keep focused on the positive, she designed a dream home. She was going to beat cancer, she and Dad would build a great new place to live, and the Hoffman family was going to get on with life. The doctors were optimistic, and it appeared the disease was in remission.

After toughing it through a hard winter, just as the flowers began to bloom, Mother became really sick again. There was more chemotherapy. June stretched into July, and we all waited and hoped for a sign that she would be okay. Nothing makes you feel more helpless than waiting. Some new tests were done, but she and my dad didn't give us the details. Mom was always so positive; she never wanted to be a burden or make us worry. She and my dad encouraged me to do a weekend demo, so Travis, Steve, and I took the semi down to Ardmore, near the Texas-Oklahoma border for the shows. Before we headed out, Travis and I spent some time with Mom. We told her we'd see her on Monday morning. We left on Friday, June 17, 1990.

We made Ardmore around midnight but couldn't find our hotel. We pulled into a strip mall parking lot for a map check. Suddenly, several police cars roared up with their lights blazing, surrounding the rig. My first thought was, "What did we do now?" I tried to remember if we'd avoided any weigh stations on the highway. Then my father's business partner Rick Kirby got out of one of the police cruisers, and my heart sank, because I knew. . . . In the middle of the night, in the middle of nowhere, we found out our mom had slipped away.

Five days after the funeral, I was supposed to go on tour. I didn't give a damn about my bike, or anything else for that matter. My dad told me I had to go—he wanted me to get on with my future, to keep my mind on other things, and to fulfill my commitments. I tried my best to keep it together, but inside I ached with a pain unlike any I'd ever felt before. There was a constant lump in my throat. I went on the road with Rick Thorne, Eddie Roman, Dennis McCoy, and Steve Swope, grateful for friendship during that tough time. My mom was in my thoughts every single day, and when I rode in the shows that summer, all the loss and loneliness I felt were channeled into my bike. I didn't care if I got physically hurt because inside my heart was numb. Emotion poured out of me and took the form of bar hop tailwhips, 900s, and 540s with any variation thrown in, pushing eight or ten feet high. I started to scare my friends with my actions and my attitude. Every time I got on my bike I threw down everything I had.

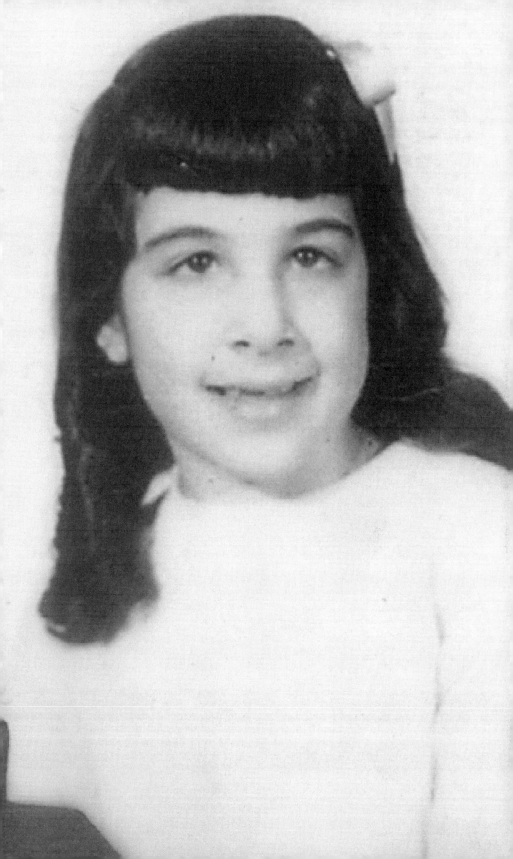

Make-A-Wish

In the fall of 1990 a European promoter brought me overseas for demos. He had a bad rep for stiffing his talent and had burned some bridges. I didn't find out the scope of his shifty ways until after the trip, but I agreed to do a double demo for him. First, I'd make a TV appearance he'd lined up in Germany, and two days later I'd fly to England for a more traditional indoor halfpipe comp with a demo afterward. The trip to Germany was fast and weird. I arrived wondering who was picking me up, where I'd stay, that sort of thing. It worked out in the end, and I wound up on a German variety show with Maxi Priest, the British musician. Our dressing rooms were adjacent, and when I saw his ornately braided hair, I thought he was Milli Vanilli. I yelled, "Hey, Milli!" and he gave me an evil look. The show ramp was sub-par, which only fueled my frustrations.

The contest in England was on a halfpipe that was pretty good. The ramp was solid and on my first warm-up run I pulled a 540 about eight feet out. The British love their twirling tricks, and so I strung an all-540 variations run together with a superhigh 5, into an inverted 5 on the next wall, into an X-up 5, into a no-handed 5. Then I gave the Brits a 900. They were pretty stoked, but there was really only one reason that I was going off. At the contest I met a little boy, about ten years old, named Matthew Jarvis. He had terminal brain cancer and had been brought there by the Make-A-Wish Foundation. His wish was to meet me. It filled me with sadness to see such a sweet, innocent kid facing his fate calmly. Being asked to ride for Matthew was the greatest honor I'd ever had. He only had a few days to live. During the demo I was crashing a lot, but I kept getting back on my bike—I hoped it wouldn't break before I was through, because there was something I wanted to do. I'd never pulled a flair before and had been trying them for months. Deeply moved by Matthew's presence, I dropped in for my last trick and blasted a big backflip and twisted it around 180 degrees. It was the first time I'd ever attempted a flair in public. I crashed hard, and the place erupted in swear words and cheers. My body and bike seemed operative, so I got back on and tried another. The second time I got off a good arch, landed it, and rode out of the flair; the first one I'd ever completely pulled. As pandemonium broke loose inside the arena, I rolled off the ramp and into the stands and immediately gave my bike to Matthew. It was probably the best reason I could imagine for pulling that trick for the first time. I would have done anything to make things all right for my brave young friend.

Losing my mother when I was eighteen messed me up for a long time. Our family began drifting apart, each of us finding our own ways to grieve and get on with our lives. The sport slipped into a recession, and it seemed like my entire world was changing, regardless if I was ready.

I lost my dependence, grew up, and started living completely on my terms all in a very short, intense time period. The one thing I felt I could trust was my heart—the thing inside me that my mom taught me how to use. I began doing things the way I thought they should be done, instead of listening to others or even to my own doubts. I questioned everything and was willing to risk whatever it took to find the answers. I wasn't governed by anyone but myself. I became my own boss. I've never had another boss since.

TESTIMONIAL

A FLAIR FOR SPONTANEITY

Mat had his secret warehouse in Edmond, Oklahoma, and was like a mad scientist. He was so removed from the Southern California–based bike industry that, unless you were in his crew, you didn't know what he was up to. I was announcing at the demo in Manchester the day Mat unveiled the flair in public. It wasn't until just before he did the trick that he mentioned he had a new one. I was very excited and nervous. If Mat was going big with something new, it could end in a bad wreck. His first attempt, he pumped a few airs and hucked this big backflip and came in 180, landing it as an air. He crashed it, but that just added to the tension. His second try, he stuck the flair. What followed was the most spontaneous natural reaction that I've ever seen—I was totally blown away, as were the thousand-plus people in the building. I get goose bumps thinking about the magnitude of that day and that one trick.

—KEVIN MARTIN, KOV CONTEST SERIES ANNOUNCER AND TOUR MANAGER

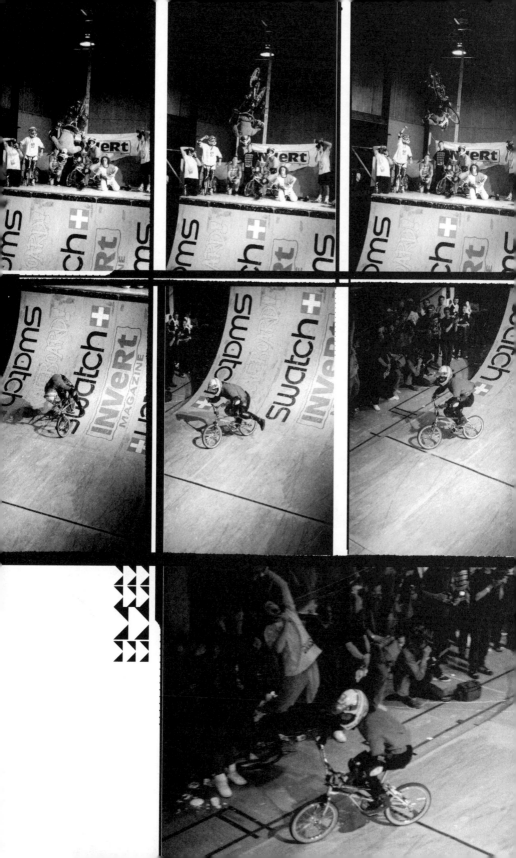

H.M.F.I.C.

With the sport continuing its downward spiral, withering and shrinking, there were hardly any events or competitions left to attend. The thriving scene of the '80s was gone. But freestyle was far from dead—it was just underground. From my perspective, I didn't really have a choice. I needed a bike, I needed contests, I needed a community. In short, I needed to get off my ass and make it happen.

The companies that still made freestyle bikes didn't seem particularly committed to, or even interested in, freestyle as a sport. They saw it as a number, and with the bike industry sales in decline, that number did not command much respect. In the past, I'd been offered a chance to have my own signature bike on Haro. I should have been stoked, but my *question everything* mind-set was provoking me to do a lot of soul-searching. If I was going to put my name on a bike, I didn't want it to be at the mercy of bean counters. I didn't want somebody's lackluster bike sale stats to control who I wanted to be. My lifestyle revolved around a sport of self-control, mastering the ability to adapt to weird environments. If there's one thing I knew how to do, it was ride transitions.

I didn't know dick about building bicycles, I just knew how I wanted mine to ride. I ransacked my Rolodex, making calls and asking questions of some of the manufacturers in the industry, researching how stuff got built, and how to translate my ideas as a rider into bent and welded steel. I got ahold of Linn Kasten, one of the greats in BMX history. Linn is the guy who basically invented the BMX racing bike. He was in charge of the first awesome BMX bike company, Redline (who also had the first great BMX team). To his credit he had the creation of the first tubular forks, handlebars with a crossbar, and high-performance Flight cranks. It was an honor to have him help show me the ropes. I started planning the way any kid with a dream does, by scribbling my frame designs on paper. I went to Linn's house where my crude drawings became intense technical discussions. We tuned the geometry in the drawing and discussed the dilemma of weight versus strength. I wanted a bulletproof bike, but it had to fly. There were incidents in the past where I'd broken three brand-new bikes in one day—and was sick of that crap. I wanted top quality, which meant using American-made 4130 aircraft grade chrome-moly tubing, the best money can buy. I was also stoked that it was going to be built in

America, which was a rarity for freestyle bikes. A couple of weeks later Linn's machine shop had built me five prototype Condor frames, one for Steve Swope, Rick Thorne, Dave Mirra, Davin Hallford, and me. Our mission was to try and break them. The Condor was good. It was quick, it was stiff, it had clean angles, but more than anything, it was built to last. I rode my prototype frame and fork set for seven months, trying everything in my power to bring it to its knees. The bike held up to flatbottom landings, rooftop drops, handrails, gaps, dirt, street, ditches, extreme weather conditions, name-calling, and giant ramps. I caused my body way more harm than my bike, and the rest of the prototypes held up, too. Midway through the testing phase, I made a couple of minor improvements and declared the design phase done. Time to see if the public would buy them.

Precision materials and craftsmanship came with a steep price tag, and I found out I couldn't afford to have Linn Kasten's shop do production. Mike Devitt of SE Racing saved the day. Mike was another old school BMX guy, and he'd been through the ups and downs of the industry with another legendary company, SE. Their machine shop could make a limited run of custom frame and fork sets. The condition was, I had to pay for half the batch up front, the other half on delivery. "Make me two hundred of these," I told Devitt and sent off the schematic for the Condor with a down payment check for $18,000.

A Batch of Trouble

With bikes on the way, I needed employees. Steve didn't even have to think about it—he was in. We set up offices in the Ninja Ramp warehouse, cobbling together desks and chairs from thrift stores. Steve and I both concurred we'd need a computer or we'd be dead in the water. We bought a new Apple II LC, 80 mhz with about eight megs of RAM, which was state-of-the-art 1992 hardware. As we pulled the Mac out of the box, neither one of us knew how to turn the thing on. I called Brad McDonald, publisher of the newly minted Ride magazine, who seemed to have his act together with computers and desktop publishing. Brad gave me a few phone tips, and Adobe Illustrator was installed. I stayed rooted in front of the screen for twenty hours a day, mousing and clicking, and two weeks later the first Hoffman Bikes product catalog was ready to take to Kinkos to get printed. While out in Los Angeles on a shoot for Dirt magazine, Spike snapped photos for the catalog for free (Spike, thanks again). Steve bought an accounting and inventory program, and he embarked on a crash course, teaching himself operational basics in a series of long nights. We were a company.

A couple months later, the UPS guy rolled up with a truckload of boxes and a big fat C.O.D. invoice. The first batch of Hoffman Condor frame and fork sets had arrived. It was a glorious day. Some were already earmarked as giveaways—I gave a few to deserving riders—but the bulk of the shipment was going to dealers. We stacked the bikes right next to the Ninja Ramp, polished them and slapped on the decals, then reboxed our booty and prepped our orders. In the time we'd waited for the payload of frames to arrive from the machine shop, Steve and I had worked the phones and faked our voices to sound older and more confident. We convinced a few shop owners around the country to carry our product line, which was a feat in itself considering the bleak bike market. Because of the manufacturing costs and high-quality materials, by the time the Condor frame and fork sets were hanging on bike shop walls, they cost around $350. At the time, a budget-minded shopper could pick up a generic, entry-level complete bicycle for around $200. But there were ample numbers of hardcore riders out there willing to shell out the clams, and by some miracle, we sold out of our first run of Condors in one month.

This cycle was repeated as fast as we could afford to rebuy another production run and get the machine shop to fabricate the next batch. It took about six months. In my opinion, that was too damn long to wait for a bike. I felt orders slipping away; I knew if I were a kid with a wad of cash in my pocket, I'd have a hard time waiting half a year to get a new bike. Another problem we had involved juggling the money—we'd bring in cash from doing demos or touring with the Sprocket Jockeys, but the semi literally burned cash every time we turned the key in the ignition. In addition, although most of our bike shop accounts were pretty honest, there were a few rubber check writers out there. Accumulating the down payment dough to set SE's machine shop into motion on our bikes involved a substantial amount of scraping, saving, truth-bending, and creative financing. A bank loan was out of the question—they wouldn't give me the time of day. I was a dropout with an eighth-grade education and no manufacturing experience. Furthering my anxiety, I had a feeling sometimes the SE guys would stop in the middle of a run and work on another company's production jobs. Delays eat into timelines, and it was frustrating. Steve and I knew from the interest we'd had with our bike shop accounts, we could sell everything we could make. We just had to supply the demand, pronto. My solution to this economic mayhem: Dig the hole even deeper.

Heavy Metal

I went to the Small Business Administration (SBA) and met a lady named Susan Urbach. I expected her to give the "you want to do what?" corporate laugh, but I thought I'd ask her advice about getting a manufacturing facility set up. She told me I needed a business plan, gave me some books, and told me how to put one together for her. I studied the materials, figured out what a business plan meant, and submitted mine to the SBA. It ended up securing us a $40,000 loan to get our operation up and running. We began checking out just how to buy all the machinery needed to start building bikes.

"Y'all want to start a machine shop, eh?" clucked the guy from the local vo-tech center. "How much money you got?" He sounded skeptical, eyeing our long hair and young faces. Steve and I relayed the good news, that we had forty grand. The guy, whom we'd come to for advice as a shop foreman, said there was no way to get all the equipment needed to cut, grind, weld, bend, drill, mill, and polish metal for forty. He said it was going to take two hundred and fifty grand, and that was for a no-frills machine shop. He chuckled again and suggested we come back when I'd saved up for another few years. I told him we had forty, so we'd just have to make that work. We thanked him for his time and bought a newspaper that contained classified ads for industrial equipment.

The critical step in our grand scheme was to lure a seasoned shop foreman to help us. There was a guy who fit the bill named Gack. He was from California and had training and technical skills in bike building. Gack was an accomplished rider, which was the main bonus as I looked over his résumé. We lured him out to Oklahoma, and with his help we sourced the tools and raw materials for our products. Through persistence and wild deal-making, we'd found all the machines we'd need to turn tubing into gold. The only machine we had to improvise on was the one that bent round tubing into an ovalized shape for the down tubes of our frames. The real version of the machine was tens of thousands of dollars. Steve, Gack, and I figured out how to get similar results using two flat steel plates and a car jack, carefully smashing the tubing until it looked oval. It was rigged to duplicate the same shape—we may have been sketchy, but dammit, we were consistent.

Within a year we quadrupled production capacity, paid back the loan, and won the SBA's Young Entrepreneur of the Year award. The machine shop became our lab, enabling us to tinker around with our designs to enhance performance at will. We built frames for flatland, dirt, and street, but perfecting designs one frame at a time was only part of the picture. We needed to crank out a prolific volume of product and do it in time to make the trade show dates and retail schedules of the industry. It was going to take manpower. If sourcing the right tools to form a machine shop was mildly traumatic, finding the folks to operate those tools was an ongoing nightmare.

The bulk of the work was not that technical, or dangerous. It was boring. Local journeymen and metal workers all wanted $25 an hour, even for repetitive tasks like pulling a lever three hundred times a day. That hourly rate was too spendy for us, so we turned to the only other option available—the unemployment office. We staffed up with a crew of ex-cons, slackers, sketchers, grifters, and various types of human driftwood. There was a high turnaround of employees, and we quickly discovered that a favorite scam of the terminally unemployed involved working for just long enough to collect benefits, then quitting for a relaxing vacation paid by the state. However, even the hassles associated with finding trustworthy employees were a piece of cake compared with the ongoing management issues we dealt with on a daily basis.

Polishing chrome-moly before it was chrome plated was the worst job in the building. Our resident expert was a salty-looking forty-year-old dude with dreadlocks. He was perpetually covered in a thick layer of dust from the polishing booth, but the guy was good at his job and never complained. He was on the rebound after a stint in prison, and you could tell he'd lived a grizzled life. I considered him one of our better employees—he showed up on time, put in a reasonably good effort each day, and he was entertaining. He constantly communicated in rhymes, and every sentence that flowed out of his mouth sparkled with the lyrical quality of a professional orator. His only flaw: The man was addicted to nicotine. I hated to come down on the guy, but after several months on the job his smoke breaks were getting longer and more frequent. It was beginning to cut into our production schedule, and a quarter of his day or more was spent on smoke breaks. I was informed to include a "yellow slip" in his pay envelope—which was the work performance evaluation paperwork that ensured if I had to let an employee go for work inadequacies, I didn't get stuck paying their unemployment benefits. The little yellow slip in this instance basically asked my polisher in a nice and professional way to cut down on the Camels and increase the work output. The guy got his paycheck and must have assumed we wanted to can him, or he really took his cigs seriously. He asked to borrow twenty dollars for a carton, which I loaned him, and then he said a rhyme and cha-cha-cha'ed out the door. We never saw him again.

On occasion, it was not a matter of keeping employees but getting rid of them. Once, I'd traded a pair of Airwalk shoes for a printout of a major manufacturer's entire customer database—about a hundred thousand names. The mailing list was huge, and valuable, but the info needed to be typed into a computer before we'd really be able to capitalize on it. Steve and I both sucked at typing, so we hired a temp to do our dirty work. She was an okay data entry person but terribly grouchy. She hated the fact that she was working in an environment of dodgy machinists and sweaty bikers and that the people giving the orders seemed to be young and goofy. To try to get her to lighten up a little and join the party, I utilized my favorite computer technology discovery—setting the control panel to play custom error messages instead of the standard *beep*. I turned the volume all the way up and recorded a message. The next morning everybody was treated to a speaker blasting swear words and curses every time she made a mistake. By the end of the day, she flipped out and stormed away.

The employee who usually made the most dramatic impression on everybody was Rocky. Rocky was our TIG welder, and he was a true craftsman. Every bead of every weld had to perfect. Physically, he was a sight: taller than an NBA forward, Rock weighed over two hundred and eighty pounds and sported long black hair and a bushy beard. He had been a Marine Corps demolitions expert in Vietnam but was discharged because even the Marines were spooked by Rocky's passion for blowing shit up. Between his size, his dubious background (he'd been shot in the back, for instance), and his fiery temper, Rocky could intimidate anybody. It was sometimes hard to muster up the guts to give him direct orders. He had a problem with authority, and he was also impulsive—I deduced this after he told me he spent $19,000 on stereo equipment, despite the fact he lived in a tiny, run-down bungalow. He also drove a car that cost about $300, in which he'd installed a single modification—a brand-new, chrome-plated chain-link steering wheel that cost $400. But for all his quirks, Rocky was a master at his job. He personally welded about half of the entire Hoffman Bikes product output between 1992 and 1997. Our other master welder was Nate Charlson—normal by comparison, but still an artist with the torch. Between Nate and Rocky, we rarely got back any warranty replacements.

With the machine shop up and running full speed, Steve and I realized the errors of our ways. Building our bikes in-house didn't solve the money-juggling problems; instead, we'd compounded the insanity. There were twenty-five full-time employees on payroll, plus rent, utilities, raw materials, shipping costs, and forklifts. The monthly overhead was gnarly. Our accounting books just didn't balance, and we were living shipment to shipment. We'd already maxed out our SBA loan, but we needed extra cash to grow the business. I figured out a way to approve ourselves for a high-interest loan: We stopped paying taxes for a few months. I didn't like bending the law, but it was either skip the taxes or shut down the business. We used the money we were supposed to give to the taxman to buy more tubing and materials, to hire more people, and to generate more income. I knew I'd have to square up with the IRS eventually, but I never would've guessed they made house calls. One afternoon the IRS agents showed up with guns and badges and demanded to see the company's records. Immediately. After an audit, the IRS informed us we were fined $18,000 in back taxes and penalties. By the time the bill was due, we'd made just enough profit to pay it off. We squeaked through a crucial fiscal year. Profit was an elusive leprechaun, and the little bastard seemed to be very afraid of bike riders.

Can-can lookback at Woodward.

Before he rocked the world as a video and film director, Spike Jonze was the master
of action photography. I love this photo.

Bar hop on the Secret Ninja Ramp. I bought that Haro off a friend for fifty bucks. I had stopped riding for Haro, and had just broken my PK Ripper, so this was all I could scrounge up at the time.

This is a great perspective of an aerial. This photo gives you a vert rider's perspective of what vert is about. Keep your eye on the coping.

This is the only photo I have of this grind. I was tempted to learn this trick to put the bash guard on my bike to the test.

This was on the Skyway tour in 1987 at the Powerhouse Bicycles shop. Every time I did no-footed can-cans, my back end just stayed vertical. It was scary as hell, but it makes for a good photo.

The Rockville BMX shows were always huge. Spike Jonze and Jeff Tremaine worked there at that time.

This was someplace in Torrance, California, by Spike's house. I was staying with him, and we'd go out every day and shoot random photos while riding.

Spike Jonze shot this for a fashion article for *Dirt* magazine. I used the vert ramp as my catwalk. Those shoes were the worst to ride in.

This shot looks like I'm doing a no-handed disaster, but it's actually a glimpse inside the heart of a no-handed 540, one of my signature tricks. I'm floating upward, twisting backward, and steering through the rotation using my hips. To make it out of the trick at this point, I've got to spin another 360 degrees, get my hands back on the grips, and bring the nose of the bike back down for reentry, straight onto the ramp.

They built a twenty-six-foot-tall roll-in at the newly designed Woodward ramp. After I was told about this I couldn't stop thinking about it. When I finally got there, I went straight from the car and rolled in to see what would happen. Since I didn't have any brakes, I just held on and blasted the first wall.

|| This was right after I learned this trick, the candy can-can (candybar, can-canned over the front of the bike). It was at the Colorado KOV, which was held in a baseball stadium. During this contest, the announcer, Kevin Martin, figured out how to access the scoreboard and gave me a new nickname in neon lights before each of my runs: THOR. Right after this shot, Spike strapped a camera on me and I took a picture from my view of an aerial that wound up on the cover of *Go* magazine.

// This ramp was in the backyard of a mansion in the San Diego area. Some kid's dad built it for him and spared no expense. The kid never rode. It was sad, but I was happy. Tailwhip with my legs kicked.

// My favorite lookdowns are the ones in which you kick the rear end of your bike past vertical, the opposite way of your air, before you pull it back. Like this.

This rail was right by the Edmond Bike Shop. This was the first big rail I ever slid.

// I originally tried this on the Hoffman Bikes Birdhouse Whoopass tour and slammed and blew out my tire. By the time I got it fixed it was too dark to attempt again. Two years later I finally got to try it again. I pulled it. The halfpipe is over-vert, so to avoid clipping the vert with your back wheel, you have to land on the last three feet of tranny, which is a pretty long, surgical drop.

// The Secret Ninja Ramp was where I lived, ate, slept, and rode. It was like a typical sixteen-year-old's bedroom, except instead of a bed there was a twenty-foot-wide vert ramp.

This was a toadstool shot on a backyard ramp in England.

I like this photo because it's right before I grab the pegs.
At this point, I have nothing touching the bike.

Superman seat grab. Woodward, 2000.

The greatest band in the world. Fugazi: Brendan; Joey; me, posing; Ian; and Guy.

Tomahawk at the Soul Bowl comp in Hermosa Beach.

Rocket Queen air. This trick, like a lot of my other variations, was conceived when the sport was at an all-time low.

Dream Team

he coolest aspect of building bikes is being able to enjoy them. When I was growing up and
ding for other companies, it was frustrating to submit suggestions to my sponsor about
roduct development or marketing and have them nod politely, with no intention of acting on
y input. If my forks broke and left me in a coma for a day, I had to deal with it as an
unavoidable occupational hazard" rather than a design flaw. With my name on the down
be, I made it a personal commitment to be a control freak about every facet of Hoffman
kes. Steve and I put together the best team we could hire. Part of it was for selfish rea-
ns—so we'd have awesome guys to ride with—but it was also for strategic reasons. The
st team meant we would also be getting the best input and could channel that
ainpower and creativity into top-notch products. When our rider Kevin Jones came up with
new head tube gusset design, we not only listened but acted. Gack came up with the idea
r oversized axles, and our core R&D team (Steve, Gack, Chad Herrington, and me) came up
ith the Super Fork. Today, all manufacturers' high-end bikes come with similar head tube
ssets, oversized axles, and forks that employ the same design as the Super Fork. An
tirely new set of industry standards were created by rider input.

rly on, we could barely afford to pay for products or get our team to events, let alone put
r riders on lucrative salaries. At first, the guys on my team got a good bike, a free place to
ay if they were in Oklahoma City, and a black leather jacket with Hoffman Bikes painted on
e back. When we lured Dave Mirra onto the team, we couldn't even afford to get him a new
cket, so I gave him my leather from the Swatch Impact tour and had it repainted with an
B logo. The black jackets were our armor against the corporate mentality.

When Jay Miron started riding for us, he abandoned his Canadian homeland and
oved to Oklahoma City. We rode together every day, pushing one another and pro-
essing. He pitched in around the offices, doing everything from working the phones
helping ship orders. Kevin Robinson was another kid who was one hundred percent
mmitted. He relocated from the East Coast to Oklahoma City for a year, just to help
t with our cause. That kind of teamwork made our operation more than a team—it
s a family. Over the years, Hoffman Bikes was fortunate enough to expand and got
e honor of sponsoring a ridiculously talented roster of ams and pros, such as Taj
helich, Simon Tabron, Ruben Alcantara, Evel Knievel, Rooftop Escamilla, Jay Miron,
ve Mirra, Psycho Hallford, Kevin Robinson, Butcher Kowalski, Day Smith, Rick Thorne,
ad Kagy, Seth Kimbrough, Kevin Jones, Chase Gouin, Pat Miller, Jimmy Walker, Mad Jon
ylor, Rob Sigaty, Brian Tunney, Leif Valin, Achim Kujawski, Daniel Randall, Edwaldo "The
" Terreros, and many others.

Full of BS

We were blind busy. Just keeping the UPS orders flowing out the door involved so mu[ch] work, my plate runneth over. Add the mayhem of operating a jacked-up semi truck and p[u]tting on Sprocket Jockeys fair shows around the country, plus whatever miscellane[ous] mission-critical projects that randomly popped up, like building giant ramps. I had no bu[si]ness taking on any other responsibilities.

"Shit, *we* should do a comp," I said to Steve. The bounty of contests had dried [up] and the sport was hurting for some action. Steve was equally as devoted and naïve [as] I was. So, at the same time we launched our bike company, we became contest promo[t]ers. Before we knew what we'd done, an advertisement was placed in one of the la[st] remaining freestyle magazines, calling all bicycle gladiators to come forth. Our conce[pt] to do a contest had steamrolled into a whole series of events, and while we were at [it,] we'd decided to rename the sport. Freestyle sounded dated and confusing. There w[as] freestyle skiing, freestyle swimming, freestyle rhyming, freestyle dog shows . . . the wo[rd] just didn't fit anymore. I proposed calling our activity BS, for Bicycle Stunts. I figure[d I] was full of BS and wanted to spread it across the land.

The motivating factor for holding a comp was not to decide who was the best, [or] keep track of winning or losing. The purpose was to gather with my friends and ce[le]brate who we were and what we did. A contest meant a place to exchange ideas and f[eel] like part of a community in which riders could groove on a sense of purpose and absc[rb] the energy generated when a mob of freaks gathered to go off. The riding was getti[ng] insane. A new jack hybrid style had emerged, demanding technical finesse and a ba[ll]to-the-wall approach. It was a mix of influences, blending trails, street, park, and ve[rt.]

The BS series made its debut at Jeff Phillips's skatepark in Dallas, Texas. I decid[ed] to call it "The Texas Chainwheel Massacre." Steve and I chose Phillips's park becaus[e it] was fairly close to Oklahoma City. I knew Jeff was easygoing and would let us hold [our] experiment there, and, most important, it was a good park. At the time, there j[ust] weren't many decent places with permanent ramps and park courses to ride.

When contest weekend rolled around, I was so sick I couldn't see straight. I ha[d a] fever of 103 degrees, was oozing poisonous sweat, and was unable to keep food do[wn.] Existing on pure nervous energy, I tried to stay focused on helping Steve handle en[try] fees, sign-ups, setting up our PA, recruiting capable judges, and getting the thing[s to] start on time. Occasionally a crisis erupted, like when Greg Guillotte transferred out [of] a ramp and landed on the roof of the pro shop. The thin fiberglass roof held up fo[r a] half second before Greg crashed through and took out the pro shop.

Between dramas and organizing duties, I lay shivering under a blanket in a germ-filled car. For the record, I have to credit the unsung heroes: The event would have never happened without the help of Dennis McCoy and Trend Bike Source, the hardcore mail-order company and long-time supporter of all things cool. At the last minute before the pro street finals, I got on my bike and hit the course. Literally. With my cloudy head I was seeing lines for new ways to use the park and pulling back-flips off everything. I envisioned pulling a flip over a spine ramp, and although it had never been done before, I was sure it was possible. In my second run, I tried a big flip over the spine and, despite being totally confident I could make it, was shocked when I landed with the coping in my guts. I took the full blow of the ramp's peak and heard the collective "Ooofh" of the crowd when I impacted. I lost my breath and spent a minute or two turning blue, unable to inhale.

The next day on the vert ramp I had my wind back and was feeling less ill. I turned out a couple strong runs: a 900, tabletop 540s, a flair, and a front-flip fly-out, flipping with my bike and landing on the deck, on my bike. At the end of a crazy weekend I found my fever had broken, the contest had come off successfully, and I'd won pro vert.

The first year of the BS series proved to be a logistical nightmare. But they were too much fun, and the experience of putting them on was the reward. We scheduled more contests, tried to up the prize money for pros, and with the help of an all-volunteer crew we took the grassroots series all over the country. In the second or third year of BS events, the rewards and reasons why we were even involved became clear.

The Kansas City BS comp was scheduled months in advance. It was planned to happen at the Big Red One Army Base, at the eighty-foot-wide halfpipe they had set up. About a month and half before the event I called to check in and make sure things were still on track. The military recreation department liaison told me the ramp had been taken down, and the location was off.

Dennis McCoy stepped in and said we could have the vert event at his house in the Kansas City suburbs, but we had to scramble to find an alternate location for the street course. Between our full-blown workload at HB, and having to build an entire park's worth of portable ramps and figure out how to get them to Kansas City, the clock was ticking at high speed. Several weeks of eighteen-hour days blurred by, until the day before the contest. I'd been booked in Europe for an appearance and flew direct to Oklahoma City from Budapest. With help from Mark Owen, our BS volunteer and crucial HB employee (he was the second guy I'd hired), we loaded up a caravan of U-Haul trucks and a flatbed trailer for the semi, which was stacked precariously with partially built park pieces. We drove to Kansas City, and the scene I found was comical. Steve was there with a skeleton crew. They were passed out on the vert ramp, tools still in hand, eyes open, and snoring. They'd been up for way too long, trying to get things ready. The lack of sleep had taken its toll—

but the work was nowhere near complete. We pulled a fifty-hour shift, some guys were up even longer, and with sign-up and start time just a few hours away, there were *still* ramps to be built.

As riders began to arrive for the event, things started happening that inspired us. Under the direction of Jay Miron, a crew of Canadians rolled up expecting to get in some early practice and found our bleary-eyed crew stumbling headlong into the work left to do. The Canucks didn't even ask if we needed help—they just grabbed hammers and started layering plywood. As more riders showed up, our participants came together and pitched in to make the contest reality. There were thirty guys helping to build the vert ramp, and another sixty putting nails and sawing the street park into place. It was madness. Nobody got much sleep, but it wound up being probably the best vert ramp, and maybe the most fun, I'd ever had at a contest. The field of pros was insane, and you could literally feel the caliber of riding had changed at that event. Three 900s were pulled, tons of tailwhips, double tailwhips, and I came close to making a triple. Dennis showed everybody what a barspin 5 looked like. Jay went off, and along with Dave Mirra, John Parker (the first time I'd ridden against him), Steve, Thorne…we had a huge pro class and everybody was ripping. In the end, it had transcended being just a contest. It was a brotherhood.

Business as Unusual

I went into business based on the different things I needed. I heard the word no about ten thousand times along the way, from people who didn't think it was possible for a guy with an eighth-grade education to accomplish whatever task was at hand. I discovered it's tough leading people, or even finding the right people who believe. I spent all the money I made keeping a dream alive and learned things about myself along the way. What more could I ask for?

Instead of labeling my work staff with traditional corporate lingo like CEO, CFO, Vice President, and more, I gave their job descriptions my own names, and in return, got the code name *HMFIC* from my staff. HMFIC is trucker speak. It stands for *Head Mother Fucker in Charge.* A bold and saucy business card title, but it was never something I'd planned.

The description sort of chose me, not the other way around.

EVERYTHING
MUST GO!
(ok... everything but, the helmet.)

HUGE
SAVINGS!
(we're not just
talking bikes
either...)

(weird?)

HIGH ENOUGH TO DIE

It all began with a phone call from Hollywood in 1990. A research intern from the *Stuntmasters* TV show wanted to know if I could jump my bike over three burning cars. Yeah, I told him, I could do that.

Within a few days, I was whisked to Los Angeles to film. The stunt coordinator was Roger Wells, better known by his motorcycle moniker, Johnny Airtime. Johnny was an accomplished stuntman with a flair for the technical. His repertoire included stuff like launching his motocross bike one hundred and fifty feet off a ramp and landing in the back of a speeding pickup truck going fifty-five miles per hour. He did another jump over a speeding train that smashed through his takeoff ramp a split second after he was airborne. Johnny had it down—he was a physics wizard and a demon in the air. He'd prep for his stunts by calculating all the various variables, factoring in height to weight ratios, G forces, speed, wind resistance, tire pressure, what he ate for breakfast. He had never broken a bone in his body.

The stunt I had to master didn't require much math; it was your basic pedal full speed, leave the ramp spinning (I'd decided to 360), and hang on tight. The distance was about thirty feet across, with a blind landing because of the smoke and intense heat from the burning cars. I was flown in a week early to practice and build up to the big leap. Within a few minutes of arriving on location, I was airing my bike over the ramp-to-ramp gap, having a good time. The producer saw what I was doing and called me over for a conference. He was worried that I wasn't experiencing enough difficulty clearing the jump. He explained the importance of a dramatic TV buildup to my test of fire. For the next four days I had to fake like I was having trouble clearing the distance, and also fake a lot of deep personal contemplation while being documented by a film crew. The set was stationed in a hot parking lot out in the San Fernando Valley with nothing much around. This was my first taste of Hollywood.

On stunt day, I had to be on the set first thing in the morning to be wrapped in fireproof Nomex clothing, and go over the jump one last time before we rolled film. I was supposed to look as serious and nervous as possible. Instead I was dazed and totally giddy. The location had been moved to a nearby site so they could film with a lake in the background. The runway was downhill. During the practice runs there were no cars, and when they parked the cars between the ramps for the real thing, it stretched the gap to about forty feet. It didn't seem as easy as it had earlier in the week. I was given a warm-up run before

the cars were ignited, and on my first try the producer got his wish—it got dramatic. I overrotated my spin during the 360 and crashed. My back wheel turned into a taco. I was tired as hell, and now, beat up.

I was watching the jump site from about one hundred and fifty feet away— three times the runway that I needed— but the director wanted a camera in a truck to follow the shot and get a close-up of my expression and intensity. They also put a microphone in my helmet. "Let's light the cars on fire!" said the director with nervous glee. With a demonic *whoosh* the cars burst into greasy flames, and I was given the cue to jump. I took my first cranks toward the target and started to chuckle. By the time I hit the ramp it was all-out laughter. There was a split second of terror as I twirled through the furnace, which I could feel even through the protective clothing. I landed the 360 perfect and touched down still cracking up. The host of the show rushed over with video cameras in tow, eager for a poststunt interview. The air was filled with the smell of burning tires and the sound of me laughing hysterically. I took a couple of seconds to compose myself, and I was greeted by the producer, who was chapped about my good humor ruining the dramatic tension of the moment, which made it even funnier to me.

The best thing that came out of the stunt, however, were the conversations I had with Johnny Airtime. We talked about something I'd dreamed of for years—a twenty-foot aerial on a bike. Airtime broke it down for me: The standard halfpipe height was a ten-foot-tall ramp with a foot of vert. Hitting that transition at full pump provided about thirty miles per hour of speed and created a vertical speed of about eighteen miles per hour. This put about two and a half Gs of gravitational force on my bike and body. On an eleven-foot ramp, I could get about thirteen feet over the coping. Airtime reasoned that by applying that same formula toward a larger transition at a greater speed, it would be approximately the same amount of G forces—the critical factor that determines the way the air feels. "Just build a twenty-foot-tall ramp and figure out how to hit it going sixty miles per hour, and bingo," Johnny said. "It'll feel about the same as airs on a twelve-foot ramp."

My mind was ablaze with possibilities as I boarded the return flight back to Oklahoma.

Notes of a Plywood Scientist

The stuff I know about riding, I learned one crash at a time. These are the things I have discovered by riding vert.

The secret is in the timing, the flow, and the rhythm. People mistakenly refer to vert riding as a very aggressive discipline. You have to be relaxed to truly flow on a ramp, and the only way to be relaxed enough is to build your confidence. It takes years of riding to master this game of staying physically loose in a very heightened mental state. Once you learn to flow, you start riding smooth and going higher. The higher you go, the more nervous you get, thus, the more relaxed you need to be because the more dangerous it becomes. If you want a new trick too badly, you can't have it. You have to possess the confidence you can already *do* a trick before you even try it, otherwise you'll be too stiff and probably wreck.

The goal is to land a fraction of an inch from the coping. That's a perfect air. You pump as you ride down the transition, milking it for all the speed you can. String a few walls' worth of perfect airs together and you go higher each time, the same way you pump to go higher on a swing set. If your wheels clip the top of the ramp on reentry, you're in for some pain. Hanging up or casing your back wheel on the coping will make you flip forward and dive into the bottom of the ramp headfirst. Usually you wake up with a flat tire. If you're paranoid about hanging up and pull out too far from the ramp during an aerial, you're also in trouble. Landing too low on the tranny or in the flatbottom causes you to lose all your speed. If you bottom out hard enough, you can break bones or bike parts. And finally, if you come in too vertical and land low on the transition, you flip over the bars onto your head, thrown into the flatbottom like a lawn dart. Some people call this one a dead sailor. It's notorious for knocking riders unconscious. Safety gear doesn't make a vert rider invincible, but it decreases the pain potential. I wear kneepads, elbow pads, a chest protector, knee or arm braces to protect past injuries from worsening, and, of course, a decent full-face helmet. After being knocked out a couple times wearing the same helmet, the foam becomes compressed and it needs to be replaced or it won't offer enough protection.

As time passes, you start to read ramps like a book. You drop in, and by the third wall you can draw a map in your mind of the ramp's sweet spots and weak points. On ramps with a lot of inconsistencies, it's always good to carry stickers and mark the danger zones to stay away from. It's tough to ride a freshly painted ramp because it throws your depth perception off. A ramp needs some color and light variance so that you can gauge your landings and when to pump. This is why sessions at sunset get more dangerous as the shadows start stretching across the transitions. Tire marks are the best footnotes for identifying lines, or just marking wear and tear.

Ramps can be built out of just about anything, and I've ridden the spectrum: Some were kinked death traps made of street signs and scrap wood; others were pieces of incredible art. The surface layer plays a huge factor in the ramp's character. Just as

James Brown knows what kind of wood a stage is made of by the way it feels when danced on, I can tell what I'm riding on by how it feels under my tires. Plywood is the most economical and one of the fastest surfaces. For skaters it's too choppy against polyurethane wheels, but rubber bike tires absorb the irregularities of plywood, and since it is hard, it's fast. Fast is good. A lot of European ramps are layered in Scandinavian birch plywood, which is the shit—seven layers thick and the hardest,

fastest ply you can get. Both skaters and bikers love Scandinavian birch. It makes you tingle when you ride it. The only problem is it's about sixty bucks a sheet, approximately five times more expensive than regular plywood. Birch plywood in the United States usually comes from Canada, and you have to settle for five-layered wood, with more filler, which is softer and slower.

Masonite is common in a lot of indoor ramp parks. It's not weather resistant at all. It warps and bubbles if it gets wet. A wet ramp is a slow ramp. Dry, indoor masonite also produces dust when ridden, making the surface slippery. There is typically a dust cloud over a park full of masonite. As a riding surface, masonite is smooth, and better for skaters. It's also softer than wood. Metal ramps are superfast but are also slippery when dusty. When the dew hits in the evening, the non-porous surface turns into greased lightning. The other downfall is that metal gets hot as hell in the sun. I've seen riders slam on metal and knock themselves out and then get third-degree burns because they cooked to the surface. For the modern era, I think Skatelite is the answer. It's got the best properties of plywood and masonite in one package: It's smooth, fast, durable, and not too slick.

Coping is an often-overlooked part of the ramp. The early bike ramps didn't have coping, so the sharp edges where the deck and transition joined were a leading cause of flat tires. The concept of coping, borrowed from skate ramps, helped reduce pinch flats. Coping also bonks your front tire out so you can time exactly when to pull up for your air. Different types include pool tile, mideighties-style PVC, and the good old two-inch-diameter black steel unthreaded pipe. The two-inch black steel has been the overall winner through the years. Galvanized steel is good and slick but grinds down eventually and gets tacky; then you have to wax it, or you'll screech to an abrupt halt on peg-to-coping contact. Steve Swope was the first bike rider to do peg grinds on coping, adapted from skateboarding. I was the second guy. When we learned to grind, we switched to metal coping. The ramp at the Paris KOV event in 1988 had the biggest coping I ever rode. It was close to six or eight inches in diameter and was impossible to get a flat on, no matter how hard you hung up.

Halfpipes have decks where the riders wait to drop in for their runs, or do platform or lip tricks. At big comps, there are a lot of distractions from the crowd on the areas of the deck closest to the stands. Decks with ladders or stairs mean lots of photographers and miscellaneous people can climb up top, so riders will also usually roost on the side only accessible by riding up and popping out. Decks are where you breathe, tune out the world, and stay focused on your bike.

The framing and foundation are the skeleton of a ramp. Everything has to fit together perfectly, be totally level, and solid. The less flex a ramp has, the quicker it rides The first quarterpipes required a couple people to stand behind the ramps and brace them, because these gems tended to slide backward when ridden. Ramps that are permanent structures are generally pretty solid and fast.

Temporary ramps built for demos or contests are sometimes assembled hastily or by inexperienced crews, and these can be a nightmare. I'll ride whatever, but it's frustrating as hell when people have come to see big airs and the ramp sucks. You just have to deal with it. It's like someone gave you a zebra instead of a bike and told you to bust an air.

I've been on a ramp where someone decided it would be a good idea to attach the two by six cross-braces (the backbone of the ramp) sideways. It flexed so badly the transitions absorbed most of my momentum, and it felt like it was layered in carpet. But the worst ramp I've ever ridden was a makeshift number for Club MTV. Downtown Julie Brown could have built it herself; from the broomstick coping, to lack of cross-bracing, to the abruptly kinked three-step transition. I think I could have bunnyhopped over it easier than pulling an air out of it. It was silly, and 100 percent MTV. By contrast, I've seen master ramp builder Tim Payne start with a pile of wood in the middle of Shanghai with seven Chinese guys who couldn't understand a word of English. We had a perfectly built vert halfpipe in seven hours. Don't ask me how.

Cement Sessions

Concrete is in a world of its own. It has no competition. Speed, character, durability, texture, and then some. It's what turns transitions into art. Unfortunately, it also takes a serious commitment to build a concrete riding environment. One of my first experiences riding concrete was a short session at the Upland Pipeline skatepark before it was bulldozed. It was dark and spooky, like a big hole. In the Combi Pool, it was an accomplishment to make it to the top and bonk your front tire on the coping. That half-day I spent there gave me a new respect for the skatepark-era riders and what it took to flow the way Eddie Fiola, Mike Dominguez, Brian Blyther, Hugo Gonzales, Jeff Carrol, and others rode 'em. It was nothing like a halfpipe. It's a whole different discipline.

The other way to ride cement is to steal your sessions. Backyard pools are fun, because the thrill of the hunt and temporary nature of your session factors in there. When my brother Travis got his pilot license we would rent a plane and fly around neighborhoods with a map and mark down everywhere we'd see an empty pool. Then we'd wait until the owners left for work, and we'd go ride it. We found a semiabandoned pool once that seemed especially ridable. We had to empty it, so we rented a water pump, drained it, and cleaned it out, animal carcasses and all. Within twenty-four hours a bunch of kids threw all the garbage back in, so we cleaned it all out again and rode it. The next day all our tools were gone from our secret stash spot, and the pool was completely filled in with dirt and leveled off. That was the last good local pool I rode.

A Massive Erection

In the weeks following the Stuntmasters shenanigans, Airtime's advice about bigger transitions was still ringing in my head. I did some calculations of my own and didn't like the way things were adding up. The building materials needed to construct a twenty-foot ramp would cost about $7,000, even if I stuck to a slim budget. I didn't have that kind of cash laying around, especially with the Peterbilt money pit. But Rick Thorne said he had a friend who wanted a Haro frame. A friend who happened to work at a lumber store and was willing to make a shady deal. A few days later, I tested the black market value of a red Haro frame and fork set I had left over from my old sponsor. I rented a U-Haul trailer (the semi was broken) and drove to a Kansas City lumberyard. The scam was, I paid for my order up front, and the crew in the back would load it up for me. (The loading zone guys all rode.) I purchased one 2x4 for four dollars, and the clerk told me to pick up my order at the loading dock. A squad of smiling bikers piled it high with sheet after sheet of 4x8 plywood, hundreds of 2x4s, 2x6s, and 4x4s. It was enough wood to build a house. The weight of the lumber made the trailer droop.

Steve and I had never gotten into anything this big before. We'd built a few ramps in our time, and Steve had worked a couple jobs as a carpenter's helper, but this was new territory. We cut the first transition, a twenty-foot radius with a foot of vert, and wrestled it upright to check out the standing height of our baby. "Holy shit!" screamed Steve. "That's taller than a telephone pole, Mat." He sounded real nervous. I took one look at it and began laughing uncontrollably, like a little kid on Christmas morning.

The ramp put up a fight, but it started coming together piece by piece, day by day. Steve and I built it near my dad's warehouse on an unused section of the property. The back of the ramp was at the edge of a landfill that had been a dumping ground for scrap iron, cinderblocks, and industrial junk. It was also where the office septic tank seeped into the ground. We cracked it when we were using the bulldozer to level out the area where the ramp sat and the whole area smelled like shit.

We'd spend a few hours each night after work nailing and framing. It was the middle of winter and constantly wet, windy, and cold. The ice-crusted ground gave us a stubborn battle as we dug holes for the four-by-four support pillars, which would provide a solid foundation. The building project took over a month, consuming most of my energy and thoughts. Finally the day arrived when we were hanging off the back of the ramp mounting the last of the decking—minutes from completion. It was pitch dark, twenty degrees, and sleeting, but Steve and I were focused on finishing. Everything was starting to ice up. To reach the top, we had stacked up three sets of scaffolds, and on the uppermost platform we had to put a few cinderblocks and a plank to make an even taller workstation. On the top of that was a chair, which is where I stood. Steve was on the scaffolding, bracing my legs as I whacked away with a framing hammer, trying to get the last sheet of plywood secure without falling thirty feet off the back of the ramp. Steve was so pissed at me. He thought we were being stupid and one of us was going to fall. But I was superdetermined, and he stayed out of obligation. I probably should have listened to him, but I was beyond reason.

I felt a deep sense of accomplishment when I finally stuck the last nail in the wooden beast. Steve and I built a twenty-foot-wide, twenty-one-foot-tall quarterpipe—the biggest quarterpipe ever made. It was time to air it.

Mission: Possible

I had to put aside everything I knew about ramps and treat it like a new form of riding. My main concern was if my body could take the G forces when entering the ramp with a sixty-mile-per-hour approach speed. For the first attempts at the ramp, I was towed while holding onto a pickup truck, but the truck couldn't get up to speed quick enough. Then some guy on a Honda street bike stopped by to see what the hell we were doing. I convinced him to tow me down the dirt path toward the ramp. On my first air, I cleared my previous record of four-teen feet by a foot. I went out looking for a motorcycle to tow me. That same week I found out I'd won "Freestyler of the Year" award by BMX Plus! *magazine. The prize was a motor-cycle. It was pretty slow street bike. I had it shipped to a local motorcycle shop in Oklahoma City and traded it in for the fastest used dirt bike I could get, a KDX 200. I held a ski rope with one hand and steered my bike with the other as Steve towed me down a two-hundred-yard plywood sidewalk. This process sent me flying out of the quarterpipe over twenty feet.*

It felt amazing. The airtime was several seconds of climbing, an exaggerated sensation of stalling out, then reentry. At the peak of my airs I was more than forty feet off the ground, higher than anyone had ever gone on a bicycle. On a normal ramp, at the apex of an air I can see the coping and adjust myself accordingly. On the big ramp, I was too high to see the coping clearly, and my perspective had changed dramatically. I could see the entire building, people on the ground, behind the ramp—stuff that you'd never notice riding a small ramp. It's a pretty crazy feeling at first. I painted logos on the center of the transition, which became the target to aim for.

Wind was a wild card I had no control over, and the higher I went, the more susceptible I was to being bullied around by air currents. It was a guessing game trying to counteract it, and eventually we started flying a flag on the deck as a wind gauge. The power of the forces at work made themselves apparent one day when I hung up my back wheel on reentry from twenty-one feet out. I was going so fast when I clipped the coping, it ripped the tire off my wheel and wrecked my rim. Luckily I didn't get hurt, but that was the tipping point for me—the moment it sunk in how serious it was. The impact speed was unreal. Bailing from the twenty-foot range (over forty feet off the ground) had major consequences, which I would soon learn. The fat trannies made it a bit less scary because their huge radius helped absorb some of the velocity, but when I did crash, I'd hit and continue skipping and bouncing across the ground for a long ways, like a puppet hucked out of a car at freeway speed.

We kept a lid on the big airs and took some photos for an HB ad. My sister, Gina, shot it. She used my mother's old camera as a tribute to mom's strength and passion for life, art, and following your heart. My heart had led me there, in a field with a few friends, testing the boundaries of everything I knew I could do, and what I dreamed I could do. The shot we picked was a boned-out aerial, twenty-one feet over coping, forty-two feet off the ground.

When the ad debuted in the June 1992 issue of *Ride* magazine, there were people who didn't believe it. Even though I had a reputation for doing high airs, I was also notorious for having a goofy sense of humor. Powerful desktop software like Photoshop had started gaining popularity in print, and eye-popping computerized effects were the latest rage in music videos and movies. The skeptics who saw the ad were critical of digital hoaxes and had a pretty strong argument: What kind of idiot would actually build a twenty-one-foot-tall quarterpipe?

The last thing I needed was to ride that thing in front of a lot of people, under pressure. It was enough of a head-trip just facing the big ramp. I wanted to ride it for myself, by myself, when the time was right. If I had some fire in me that day, I could go get it out by riding the ramp, but it took Steve to pull me. I could talk him into it, and trusted him with my life, but knew that he didn't always like what he was doing. He didn't want it on his conscience that he'd towed me toward my own demise. I decided to build a ramp I wouldn't have to rely on anyone to ride. I began plans to turn the quarterpipe into a halfpipe.

It took two years of planning and saving before construction on the world's tallest halfpipe was nearly finished. To pump a twenty-foot-tall tranny, I'd need speed. Tons of it. Without motorcycle assistance, the next best thing would be a giant roll-in, like the takeoff for a ski jump. I went with a forty-six-foot-tall platform that shot me into the ramp at a sixty-degree angle. The halfpipe took two months to build and, like its predecessor, was also a winter construction project. One night when I was close to completion, I could see the proverbial light at the end of the tunnel. I was out there alone. It was mid-January and just after midnight. All I had to do was get the first layer of plywood on the roll-in. I didn't have a deck built on that side of the ramp yet, and the roll-in connected to the roof of my old warehouse. I made my way up the roll-in, laying down one piece of ply at a time. I'd nail a short block of two by four sideways into the transition, to act as a step, while I attached the next piece of plywood up the ramp. Finally I'd gotten every sheet on except the last piece, which needed to bend sharply at the top of the roll-in. As I tried to get the plywood properly positioned, it popped off and began tipping sideways. I got out of the way and watched it slide down the ramp. The wood acted like a wedge, knifing under the top block of my wooden stairway to heaven. The block popped out with a chunking sound, then the sheet dropped down to the next step. Cachunk! And the next . . . chunk! Chunk! Chunk! Cachunk! Chunkchucnkchunkchunk! I stood at the top of the roll-in and stared down at nothing but nails sticking out where the blocks had been. It looked like a runway of golf spikes, all the way down the sixty-degree wooden slope. I sat there for a while, dazed and thinking how in the hell something like that could happen with such flawless, total destruction. Then it dawned on me that I was stuck at the top of a forty-six-foot-tall structure and the only way down was to slide through a field of nails. I could wait until morning, when people would show up for work, and they could get me down. That was in eight hours.

Twenty minutes passed, and I was freezing. It was windy, and I'd stopped working, so my body temperature was dropping. I knew I'd be a Popsicle if I waited much longer. I stood there, no foot planks, looking down the barrel of the roll-in until I felt the *Geronimo!* instinct kick in. Because of the cold, I had on superthick Carharrt workpants and four layers of clothes, I went down the slide and the nails ripped my clothes to shreds. I got to the bottom, breathing fast, pant legs in tatters, and thought, "All right, we'll call that a night."

When the ramp was all finished, I stood on top of the roll-in with my bike. I could clearly see downtown Oklahoma City, ten miles away. The halfpipe resembled a giant boat. The stomach-floating effect of taking the roll-in was the same sensation as bungee jumping. I could drop in and clear eighteen feet on the first wall.

The only problem was, my bike was too small—the wheel base was three feet, and the twenty-inch wheels would quickly reach their maximum velocity. After my first air, the transitions would slowly bleed my speed no matter how much energy I put into pumping the walls. I went from eighteen feet, to fifteen feet, to thirteen feet. I'd need another solution besides the roll-in.

Operation Weedeater

People sometimes ask me how I can stand living in Oklahoma, when the riding scenes seem to thrive in other places like California, Texas, or pockets of the East Coast. I've always let the space in my brain exist as its own environment. My body might be in Oklahoma, but my mind's been someplace else the whole time. I've never really needed to subscribe to another social circle. I always had a ramp, I had a family, and I had weird projects running around in my head. All I need is a place to let them out. Oklahoma has been the cheapest laboratory I could find. For the record, Oklahoma is also probably the best place in the entire world to convert a bike to run on a reverse-engineered weedeater engine. Nobody involved ever questioned the ridiculousness of it. The general attitude was, "Yeah, that sounds cool, man. Let's get it on." After some research into various motor types, I bought the biggest weedeater I could get. My friend John owned Road and Track, a local performance motorcycle shop. With John's help, I repositioned the points so the little engine would run backward, driving my rear sprocket. We machined a drive shaft for it, welded motor mounts to the frame, and duct taped the gas tank on. I had to use a tiny 13-tooth sprocket on my front, and a 122-tooth freewheel. There was no chain, so I tightened my cranks and pedals in place. We set up the throttle cable through my Gyro, so I could spin the bars and keep the throttle cable from tangling. After completion, I'd set up on the roll-in, grab the throttle and dive into the ramp with the engine whining at seventy-two hundred rotations per minute, full speed. The first airs were in the nineteen- to twenty-foot range. The bike had a weird gyroscopic effect in the air, and the engine, fuel, and extra metal on board put the center of gravity way off to one side. My back end would lag every time. It's also weird getting used to the timing of a bike that doesn't naturally decelerate; I'd reenter the ramp with the throttle fully cranked and have to let off before the opposite wall. What I was doing lost a lot of the elements an aerial has; on normal twelve-foot airs you can look over your shoulder and see the coping as you start steering the bike toward reentry. On twenty-foot plus airs, I would go fast and launch straight up like a missile, and try to turn around after I'd slowed down at the peak height. I had to wait until the bike has stopped upward momentum, and if my timing was off, I didn't turn. I fell.

It took a few sessions, but I got used to it, and began working up until I was clocking airs in the twenty-three- and twenty-four-foot range. Then *MTV Sports* called and asked if I was working on anything new.

Crash and Learn

Maybe it was karma's way of getting back at me for taking advantage of the deal on heavily discounted wood in Kansas City, but the bill was about to arrive. MTV sent a skeleton crew of two guys, a producer/sound operator, and a camera man. They were in town for only two days. The first day was too windy to get high airs, and the next day it was gusting about twelve miles per hour. Any wind speed above five miles per hour made it really difficult to ride the big ramp because the higher altitude seemed to magnify the wind many times over. Having a weird bike with a weedeater engine didn't make it easier. But I wanted to show them what I could do on the thing, and so I rode anyway. We taped for a few minutes, and the airs were getting higher, consistently over twenty feet. Then I missed my timing on one and didn't rotate enough. I went from rocket to rock.

I tried to keep my head from hitting the ramp and took the force of the blow with my ribs. I saw stars, but didn't get KOed. Sometimes when you hit that hard your body just starts throbbing, but you can't really diagnose what's wrong. You have to chill out and let everything settle down and figure out if you need to go to the hospital. I got up and walked it off, pretty shaken, and went inside the warehouse to relax a little bit.

We watched the crash on video, and it didn't look that bad. I knew I'd slammed harder, even on smaller ramps. This was a smack-n-slide crash. My midsection got it pretty good, but I also caught quite a bit of the fat transition, which helped lessen the impact. What I didn't know was what was happening inside my body. I'd been beating on my spleen all year, taking crashes in shows and practices. The organ was in a constantly swollen state, and the impact from over twenty feet was enough to burst it. We were still talking about filming more high airs when I noticed my collarbones began to ache. I hadn't taken much of the fall on my arms or shoulders, and I couldn't figure out why they were throbbing. It was pressure from blood hemorrhaging inside my abdominal cavity. Before long I began to get dizzy. On the way to the water cooler, I leaned against a wall for balance, and the floor rushed up to greet me. Steve, my girlfriend Jaci, and the film crew knew this was not a good sign. I was only out for a few seconds, because as soon as my body got in a horizontal position my heart could generate enough pressure to get blood moving to my head.

The paramedics were called, and a few minutes later, when they arrived, I was worse. I'd passed out again from trying to stand up, and people were starting to get that crisis situation panic about them. The paramedic put a blood pressure cuff on me and took my pulse. He said it didn't register but told me not to worry because his medical gear had been malfunctioning earlier. Steve asked about internal injuries, and the paramedic told him I'd have bruising and discoloration, from the blood pooling inside. I didn't. As I lay flat on my back, the medic tried his blood pressure cuff and got a weak pulse. I didn't have $500 for the ride to the hospital, and my health insurance was a shake of the dice, regarding what they'd cover and what they wouldn't. We told the ambulance to go away, and Steve and Jaci brought me in.

You turn into a mumbling, happy fool when you are about to die. And you don't care. The human body is amazing the way it heals itself, reacts to trauma, or prepares to shut down. Your pituitary gland unleashes a flood of endorphins, which takes the edge off anything and calms you down. Pain, stress, and fear start to melt away. "I need my keys," I slurred to Steve as they tried to get me in the backseat of the car. "Don't let me forget my keys." I was talking gibberish; what I needed was a surgeon. En route to the hospital I was mad because Jaci wouldn't let me go to sleep. The ER doctor examined me and told Steve I'd need an emergency spleenectomy to save my life. Inside, my ruined spleen was leaking massive amounts of blood—I had lost four pints. He said another twenty minutes and I wouldn't make it.

A spleenectomy is one of the crazier abdominal surgical procedures. The doctors remove all thirty-something feet of your intestines and put them in a bowl next to you while they mop up the blood and remove chunks of broken spleen floating around inside you. Your spleen produces white blood cells, which helps your immune system fight off infections. But it's also somewhat of a bonus organ. Your body doesn't need a spleen to keep on living. After the ruptured spleen is cleaned out, the doctors check your intestines for holes by hand, like looking for a flat tire in a bike inner tube. The surgery takes a couple hours, and the recovery time is pretty fast thanks to modern medical techniques.

The first thing I saw when I woke up was the MTV producer. I'd just had my colon fondled from the inside, could barely open my eyes, my brain was spaced out on anesthesia, and my whole torso was throbbing from the trauma. "Hey, Mat. I know this is a bad time, but, could you sign this, ah, liability release form for us?" I couldn't even hold a pen. I tried waving him off by mumbling that I accepted full responsibility and would never sue anybody for something I did on my own. He said his job was on the line, because he'd forgotten to get a signature before we started filming. I signed the paper and haven't worked with MTV or attended any of their sporting events since.

A Big Ramp Inside

We all want something nobody can take away. A personal mark that stands for a time when you did your best. I believe this desire is inside everyone. It's there the day you are born— your true calling. It takes experiencing life to reveal that purpose. You have to realize your potential, then challenge it. You must give everything you've got to get there. If it were easy, it wouldn't mean so much. By accepting whatever consequences may arise, you're free from having to worry about getting validation from others, or permission. Approval or failures don't matter. All that matters is that you pursue what you have inside you. Once you're on that mental plane, anything is possible.

I knew my mission was to go higher than anyone. I was willing to break rules, break convention, break my bank account, my body, and whatever else it would take to reach that place. I had already gone about fourteen feet out of a ramp, but I felt there was more. I listened to people who told me a twenty-foot aerial was impossible, and then I listened to my heart tell me that without challenge to what is known, there is no progress.

My true calling manifested itself as a twenty-one-foot-tall ramp. Everybody has some form of big ramp inside them, waiting to come out.

What's yours?

ADDICTED TO AIR

There's one last chapter to the twenty-one-foot quarterpipe saga. We were putting on a BS contest on Labor Day in 1994. Mat's shoulder was really screwed up at the time, and he was going in for surgery just days after the contest. Mat had never ridden the big ramp in front of crowds, and even within the community of hardcore bike riders, a lot of them just straight out thought it was fake. The BS contest was at the Hoffman Bikes park. Mat had a friend of ours with a tow truck drag half of the twenty-one-foot halfpipe over to an area where Mat could set up a runway. The ramp wasn't set into the ground with a solid foundation. It was totally rigged. At the contest, there were some skeptics who came just to see if it was real or not. It had been a year since he lost his spleen, but Mat wanted to ride and prove it was possible to crack twenty feet. On Saturday it was a really nice day with no wind at all, and he did a couple of no-handers and some very high airs on it, over twenty feet. Mat decided he could top it and declared Saturday was the warm-up day, and Sunday he wanted to fire off some huge airs. I was the guy in charge of towing him on the motorcycle.

After he got warmed up on Sunday, he turned to me and said, "Steve, go *as fast as you can.*" I knew there was a good chance he could die if he crashed from that height, but Mat was so fixated on it that I said, "Screw it. If we're doing it, we're doing it." I laid on the throttle and went as fast as I could.

He went twenty-three or twenty-four feet high, beating his previous height and blowing everybody's minds.

After that day, Mat got his shoulder surgery and later went out of town. While he was gone, a windstorm came and knocked the remaining pieces of the big ramps down. They were the only structures in the Hoffman Bikes park that were damaged.
—STEVE SWOPE, FRIEND AND BUSINESS PARTNER

new transitions

NEW TRANSITIONS

She was pretty. I was shy. Love is stupid. It hits you like a blunt object and converts the rational mind into emotional mush. And the beautiful part about it is, you don't even care because it feels so awesome.

Jaci worked in a store. I came in Christmas shopping and there she was, looking kinda bored, but with a spark in her smile. I wanted to ask her out on the spot, and at the last second, I choked. I left, kicking myself all the way home. I returned the next day and bought a pair of sunglasses, just so I could interact with her again (and ask her out). She floored me and put me in a state of heart-pounding, rubber-legged confusion. We chatted for a minute, but I seized up once again. I forgot the sunglasses and exited without her digits or a date.

Within twenty-four hours I'd mustered up the nerve to march back in and be direct. This time I emerged with her phone number and plans to rendezvous, Edmond style: I was taking her to Braum's, my ice cream connection. Our first date went well. I impressed her with my vast knowledge of toppings, nuts, and flavor selection, but she was fronting slightly and ordered a low-fat sandwich instead of caving in to the decadence of pure sugar. I got a big brown shake, but I was fronting, too—what I really wanted was a kiss, yet didn't have it in me to ask. Our date wound down to that awkward little parting moment, and either she read my mind, or she wanted a taste of my shake. Jaci leaned over and gave me a smack on the lips. As she drew away, she said—and I'll never forget this—"*Mmmm, chocolate.*"

That's my girl.

When Jaci was younger she'd been part of the punk rock scene. We'd even briefly met, when I was twelve and she was fifteen. But in the years that had passed, she'd dropped out and joined a circle of folks who were even weirder than the punks: She was a professional ballet dancer. Jaci had passion, poise, and sophistication. On our second date, I asked her to accompany me for some fine dining and the theater. We met up with Steve and six other bikers for greaseburgers and meat-based humor. Then, we took in the evening's entertainment, the Charlie Sheen classic *Hot Shots, Part Deux*. The movie was a total cringe-fest, but with the Sprocket Jockeys cracking jokes throughout the film, Jaci had a good time. Date number three was a party at my house,

and Jaci was the lone girl amid a roomful of loudmouthed dudes in sweaty T-shirts, bingeing on giant Costco-sized boxes of Ding-Dongs and Fritos. But I knew how to show Jaci I had some class. I cracked open a bottle of champagne for us to share, and at the sound of the cork, the Sprocket Jockeys posse all began yawning and checking their watches, leaving us alone. It was almost as if they'd been waiting for a signal.

She was the one. After seeing each other for a couple of months, my soul mate radar was lighting up, big time. Historically, my track record with girlfriends was the same—whenever things got too deep or complicated, I hit the "eject" switch. But this time was different. I was crazy about Jaci. I could see the cute house with the white picket fence, the 2.5 kids, the fancy little soaps in the potpourri basket in the bathroom. The more time we spent together, the closer we became. Jaci was the first person I'd been able to open up to since my mom had passed away. She helped defrost my heart, and I was finally able to be happy inside again. Everything was going great . . . and then I got jacked: Jaci was asked to dance for the Ballet Mississippi. She'd be gone for several months. I knew better than to try talking her out of it, because she was as passionate about dance as I was about bikes. In fact, that was part of the reason we got along so well. Despite the surface differences between bikes and ballet, the two activities shared a similarity at their core: Each attracted a certain type of totally committed freak who was determined to find the balance between mental and physical worlds. Jaci's move to

Mississippi was a great opportunity, one she couldn't pass up. The downside: Between her schedule and mine, we were looking at months of separation. Rather than break off our relationship, though, we decided to stay a couple, distance be damned.

I visited Jaci a few times while she was dancing with the ballet company. I'd go out and ride the streets of Jackson, toting a Polaroid camera with me to take photos of the handrails I was trying to slide. I would place a picture at the bottom of the rail. My technology was simple: If I fell and got knocked out, I'd come to and see the photo there to remind me who I was, and why I'd woken up lying in the street next to a bicycle.

The King of KOs

I was starting to have a real problem with getting knocked out. After I learned 900s, I put it on my to-do list, once a week. Then it became once a session. On vert, you can't get more gnarly than a 9. It's pure commitment, and if you fail, you take the brunt of the impact with your head and shoulder. You know there's only a fifty-fifty chance you'll make it, but you have to convince yourself to try 100 percent. The more 9's I spun, the more frequently I found myself waking up in the flatbottom.

I suffered a serious incident with a 900 at the BS contest in San Jose, California, in 1992. I was the last rider in the final class of the weekend, pro vert. It was the closing trick of my last run, and I rolled in focused on firing off a 9. I didn't make the spin, came in backward and sideways, and channeled the full momentum of my upper body into the flatbottom. I spanked the ramp with my head and knocked myself out, bad. The contest energy in the building came to a grinding halt. The music shut off, replaced by an uneasy lull as everybody wondered what just happened. As Steve later put it, "we watched Superman fall out of the sky and get knocked out cold."

My friends brought me around, trying to make sure I was okay. I came to amid the confusion of the contest environment and couldn't remember who I was, why I was there. I'd lost all my recall, and the first thought to return was the most powerful memory—that my mom had died. Totally out of it and in a concussion daze, I broke down and started crying. In my mind, the scars reopened, and I had to again go through the most terrible thing that had ever happened to me. Riders were milling around to find out what was up, if I was okay. I couldn't grasp the concept that it was *my* contest, and I was in charge. People wanted to know what the scores were for the finals. Until the results were tallied, nobody could get paid or know who won. I was being asked questions I had no idea how to answer. "Somebody go find Wilkerson," I said, half-sure we were at a King of Vert comp and the year was 1988. Thank goodness the riders on the scene were understanding enough while I got my wits back. The incident really freaked me out, and for a long time thereafter the first thing I would try to remember when I came to after knocking myself out was, *Don't try to remember anything.* Steve, Chuck D, and the BS contest crew had their work cut out for them that day, taking care of me, trying to maintain control of the event, and closing things down afterward.

Broke and Broken

Dennis McCoy has had an excess of success during his career for being consistently one of the best overall riders—a true testament to his riding skills. Dennis was the first guy to rule ground, street, and vert all at the same time.

Dennis and I both got the same stamps in our passports three times during a six-month span in 1992. First, at the World Championships in Budapest, Hungary. It was there that he took the worst slam I've ever seen anyone suffer. He slammed a flair and his body bounced at least one foot off the flatbottom after the impact. I joked with him later that it looked like he was trying to do a loop on the halfpipe and reenter down the opposite transition. He somehow got up under his own power, but later at the hospital it was discovered he'd broken his back. During my run I got a flat tire and had to borrow his bike. It was so small and set up so weird I could barely ride. Getting on a strange bike and having to adapt as you roll into a ramp is like trying to do cartwheels through a car wash holding a watermelon: It's awkward. Using Dennis's Mongoose, I dropped in and aired a couple feet out feeling incredibly dangerous. I got a pump off the wall and threw a no-handed 540, half-expecting to go down in flames. I pulled it by some mystery, linked a couple more tricks in my run, and decided it was best not to question that miracle. I ended up winning the contest, and as an odd bonus I was declared the world champion of mini ramps.

Our next overseas travel adventure was the Rider Cup in England. The Cup was one of the first contests to blend skate and bike events together under one roof, with a street course and vert ramp. Riders and skaters from all over the world were there. It was a bad contest for me for a couple of reasons. First, it started out bad—I'd blown up the transmission in my car on the way to the airport. But by the time I'd arrived in England, I was ready to work out some tension. I found the vert ramp to my liking and was quickly clocking airs fourteen feet out, doing high tailwhips, 540 variations, and keeping my legs busy kicking through, around, and over my bike. My runs were interrupted by a steady stream of shoulder-shearing slams, flat tires, and more bike borrowing. At the end of the day I took myself out for good with a flair to chainring hang-up—I pitched forward into the flatbottom and stuck out my arms to break my fall. Bad move. I didn't know it at the time, but I'd completely torn the rotator cuff and inherited arm and shoulder problems forever. I'd already had one surgery to repair my right rotator cuff, so I had a sinking feeling I was in for some more time under the knife.

The other pain was the promoter of the event. He'd stiffed me the last time I was flown over to England to do a demo, and he fed me the same "I'll mail your check" promise this time. I told him I needed cash before I got on the plane, or I wasn't leaving. "There are no ATMs at this airport," he pleaded, trying to brush me off. I got very firm with the guy and informed him I would be staying at his house, on his couch, eating his food, and using his telephone until I was paid my $1,500. That did the trick. I got my money and hopped my flight with a throbbing arm. On the eight-hour flight over the Atlantic, I was bored and sitting by myself in coach class. I put on the headphones as they started the in-flight TV service, and a documentary film came on called *High Five*. I vaguely recognized the host, and while I tried to figure out where I'd seen the guy before . . . *shit* . . . video footage from the Ninja Ramp flashed across the TV screen, and I did a stretched no-handed air. The thirty-minute documentary was about *me*. I eased down low in my seat and peeked around to check the other passengers watching TV. Nobody knew, noticed, or cared that I was sitting there in seat 43A. I stayed ducked down and watched the film with mix of mild embarrassment (hoping nobody recognized me) and a stoked sort of fascination.

After such a strange and taxing trip, it felt good to be back home and in Jaci's waiting arms. My schedule didn't allow us much time together, though; I was booked to do another European demo with Dennis, this time in Germany. I couldn't cancel it, because I needed the money to pay for my shoulder surgery. I rigged up an arm brace, bags were packed, and a few days later I met Dennis in Munster. We were the half-time entertainment for the Eleventh Annual Munster Monster Mastership, one of the biggest and longest-running skateboarding contests in the world. Nearly all the top contenders in skateboarding were on hand, and I was looking forward to showing them how bike riding had progressed since my demo there the previous year. The halfpipe was insanely great, one of the smoothest and fastest ramps I'd ever ridden. It had been varnished with some supersmooth, superstinky toxic lacquer, which made the arena smell like nail salon fumes. It gave you a headache just being in the building. The promoter wanted to make sure we didn't gouge up the vert ramp before the skateboarding championship contest, so Dennis and I were told to do a demo on the street course. There were several thousand people watching us. Since backflips were still pretty new, I wanted to bust a few in our demo, including my newest invention, a tailwhip backflip. I saved the tailwhip flip for the finale. Dennis and I decided to launch from the box jump in 1–2 formation and both pull flips. We raced across the arena toward the box and hit the lip. I spun my tailwhip flip and Dennis did a regular flip. We landed to the sound of thousands of people totally losing it. It sounded like a riot in progress. The halfpipe decks were packed with skaters and spectators, who began pounding boards and fists, and stomping their feet on the plywood. Without warning, the entire halfpipe collapsed from the stress of the stomping. One second it was there, the next instant it had imploded in a cloud of screams and splintered wood. I saw some guy leap off the back of the deck and grab a World Industries banner that was suspended from the ceiling, and swing to safety holding on, like Tarzan. The fire marshal of Munster showed up and declared the area a disaster zone. Fourteen people were sent to the hospital with broken bones, cuts, and bruises, and the vert contest was canceled.

Munster is an awesome city for bike rides—they've built mini freeway systems

with twin lanes and overpasses specially for bicycles. Dennis and I took advantage of it and went out street riding all night, so we could board our plane the next day and sleep through the entire flight home. We rode, explored, and sessioned Munster after midnight. Around four in the morning it started raining, so we took shelter in a covered bus stop. The morning newspapers had just been delivered, and we sat down on a stack to rest our bones and discuss the wild events of the demo. "Do you think they'll invite us back to another one of these contests?" I wondered aloud. Dennis pointed to the front page of the newspapers—the bold headline said stuff in German, with the word "HALF PIPE." We could make out our names. There was a photo of a bloody fan being hauled out of the skate contest arena on a stretcher. Whoops.

I returned home and gave Jaci a sore-shouldered hug, and a couple days later went in to have my rotator cuff repaired and my bank account cleaned out.

German Voodoo

I think the Munster event started a streak of German voodoo, because I began to have bad luck whenever I was in the country. A few months after Munster, I returned to Germany for a demo at an event called Sub Culture. I thought it would be an in-and-out show. The ramp had different ideas. I fell during practice the day before the demo, and my weakened postsurgery shoulder dislocated (the first of what would become many times). I wound up in a German hospital, alone and unable to sprechen sie Deutsch. I knew it was out of the socket and kept asking them to put it back in for me. They x-rayed it and discussed the problem in German, and I kept trying to communicate with them to just help me get it back in the socket. It was like a game of pain charades with Dr. Dieter and Nurse Nein. I sat there holding my throbbing arm for another two hours. A nurse came in and stuck an IV drip in my wrist, and I started to panic—I told them I didn't need an IV or surgery, I just needed . . . I don't even remember being put to sleep. I woke up around five the next morning with my arm strapped to my body in a room full of other patients. It appeared they hadn't operated on me. I got dressed one-handed without waking anyone and slipped into the hallway to find an exit while dodging swing shift doctors. I snuck out of Das Hospital and walked back to the Sub Culture event site. I waited until the promoters showed up with my bike, and later that day I rode in the demo. I needed to get paid like Ruben Kincaid. I couldn't even bunnyhop my bike up over the coping to roll in, so I had to footplant in every run. I ended up getting a camera strapped to my body, and used the thumb-activated shutter cable to shoot a two-page spread for Freedom magazine of an aerial from my perspective. I had a feeling once I got back to the States, I'd be spending my demo money on surgery, again.

I Do, You Do

In the summer of 1993, I was in New Mexico riding in the state fair shows with the Sprocket Jockeys. While we were on our bikes during the shows, we were having a grand time. At the end of the day, once we were back in our hotel room, our jolly group of Jockeys morphed into a bunch of semimiserable schmoes. We each took turns racking up enormous phone charges calling our girlfriends and getting in long, drawn-out "I miss you" type conversations or silly arguments, magnified by distance. I was on the phone with Jaci and we were both bummed, missing each other, and frustrated. "You know what? We should just get married," I said to Jaci. It wasn't a proposal, it was a call to action. Probably the lamest way to propose, ever. Jaci felt the same way I did: We were meant for each other, so what were we doing dating? It had been two years since our first date. I knew she was my wife, and I was her husband. We just needed to make it official. I had a couple days off, and I flew Jaci down to meet me at the fair. I made her ride the Zipper, one of the scarier, shakier carnival rides on the midway, to seal the deal. After the fair shows were over, Jaci drove with me back to Oklahoma City, and our first stop was at Braum's to celebrate. We got banana splits.

On December 30, 1993, Jaci and I exchanged our vows. I gave her my only treasure in life, my mom's wedding band. We had a simple, beautiful ceremony. Jaci's friend Marcus, her ballet company's costume designer and resident drama-magnet, made Jaci's gown and the dresses for the bridal party. As the ceremony started, Marcus was following behind the procession with a needle and thread making the final stitches as we tied the knot. The day started in slow motion, turned into a heart-stopping rush, and peaked when we said our vows and kissed, husband and wife.

It was a little like rolling into a giant ramp.

My early experiences with ESPN were as a rider. It was a great way to learn how dangerous the power of TV can be.

Let's rewind to a bored afternoon backstage on the Swatch Impact tour, in Philadelphia, circa 1988. It was a media day. The rest of the athletes and I were all waiting for a local newspaper or TV news station to arrive and interview us. Often the journalists outside our sports had no idea what we did and made rookie mistakes like calling the halfpipe a "half-pike." The show business philosophy about coverage is, "It doesn't matter what you say about me, just make sure you spell my name right." To ensure accuracy in this matter, Swatch set up our backstage area with a chalkboard, and written neatly on this board were the names, ages, and hometowns of each skater and biker. On this particular day as we waited for the press, one of us noticed that the only guy with a flashy nickname was Mark Rogowski, who went by the moniker "Gator." I think maybe it was skateboarder Chris Miller who picked up the chalk and began scrawling up some new nicknames on the board. We all began chipping in, and "Gator" was changed to "Carl." A variety of animal names were conjured up for the rest of the riders and skaters: Chris Miller was "The Chimp," Brian Blyther became "Pterodactyl," and me, I was labeled "Condor." We laughed and joked and thought our silly pranks with chalk were awfully clever.

Six months later in Canada I pulled the 900 at the Ontario KOV contest. By fate, an ESPN crew had showed up to film the comp—it was the sports network's first foray into televised freestyle coverage, and they were out of their element. The ESPN announcer looked like a TV meteorologist, and because the film crew wasn't part of the scene, they didn't know who was who or what tricks were hot. To them, we were just nutty kids riding little bikes on a wooden boomerang-shaped structure. But after I pulled the 9, they sensed from the crowd reaction that something important had just gone down. The producers began asking about that kid who did the spin. Brian was the first to answer and offhandedly remarked, "Yeah, that's the Condor." Never ones to overlook the allure of a spicy nickname, ESPN latched onto *Condor* and ran with it, introducing me to the world as the incredible twirling bird, Mat "The Condor" Hoffman. I've never lived it down. The lesson here is, be careful of sharing your inside jokes with TV crews.

My next contact with ESPN was six years later, in 1995. They'd launched a new spin-off network, ESPN2, with a mission to cover sports that were younger, faster, edgier, and more action-packed—an umbrella encompassing everything from lumberjack grand nationals, bungee-corded kayak drops, rodeo clowing, modified snow shovel racing, and of course, bike stunt riding. The network initially contacted me to do a commercial to promote some vague event they had cooking. I was excited that somebody wanted to put bikes on TV—a rarity at the time—so I didn't really ask questions. The shoot was at Muscle Beach in Venice, California. It was blistering hot, and the sun reflected brightly off the blinding sand. At the director's request, I did one hundred consecutive backflips that day. Before each one I squinted at my friend John Pova and uttered the same line, "Watch this, I'm going to do a backflip!" It was a long day and doing the same trick over and over was pretty boring, so I had to find a way to entertain myself.

In the weeks that followed I found out just what ESPN2 was up to. The thing I'd helped advertise was their concept for a new contest series, called the Extreme Games (later shortened to X Games, when the network discovered they couldn't copyright the word *extreme*). The comp was to be a modern-day made-for-TV mini-Olympics, with skateboards, bicycles, in-line skaters, wakeboarders, and a fistful of risky and frisky sports. The inaugural Extreme Games contest site was in Providence, Rhode Island, a tourist-attraction-type town known for being the home of the nation's first circus. ESPN2's plan was to set up a bunch of ramps, TV cameras, bleachers, and banners, then invite a few hundred pro skaters, bikers, and miscellaneous freaks to converge on the sleepy city, creating a whole new definition of the word *circus*. The bait was a pile of money and a challenge: Try and get it.

From the word *Go,* it was apparent the contest was going to be an extreme learning experience for everyone involved. The network had the almighty power of Mickey Mouse–based media dollars behind them, but it was clear the Disney subsidiary didn't know shit about skaters, bikers, or holding a fun event. The contest was at its best, a big TV show where athletic rivalries were fictionalized to fit in with the network's approach to dramatic sports coverage. At its worst, the contest site became a ticking time bomb of tension between the participants and the appointed glad-handers, producers, cameramen, security guards, and various production staff involved. I was one of hundreds of athletes competing in the Games, and I used my personal experience as a benchmark for how stupid things could get. Before the games even began, competitors were notified not to wear logos on their clothing—ESPN didn't want to conflict with their TV sponsors. I printed up a Fugazi-inspired shirt with large, THIS IS NOT A HOFFMAN BIKES T-SHIRT typography across the back. I went to Rhode Island braced for trouble, and sure enough, it found me. I got kicked out twice in less than twenty-four hours by the same rude dick.

The first ejection was because I was helping Dennis McCoy's wife, Paridy. She was being hassled by a beefy jerk, who wouldn't let her into the rider staging area because she had the wrong color badge. ESPN was very big on badges, wristbands, levels of access, and security. I stepped in to ask the guy to have a little respect. I introduced Paridy and said her husband was starting his run and she needed to be close by in case he got injured on the dirt jumps. "Not without a badge, buddy," said the sucker with authority. I took my badge off and handed it to Paridy right in front of him. Paridy tried to pass through and he became a little aggressive with her, so I got up in his face. Guards were called, and I was escorted off the grounds by the elbow.

The next day was the vert contest. ESPN2 had provided the biker group and skater group with their own vert ramps; there were strict practice and contest schedules. I dropped into the designated bike vert ramp and noted they'd put sand in the paint; their logic was that bicycle tires would stick to the surface and allow us to pull off even wilder stunts, which would make for better TV. It was a good idea in theory, but in practice, it sucked. They never considered what it would be like to fall and slide down the tranny. Warming up, I slammed a couple times and the surface ripped my pads off and ground my skin like a giant piece of sixty-grit sandpaper. Before long, the bikers had dubbed the ramp *The Skin Eraser.* "Screw this," I finally said, noticing there were only two skaters riding the skate halfpipe. Their ramp was built sans sand. I went over and asked the skaters, Mike Frazier and Neil Hendrix, if I could join them. They were cool with me riding, so I dropped in and took a run. Suddenly the same jerk who'd kicked me out the day before was back, squawking at me to stop immediately, because I was practicing on the

wrong ramp. I kept riding, hoping he would go away. The guy was too stout to make it up the rickety ladder to the decks, so I stayed up there and pretended I hadn't noticed the scene he was making. Neil, Mike, and I continued sessioning, and the rule enforcer was getting more frustrated. Finally he strode into the flatbottom of the ramp to "block" me from riding across while he continued yelling. I did airs around him—a 540, a couple of high pumps, to a tailwhip. I did a fakie and rolled backward, taking us both out. I was marched out of the rider's area by security once again. The rest of the bikers cut the organizers no slack, complaining loudly and bitterly about the bicycle halfpipe sucking. Several of my friends protested that I'd been collared and tossed out of the contest area and sarcastically asked the producers if they'd throw Tiger Woods off a golf course. ESPN recognized they'd goofed, and I was un-kicked out. By that point I was so pissed, I converted my anger into energy and won the vert contest. It was held, by the way, on the skate ramp.

Standing on the podium with a gold medal around my neck, I had another reason to be revolted: I was handed a giant check to pose for the cameras and noticed it was for $12,500 less than the check given to the guy who won the mountain bike event.

To Serve and Protect

After their first contest had been broadcast, ESPN2 got an earful of criticism from the athletes and the action sports industry. The network also found out Steve and I had been putting on the only national bike stunt contest series for the past four years. They were real curious as to what we thought of the Games.

I got a letter from the same jackass who'd kicked me out of the contest. Without acknowledging that he'd booted me, the producer stated in a chatty tone they wanted me to be a consultant with their organization, run the bike events, and help them put on the Extreme Games. He ended his chipper correspondence, "Extremely yours" followed by his signature. I just about heaved. I was concerned all the work we'd put into running the BS comps over the years were going to be undone by a group of clueless TV execs. I could ignore them, but they weren't going away. And on the bright side, at least I now had the name of a guy on the inside—I didn't have to battle a faceless cable television monolith.

I barraged my extreme friend with a long list of everything that was wrong: From blaring Top 40 music (and, sometimes, no music) during runs, to pointless ramp placement and park setup, sand in the paint, low pro purse money, and lack of respect for the very talent they were featuring as their entertainment. There was no sugarcoating. I included a list of conditions on which my involvement hinged. And I signed my letter "Fucking yours." Yeah, I was an ass—but I needed to let them know I couldn't tolerate overt stupidity in my sport for the sake of TV industry meatheads chasing snack food sponsorship dollars.

Ron Semiao, the creator and developer of the X Games, is one of the true visionaries at the network. He read my letter and said, "You're right." Ron was smart enough to realize that action sports could be groomed into the next big sporting category. He also understood that the network could do a lot of things well, but they didn't know enough about the new sports they were covering to walk in and be accepted as an authority. To establish themselves as part of the action sports culture, they needed support from within. And first, they needed to prove themselves.

ESPN2's primary concern was to create a product that was living room friendly; that is, basically remove all the slow, inconsistent parts of a contest and create a pure adrenaline, high-action TV format. My concern was to make sure that while they did their job, they didn't accidentally or purposely suck the life out of my sport by trying to edit it for television and change the focus for a new, broader audience. I saw right away the positive and negative aspects of a network. For the first time, the bike riding community didn't control things. I was fine with Ron and Co. saying they wanted to make history—as long as they were careful not to *overwrite* history that I'd been part of since I was twelve years old. But if Ron's vision was done right, we could evolve the BS series into the qualifying events for the X Games, bring in more money for the riders, put

together dream courses and ramps, and still have a great time while giving some exposure to an underground activity. There would be a learning curve as the corporate side experienced our culture and we interacted with their world.

Steve and I started working with ESPN2 to run contests. We felt an overwhelming need to make fun of every policy that was uncomfortable, too strict, too pointless, or too stiff. At the first BS/ESPN2 comp, I printed up T-shirts for the riders that featured the slogan *TV IS YOUR FRIEND*. The shirt artwork also featured a receipt with a list of tricks, and the cash equivalent those tricks were worth. Every chance we got, we poked fun of ourselves and the network. For every rule, we made up an antirule. If the network proposed anything too outrageous—like when they said they wanted to discontinue flatland coverage—we told them no way and gave them a long list of reasons why they were obligated to support the ground guys. When they said they wanted to eliminate the entire amateur classification, we pointed out that without an am class, there would be no pros. Even in the planning and organizational phase, the

network was constantly scratching their heads when dealing with Steve and me. For our first dirt jumping event, Steve sent ESPN2 a materials list for the things we'd need. The list included dynamite, gasoline, beer, a steamroller, and strippers. Over time, the network began to understand our stupid humor and passionate arguments, and the events improved. We never did get any dynamite, though.

But even by making the contests better, I realized that it would only get me so far in my fight to portray and explain bike riding to a mainstream audience. If I was going to succeed in making the masses understand our sport, I'd need to learn TV production and be able to show there was more to life than contests. I began to bug Ron about taking a lifestyle approach in their coverage, to show the personalities and inspirations in action sports. He had begun to trust me enough to know my motives and instincts were pure and that whatever complaints I had about the way ESPN2 did things were ultimately for their own good. His response to my request for a lifestyle show was to give me the rope to hang myself—he offered air dates in a prime-time slot.

Kid in the Way

With the green light to produce a TV show for an audience of millions, I was in trouble. I didn't know how to program my VCR to get the clock to stop flashing. But I could use a computer and knew the basics of video camera point and shoot documentation. What I needed was something to practice on, so I concocted a project to bring me up to speed on making lifestyle-based entertainment that would bridge the gap between the bike stunts crowd and a broader audience. I set up a Media 100 editing system in my basement and told the Hoffman Bikes crew to get ready to do some filming. "Order a monkey costume," I said to Steve. "We're makin' a movie."

As an action sports production, *Until Monkeys Fly* confused the hell out of most bike riders. Hoffman Bikes had the best team in the world, which meant it would have been a no-brainer to pack sixty minutes full of sick trick clips cut together to a thumping soundtrack and progressive graphics. Instead, there was Rick Thorne using handlebars as kung fu weaponry to pound down a jock with a mullet. I had Kevin Robinson rock it like Sonny Crockett, wearing no socks and a sport coat, driving recklessly to *Miami Vice* music and beating up patio furniture. I insulted vegans and animal lovers alike by having masked vandals graffiti "Eat Meat" on cows. Taj, one of the best jumpers in the country (and a devout vegetarian), was relegated to portraying a shoeless, dirt farming hick. For most of my own appearances in the production, I sported a galactic space helmet/salad bowl and a flamboyant fake moustache. Adopting a gruff accent, I commanded a time-traveling primate to steal bike parts in a plot that revolved around the central character, monkey boy. Steve was forced to dress up as monkey boy and partake in a variety of ridiculous scenarios, including humping legs, playing Tetris, break dancing in public, and at one point invading a karaoke bar wearing the suit and screeching wildly (the bar patrons were *not* thrilled). The humor was beyond corny—it was cornography. Despite the video's flaws, there was also some decent riding in between the skits. But I took a heap of flack from the bike community upon the release of *Until Monkeys Fly*. Which was perfectly fine with me. I'd learned what I set out to do: make a TV show.

My pitch to Semiao was to showcase the pioneer spirit of people who ruled—whether they were into snowboarding, bikes, skateboarding, music, or miscellaneous danger. I wanted interviews, documentary footage, travel coverage, humor, and music reviews in the part of the mix. At first, the network execs balked when they read my treatment. "This is ESPN2, not MTV," they said, concerned about bringing music on the strictly-for-sports-nuts channel. I asked Ron to believe in me and told him I'd create the program for free. He backed me up with his "show me what you got" attitude, on the condition the network reviewed all materials before airing.

During the contract negotiations, the phrasing and legal boilerplate stated the network wanted my soul, my blood, my firstborn child, and worldwide rights to everything associated with my show, forever. Somehow I was able to delay and argue and revise the contract long enough until they just gave up. As for turning in the finished tapes so they could review each episode before it aired, I was afraid the Connecticut crew (ESPN's home base) would tinker with the tapes and muddle up my work, so my tactic was to turn in the tapes a day before show dates. If they hated something, they could cut the whole show or go with it untouched.

In one season, with *Kids in the Way* as my platform, I was able to change the way ESPN2 approached action sports.

The debut of *Kids* featured an interview in a laundromat with a band called Man or . . . Astro Man, who claimed they were messengers from outer space. I can't imagine what the network heads were thinking when they saw the band jumping around in NASA jumpsuits, with the singer wearing a flaming TV set converted into a helmet while cavorting herky-jerky across the front of the stage. The only instance the network ever intervened and cut content from the show was an eight-second clip of fully clothed porn actress Jasmine St. Claire introducing a segment on Mike "Rooftop" Escamilla. I hadn't expected the network guys to recognize Miss St. Claire, but there must have been some pervs in the standards and practices department.

Over the course of six episodes, *Kids* opened the door for shows like EXPN's popular *X2Day* series, which is one of the most recognized features on the network today. *Kids* also helped expand the networks' collective minds to recognize that music and action sports thrived on the same creative energy, and that through expression and artistry, our sports were about more than just a score; they were a way of life.

But my biggest reward for doing the *Kids in the Way* was getting to befriend one of the greatest living myths.

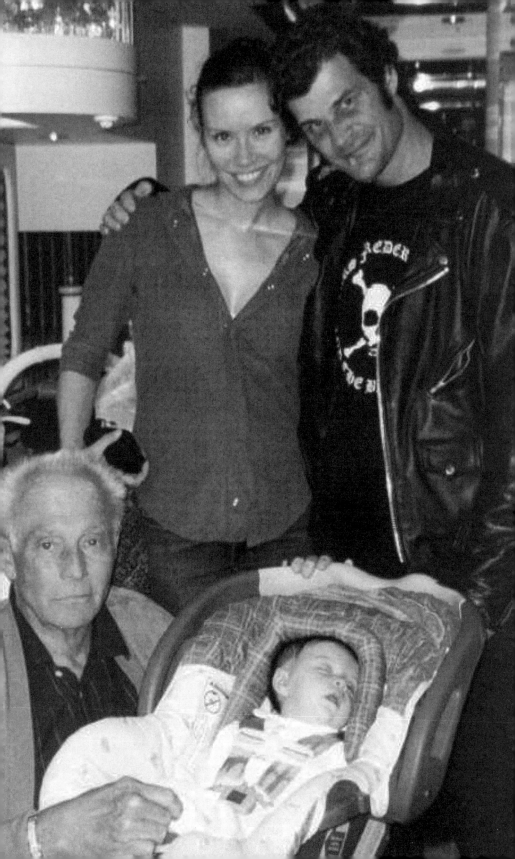

A Touch of Evel

There is nobody in the world like Evel Knievel. His career as a motorcycle daredevil defies belief—that he had the skill and guts to pull off his stunts, using the equipment he employed. The other incredible part of his story is, of course, that he gave so much of himself and kept coming back, that he survived the falls he took. Evel is the original Never Back Down, Take No Shit superhero. An international icon and a man of solid principles, Evel's legacy inspired me for many years. It was perhaps the ultimate reason for doing a TV show—so I could figure out a way sit down and talk to the man.

I got word that Evel was going to be signing autographs at a boat show in Los Angeles, so I hit the road with a cameraman in tow with the hopes of securing a legendary interview for *Kids in the Way*. I'd prepared and overprepared, and by the time I got to the boat show I was jittering with nerves. Just approaching Evel was not easy. He can be a hard bastard, mainly because he's earned the right to command respect from his fans and the media. I stepped to him as a little bit of both. He was sitting at a table signing pictures when I approached and asked for a minute of his time. That's about what I got, sixty seconds. It didn't go well.

Evel had already been signing things and sitting there for a while and was getting tired and testy. His terse answers took me off guard. I don't know what I expected, but I quickly learned nothing can prepare you for the Evel experience. He lives so *in* the moment, there are two ways he approaches any situation: He's either superstoked or superpissed. There is no in between.

His business manager suggested we cut things short, and Evel shut us down and made his exit. I was so bummed; I'd flubbed up the chance to talk to one of the few guys in the world I really respected and with whom I felt a connection. Wandering around the trade show floor, I half-heartedly checked out jet skis and fishing boats, then drifted toward the lobby. Time to go. As luck would have it, I bumped into Evel. Without the camera present, I had a more casual convo with him, and he began to open up to me a little. I knew his history included a long list of line extensions (Evel grossed over $30 million dollars at his peak in the 1970s), so I was curious about his involvement with bikes. Evel had licensed his name to mass merchant companies to create entry-level BMX-style bikes in the past, and I asked if he'd ever considered doing a high-end, collectable signature bike, with top-of-the-line components. I mentioned I had a bike company and gave him my card before we parted ways. I returned to Oklahoma City, rejected but somehow enlightened.

Not long after, I got a phone call. A familiar, salty voice said, "Mat, it's Evel. I'm going to Vegas to watch my son Robbie jump and break the world record. You want to come?" Not the kind of question I needed to be asked twice. I was on a plane immediately and spent three days in Sin City with the guy whose name was synonymous with the fountain at Caesar's Palace, among other locations. We watched Robbie rocket into the record books, we gambled, and we drove around. At one point I was sitting in the backseat while Evel and one of his lifelong friends—his getaway driver—cruised through town reminiscing about back in the day. It was surreal, hearing the stories I'd read about for years, from the guys who'd lived it. The weekend was like a gift.

Together, Evel and I designed a couple of Evel signature bikes, which Hoffman Bikes released to commemorate historical stunts. I went to his wedding. Sometimes I get phone calls at two in the morning, and it's Evel . . . just calling to shoot the shit or tell me he busted a rib. He pitches me his inventions, which I am not at liberty to discuss, but I can tell you they're totally insane and amazing.

Because I was a "Kid" who'd figured out a "Way," my dream to meet and interview Evel turned into reality. Then it kept progressing into something even better, friendship. It's so weird, being friends with one of your idols. But it's good-weird. I think the reason Evel and I hit it off so well is because we share the same wavelength—we know what it's like to sacrifice and take pain and risks to experience the pleasures and success in life. Although he's over sixty years old, Evel is as wild and hyped up as any twenty-five-year-old.

I can only hope that when I'm pushing sixty, I've got that kind of legacy to look back on, and that pure energy to propel me forward to whatever challenges the day brings.

GROWING PAINS

Things began to stabilize at Hoffman Bikes after our first couple of years in business, but there was never a shortage of crisis situations. We were constantly strapped for cash and pushing to grow, but sometimes my team riders grew faster than we could as a company. While Jay Miron rode for Hoffman Bikes he got good—supergood. There were casual practice sessions at the Ninja Ramp and at the ramp park outside the warehouse that were no holds barred, some of the craziest shit I've ever seen done on bicycles. The top three spots at contests usually became a battle between Dave Mirra (our other HB star), Jay, and myself. Jay's bag of tricks included Mironized no-footed 540s, a tailwhip air where he'd kick his legs into a superman, and total coping control with a slew of sick lip tricks. His surgical style of front- and back-brake-based bedlam helped popularize new ways of using the entire ramp—from the decks to the side railing. Jay constantly pushed the limits of his riding, and he was anxious to get some payback for all his efforts. The most I could do was offer a modest salary and line up as many Sprocket Jockeys shows as possible, keeping our team busy on the road getting paid at fairs. Jay was annoyed, I think, because of our loose game plan. He wanted stability and a sponsor that had everything figured out—not the fly-by-night style Steve and I utilized during our entry in business, as we learned the ropes.

As was often the case, I'd be out of town or overseas doing demos. Steve and Jay would be dispatched to drive the semi truck to the fair shows. Sometimes they spent weeks on the road, packed into the cab of that Peterbilt. The lifestyle of a Sprocket Jockey was a demanding one, and over time, the close friendship Steve and Jay shared began to unravel. To complicate matters, Jay had the metabolism of a field mouse, and we could only afford to pay him $15 per diem. I've seen him consume $60 worth of food a day (we're talking road grub, too—not spendy New York steakhouse fare), and he'd still be famished. And if Jay's daily caloric intake was insufficient, he'd get hypoglycemic and a scary transformation would occur. We called this personality phenomenon *Larry*. When Larry made an appearance, hotel rooms got trashed, swearing was rampant, and destruction reigned over everything. Nobody was fond of Larry. After a grueling tour and months of stress, Steve

and Jay were getting along like two cats trapped under a laundry basket. In a Texas hotel room, Jay announced he was quitting the team; Steve agreed it was probably best for all. Later that evening, psychotic Larry made a confrontational midnight entrance. There was urine involved. Push came to shove, and Steve, blind as a mole without his glasses, got clocked in the head.

Jay was gone the next day.

He got picked up by Schwinn, one of the bike industry giants who had a spotty track record when it came to supporting the sport—but they had money and were gearing up to build a new BMX and freestyle team. I was glad Jay got the sponsorship opportunity he'd been searching for, and after hearing about Larry and Steve's hotel room showdown, knew it was time for Jay to move on from the HB family. I wasn't that stoked Jay took the bike design we'd been working on with him. We built a beer bottle opener into the frame near the seat mast. It was supposed to be his signature frame. The design carried over to his new Schwinn model, minus the bottle opener. But whatever.

When Dave Mirra wanted a pay hike, it also came at a time when every extra cent we generated was already going to my team riders; I couldn't afford to cough up much more. I was already paying Dave

$1,000 a month when he came to me and asked my advice—he had an offer from Haro on the table. I told Dave I could maybe go up to $1,250 a month, but even that was really out of my league. Haro was bidding $1,500. But I didn't want to forfeit to Haro by $250—if I was going to lose a good rider and friend, I wanted to lose big. I told Dave to tell Haro I was paying him $2,500 a month, but also said that if Haro didn't try to top that fictitious salary, I wasn't going to be able to swing it. It was shady, but Dave was up for it. Haro bought the story and "matched" his salary of $2,500 a month. I was bummed to see him go but happy that I'd helped boost his starting wage—Dave deserved every dollar he earned, and he quickly proved himself a valuable asset to Haro's team roster.

Warehouse Warlords

The formula for success at Hoffman Bikes has always been to find people I could trust, who were ambitious and energetic, and empower them with all the tools they needed to kick ass. Finding trained, groomed workers was never as important as finding the people who had the passion and were willing to commit to the cause. I've picked up an incredible staff using this hiring approach.

The second full-time salaried employee I brought on board after Steve was a guy whose real name, for the longest time, I didn't even know. I called him Chuck. Chuck was a pale, freckled, red-haired guy who stopped by to ride with us at the Ninja Ramp—he lived out in the boonies and we didn't see him around often. Chuck found out about our plans to start a company, around the same time we got the BS series off the ground. Chuck offered to help us put on our second BS comp, which was in Arizona. We didn't know the kid too well but figured, what the hell, free labor. We left Oklahoma on Route 40, one of the longest, driest, most boring, desolate highways in the United States. Just a couple of miles into our twenty-hour minivan journey, Chuck got violently ill. Steve and I exchanged, "Aw man, who *is* this knucklehead?" glances as our volunteer bent over on the side of the road, heaving his guts out. It was going to be a *looong* weekend. Since I'd already experienced the nauseous joy of putting on and riding in a BS contest while extremely sick, I had no desire to repeat the experience. I told Chuck to stay a couple seats behind me in the van. We frequently pulled over to the side, with the hazards flashing, while Chuck got his heave on. Between bouts of vomiting, he asked me why I kept calling him Chuck. I didn't want to tell him it was because I'd forgotten his real name (which I later found out was Mark Owen). I'd come up with Chuck because he reminded me of a red-headed kid in school who used to beat me up. However, I didn't tell him this, either—I told him it was because he bore a striking resemblance to Chuck D of Public Enemy. "Oh, okay," Chuck said and folded back in half to let loose another roaring torrent of regurgitated Burger King Whopper slop.

Chuck proved himself at the Arizona BS contest. By the time the comp was over and Chuck's bout with food poisoning had passed, Steve and I knew he was employee material. He was cheap, worked hard, rode bikes, and understood what we were trying to do: change the world. Chuck moved in with Steve and began working at HB as a jack-of-all-trades. When he started, he couldn't turn on a computer—he went on to become our in-house bike designer. He taught himself computer-aided drafting (CAD), learned to source materials at machine shops, and eventually became the guy who oversees all bike production. I call him the "I can do Anything" guy, because that's what he's capable of. Chuck also volunteered to work at every single contest we held and gradually became known to us as Mark Owen. If you've ever been to a BS contest, you have to give it up for Chuck. I mean Mark.

Other guys from our Edmond riding posse, like Page Hussey and the Collins brothers—Mike and Chris—came into the fold and made vital contributions, too. None of the friends I hired had much training in the jobs they would eventually master and excel at, but they were highly resourceful. They lived the lifestyle of 100 percent riders and action addicts. The ramp park in the back of the warehouse attracted people from all across the country, and sometimes this plywood playground acted like a Venus flytrap, snaring many potential victims . . . I mean, employees. Street pro Keith Treanor came to ride the park and ended up working with us for a spell. And there was a helpful Hawaiian named Big Island who had a trustworthy face—he was tapped to handle the cashbox at the door and the sign-up table at BS contests. Eventually I stuck Big in front of a souped-up Mac and we discovered he had skills as a designer. I could use all the help I could get in the art department—the graphics for the first batch of Hoffman Bikes were press-on letters from the art section of the local Kinkos, which looked like it spelled "Condo" instead of Condor. I enlisted the aid of HB team rider and artist Davin "Pyscho" Hallford to help craft better logos and also found a guy named Bryan Baxter working at Massive Graphics, my T-shirt print shop. Bryan rode, played music, and was an artist, so I had to steal him to work at HB. He was our first art director, and when we started doing video production and websites, he took over that territory. Big and Chris Collins became the new art department regime and began designing ads and art directing the materials. With a Web presence, slick titles and video production, and good graphics on our stuff, the HB image smoothed out and started looking pretty pro.

Turning to Taiwan

Sales were super, but after four years in business we were spinning our wheels. To grow and keep up with the demand, we'd need to expand into the territory claimed by the well-distributed manufacturers like GT, Haro, and Schwinn. In short, we'd need to take our bike line from strictly hardcore vert, street, and flatland fare into the realm of budget bikes. The idea was that since most bikes sold are entry-level rides, we could get new kids into riding, gain presence in our shops, and once the shops saw how fast the low-budget models moved off the floor, they'd order some of the more serious equipment.

Building an economical bike couldn't be done with our in-house machine shop—we were cranking out product as fast as we could get raw tubing on the shipping dock, but it was walking a razor's edge just to stay afloat. To cut the margins and try to make things cheaper would sink us for sure. The key was to source a competent manufacturer in Taiwan, where the prices were more affordable. But even setting up that program cost a lot of money, because the Taiwanese factories had minimum orders and needed down payments before they would do a production run. Mike Devitt, my old friend from SE, mentioned the T-word to me and I brushed it off, saying I couldn't come up with the down payment money. Mike suggested I get a letter of credit from a bank and that would work as a cash advance for Taiwanese companies. I had a better idea. I got my international distributor accounts to preorder and send me letters of credit from *their* banks. I sent these letters to my Taiwanese manufacturer to finance my order. Whatever profit I made from these preorders I used to finance additional bikes for me to stock. It was a way of covering the fact that I had no money, and to my surprise, it worked. With the profit I made from selling these bikes, I was able to order an additional container. So, for no money out of pocket, I got two-for-the-price-of-none and was able to bring a new bike to the Hoffman lineup. It looked like a rare occasion where math was working in my favor.

We called our first Taiwanese bike The Egg, because we just knew they were built to crack. The geometry and componentry were okay, but the frame and fork sets, compared with the heavy-duty Condors, were merely high-tensile steel tubing. It had an affordable price of just $199.99. Perfect for the beginning rider for transportation to school and back. Unfortunately, our reputation preceded us, and despite our best efforts to alert bike shops that The Egg was *not* the same style bike as our infamous American built, high-end, high-performance lineup, a lot of the hardcore riders bought Eggs. They tried to jump them, street ride them, take them on vert, and literally scrambled the Eggs. We got back tons of cracked frames and choppered fork sets; it was clear we had to do something before our reputation was destroyed. The Egg sold out but cost Hoffman Bikes a chunk of credibility. I knew we couldn't make the same mistake twice and had to find a better way to get bikes made in volume.

Taiwanese manufacturers had machinery I would drool over. With their equipment they could build more consistent bikes than what I could do in my shop. They just needed somebody looking over their shoulders, to make sure everything was done to our specifications. With the help of a friend in the industry, we found an agent to help us find the cream of the crop in Taiwanese manufacturers. Our agent could source a shop to build anything we needed and would make sure it got done the way we wanted. I would also send Mark Owen over there to peek in and make sure they didn't cut any corners. With the new system, a complete bike was not coming from one company but several smaller and medium-sized facilities: the tire guys, the seat guys, the crankset guys, the handlebar guys, and so forth. We just cut a check, and several weeks later the finished product arrived at our warehouse. We had a dependable lineup of small Taiwanese shops staffed by craftsmen who could create the bike we wanted to meet the demands of the hardcore riders and could make lower-end units, too. It took a ton of pressure off of us back in Oklahoma. I wound down the in-house machine shop and phased out the headaches of running a massive staff.

One of my favorite things about owning a company is I got to name the bikes. I decided my fat cat, George, was too awesome to not have something named in his honor. The Hoffman Bikes George model was questioned by a lot of shops because it sounded like a stupid name for a bike, but most of the Georges sold. One day my agent in Taiwan called me at home to notify me that the tire company that was developing our new line of tires could put a signature or fancy name embossed on the sidewalls of the tires. She wanted to know if I wanted *Condor* on there or if I had any other ideas. George had just crapped on the stairs at home. "Hmm," I said, staring at George's steaming mess on the white shag, as he dragged his ass across the carpet as toilet paper. "How about Skidmarks?" Six weeks later the first batch of Skidmarks tires arrived on U.S. shores, and they've been Hoffman Bikes' standard tires ever since.

Another pet-inspired product was the Hoffman Bikes Deebo, and a slightly smaller model called the 'Lil Deebo. These bikes were named after my spastic dog, who was in turn named after my favorite character from the film *Friday*. A drunken night at a bar in Malaysia with the HB team resulted in a product called the Spice Dog 4 (a nickname I was given for the night), which we later abbreviated to SD-4, for coded purposes. It's funny what a name can do for a product's sales—even the name of a color. We got a batch of bikes in stock that were brown. When our sales staff would describe it to bike shop buyers over the phone, we determined that nobody wanted brown bikes. Fearing a large inventory of earth tone product sitting on the warehouse shelves, I told the sales staff that brown was now being called "burnished bronze." This worked like a charm, and the brown, err, bronze bikes sold out.

After a couple years of importing product from Taiwan, despite the ongoing obstacle course of business, we were paying off our debts and things were looking up. Our lease option was running out on the old warehouse; my dad had moved out and the new landlord was trying to jack me around. I was pissed and went looking for a new place. I found some property that looked perfect. I didn't even know if the building was for sale and walked in the door with my checkbook. The owner and his wife had occupied the building for over twenty-five years. His wife had been wanting to move for the last ten years, but they never had a good enough excuse. I was that excuse, and by random luck scored a deal on a new space. I designed the new offices and built fixtures using scrap wood from the old twenty-one-foot-tall quarterpipe, and various parts of ramp park scraps. The decor was one of the things I focused on in my downtime during my numerous riding injuries. As the boss, I also liked making up the rules. I'd heard of Casual Friday business attire, so I ran with that idea and made up my own version. I called it "Speedo Wednesdays." We had a brand new intern starting the day I put that rule to the test—I walked into our Wednesday morning ten o'clock meeting in the conference room, put my feet up on the table, and asked everybody to fill me in on their departments' progress for the week. I was wearing nothing but a silky black Speedo.

Mad Math

My sister, Gina, married an investment banker named David Lindley. David was suave and savvy, a BMW-driving numbers ninja. After some coaxing on my part, he agreed to take on the adventure of becoming the Hoffman Bikes chief financial officer. "Say, you know, since you're naming these products after your pets, you can legally write them off as tax-deductible corporate mascots," was one of the first insights David noted when he came on board. I liked his thinking.

However, David quickly had his work cut out for him when he walked into a minefield the first couple of months on the job. Steve and I had signed a huge distribution deal with one of the oldest and most respected distributors in the bicycle industry. The company had been around for thirty years and had solid channels into retail accounts all over the United States. We figured if we could rely on a company to sell our bikes to shops, we could focus our laser beam of expertise on designing better products, running a bigger team, and making cooler stuff. Things were looking up. Until our distributor filed for Chapter 11 bankruptcy protection holding a massive order of our bikes—bikes that I'd maxed out my credit line to get built, and I was counting on a substantial check from the distributor to pay off the loan. Ugh. I was left holding the bag, several million dollars in credit debt, with all my bikes tied up in asset forfeiture limbo with the distributor's creditors. It sucked. Rather than write off my own losses and take the cheesy way out, I assumed the massive debt and begin rebuilding the company one sale at a time. Even with David Lindley's master spreadsheets, I was looking at a slow crawl out of debt and back to normal. But I'd rather dig ditches than welch out of what I owed.

Around this time, the official HB company motto became Rise Above. I ran the tagline in our ads, on our T-shirts, and signed autographs with it. The more I thought about how lame the situation was, the more it hardened my resolve to not give in.

David got HB out of another bind. It was an epic fuckup, and to make matters worse it came via a good friend whom I'd employed. There was an error in the way a batch of bikes had been built in Taiwan, so because they weren't made to spec we didn't have to pay for them. Basically, they were free bikes if I could find out how to get them to the United States cheaply. Christmas was approaching in about a month and half, so I asked my friend/employee to get a cost on having the bikes shipped to us, and we could give the bikes away to charities and boys' homes. The shipping by sea freighter was $4,000, which was more than I'd hoped to spend (or could afford), but it was for a great cause. The boat would take twenty-eight days to arrive and still give us time to

get the bikes to their new homes.

Two days later, the UPS truck pulled up out back. "Here you go—sign here." My buddy had accidentally checked the "second day air" box on the shipping instructions. We'd basically just express mailed one hundred and fifty bicycles from Taiwan via the fastest possible method. It was also the most expensive method—a whopping $25,000 over the original price. David quickly set to work and got UPS to reduce their costs, basically reeling them into the fiasco by crediting them as codonors of the gift. It still cost me ten grand, but sometimes you give until it hurts.

For all the troubles and headaches and sleepless nights, even the worst day at Hoffman Bikes is probably better than the best day just about anyplace else I could work. And when things get *really* bad at HB, I've still got two words that keep me coming back, and keep me moving on.

Rise Above.

B.A.S.E.HEAD

I love a good view. I also love jumping off of things.

Edmond, Oklahoma, is pretty flat. In my years as a curious preteenager, I found and climbed the tallest thing in town—the local NBC affiliate's fifteen-hundred-foot-tall TV antennas. My mission: just to see what the air looked like from up there. By the early eighties, air was supplied by my bike, which had become my hobby of choice. In the late eighties riding was my sport, and by the nineties, it became my art—an art that had begun exacting its toll on my battle-scarred body.

In the first few years following the death of my mother, I entered an experimental era of backflips, 900s, twenty-three-foot aerials on the big ramp. I also started skydiving and B.A.S.E. jumping. I was constantly searching for a new impossible experience.

"Aren't you scared of death?" is a question that comes up often. In 1995, my typical reply was a sarcastic quip, like "Death is just a moment when dying ends." Sounds like a tagline in a Van Damme movie, but I had seriously reached a point in my life where I *wasn't* scared of death. I was driven to challenge my own potential, to map uncharted territory and test possibility. *Can I take my hands off during a flip? What if I tried tailwhipping it? How high can I really go?* Over the years these experiments resulted in many encounters with pain and fear. Panic is replaced by *Aww, shit, how can I fix this before I hit the ground?* You develop an inner calmness and build up a tolerance to crisis situations, and begin losing your perspective on mortality.

I started skydiving because I was superfrustrated with my physical condition. I had to compromise my riding, based on the current status of my body. Every time I pushed the proverbial envelope, a bone would break or a ligament would give out. I'd be forced to percolate and recuperate, unable to ride, yet dreaming up even harder stuff to pull off next time. I was discovering a dark truth: What I wanted to do on my bike and what my body could handle were two different things. Sometimes I was in this injury purgatory for months at a stretch. Skydiving became part of my rehabilitation. It revitalized me.

The most obvious thrill of falling from the clouds is the pulse-pounding ground rushing view and incredibly surreal sensation of being alone in the sky. There is also the more sublime element of pure freedom. You have no gravitational restrictions, and jumping from twelve thousand feet translates to just over a minute of pure playtime. Front-flips, gainers, 360s left and right, docking with other skydivers, or just complete dork sessions—you name it, I've indulged.

For the first couple of years, it was a weekend kick. I'd drive out to the airfield, pay $80, and experience the view as I hurtled toward earth at over one hundred miles per hour from ten thousand feet. After a while it becomes heroin. Skydiving was the most thrilling and intense activity outside of riding I'd ever known, at a fraction of the cost on my body. It was the way I could recuperate without going crazy. The more time I spent wearing a parachute, the stronger my skills grew, and the more I realized all the possibilities.

Jump from an Airplane

I only had eight hundred bucks, so I had to go ghetto. My friend John Vincent had a buddy at the Deland Drop Zone in Florida who wanted to get rid of it. I never questioned why. It had thirteen hundred jumps on it, didn't fit me, and had been dyed about fifty times with acids. Even the style of the canopy had been discontinued twenty years earlier. It was sketchy as hell, but it was mine: a Pegasus parachute. My friends used to joke and call it a pawn shop special or claim it was originally a camping tent that had been retrofitted and resold as a skydiving rig. But I trusted this twenty-pound sack of strap-on nylon and polyester with my life.

Skydiving has something in common with mountain biking, and that's the dress code. There's a certain style that consists of sheer gear. You know the look: covered head to toe in technical fabrics and colorful prints, full-on pro shop ensembles that proclaim your status. I've always been the guy in the black T-shirt and cargo shorts who looks like he wandered in off the street and accidentally ended up getting on the plane. Occasionally, I will dress for the part, like when jumping in winter.

If you don't have enough current jumps in your logbook each year, you have to start over if you want to keep advancing. To avoid losing my certification, I've gone skydiving in the dead of winter, when it was a cool eighteen below zero where you exit the plane. You can't wear thick gloves, because you have to be able to grab your pilot chute and control your canopy using steering handles, called toggles. So for these jumps I wore snowboarding pants and a parka and still felt like a free-falling Popsicle.

You learn the basics first, such as how to exit the plane. Nothing makes you feel more like a dumb ass than tumbling out of a speeding airplane and conking your head on the wing, as I deftly demonstrated one fine November afternoon. The other crucial, yet basic, skills you pick up during your early skydives are things like how to manipulate your body to move yourself around, dive fast, slow down, and track toward objects such as your landing zone. Oh, and landing. That's pretty important. One of the first "think fast, pop quiz" situations to test how well I had learned the basics came courtesy of my sketchy right arm and my equally sketchy old Pegasus rig. Together they scared the crap out of me, but afterward I knew what to expect in case it happened again.

It was over the GCS Metro airport in Skiatook, Oklahoma. The mid-July skies were sunny and bright blue. It was my thirty-ninth jump as a skydiver, and I was getting comfortable in the air. A C-182 turboprop took us up around eight thousand feet and I exited with a triple front-flip and a huge grin. I locked into a standing up straight position, which gets you cooking pretty fast, plunging feet first toward earth at about two hundred miles an hour. I felt like Superman. My temperamental parachute was engaged by throwing a pilot chute—essentially a little parachute that you release into the air first. The drag it creates pulls out the main canopy on your back. My main canopy never worked very well. I'd throw my pilot chute, and instead of immediately engaging my main canopy, the thing would just snivel for a while and take about twenty seconds to open.

I have trouble waiting twenty seconds in front of a microwave for a burrito, so trying to sit and wait calmly for my chute to pop while sizzling toward earth can be a test of patience. This time my pilot chute seemed to be whistling and sniveling above me for an extra long time, so I raised my right arm up to shake the risers (the ropes connecting my chute to my body) and see what the . . . WHOMP! My chute deployed and jerked my body violently, the force from the risers instantly knocking my right arm out of socket. It was one of those Homer Simpson "Doh!" moments as I floated through the sky, unable to steer my parachute and in an awkward situation. After considerable struggle, I popped my arm back into socket and regained control. I steered in and landed without further incident, then spent the rest of the day in an endorphin overload daze.

A week later I was jumping at my home field, Paradise Paracenter in Norman, Oklahoma. I had a new rig. This one was a Sabre 150, state of the art. It flew like a Ferrari drives. You could crank off lightning turns, and if you pulled one toggle down to your foot, backflips were possible with the canopy open. The difference between my old Pegasus and my new Sabre was that the Sabre's pilot chute was hooked up to a kill line. After the pilot chute popped open the main canopy, the kill line disengaged the tiny pilot chute. With only one canopy open, you were free to haul ass and zoom around until it was time for what you hoped would be a gentle, pinpoint landing.

"Look for the red canopy," I told Jaci. She'd come down to Paradise with me while I got in a couple of quick jumps. I had a jumpmaster assemble my rig, including the kill line. With the rigging taken care of, I carefully folded the canopy and packed it into the backpack-like apparatus called a container. Then I put it on, adjusted the shoulder and thigh harnesses, and was ready to jump.

After exiting the plane, I spent fifty seconds lofting my jive and was ready to release the pilot chute. Without warning, my kill line collapsed before it pulled my main canopy open. I was free-falling, towing my bag behind me as I tried to sort things out in my head. Now what the hell? I considered shaking my risers but remembered the out-come from the previous week. As I attempted to solve the problem, the solution became clear: Cut away from the defect chute and deploy my reserve chute. My altimeter was bleeding off hundreds of feet, and I'd hoped my arm didn't pop out of its socket as I fought the wind and my parachute. It was like one of those Extreme Magic specials on Fox TV, only not fake. I normally pop the canopy around the twenty-five-hundred-foot mark, but when I looked down I was at fifteen hundred and falling fast. I ended up cutting it away and got my reserve open at eight hundred feet. That's about eight seconds before I hit the ground like a sack of turtles, roughly the same amount of time it took you to read this sentence.

I drifted in for a landing with the reserve canopy, which is silver. Jaci was on the ground, looking nervous and squinting up toward the sky, still searching for the red one.

Immediately the jumpmaster guys were on the scene, heckling me. With less than fifty jumps in my logbook, I was still a rookie. I had no idea what happened, but the jumpmasters suggested I failed to cock the kill line, something you're supposed to do as you pack your chute to ensure proper deployment of the canopy. I had cocked it, definitely. I was positive. So what had caused the mishap? As I gathered up my chute another veteran jumpmaster walked over and examined my rig. "Hell, this thing was put together wrong." He said. "You jump this again, it's not opening a second time. You're jumping out of a plane with a parachute guaranteed to malfunction." His words hung in the air. For their error, they offered to pack my reserve chute for free. Apology accepted. I saved $40.

The next high-risk exam hurt. I was out the door at ten thousand feet with another Oklahoma local, Joe Bill. We were doing relative work—basically just practicing flips, we docked together, and then broke away. I threw my arms back into a delta track position to maneuver in closer to Joe and pandemonium broke loose. My right arm obviously didn't get the interoffice memo to *stay in shoulder socket while free-falling*. The roaring wind blasted my arm, and I felt it give out. Instantly I careened out of control like a rag doll, arm dangling and flapping uselessly out of the socket. The whole point of skydiving is to become a wing. Your limbs are crucial in maintaining body positioning when you're free-falling, so if you lose command of an arm or a leg, it's like a plane without any aileron rudders. No control at terminal velocity means you're a human ball of laundry inside a clothes dryer, set to tumble high. This in turn affects your equilibrium; your only real reference point up in the middle of nowhere is the plane (long gone by then) and other skydivers.

I had no idea where Joe was, but I had other concerns. First, get a hold of my flopping arm and pin it down to my chest in "National Anthem" position. This helped stabilize me, a little. I'd burned about a thousand feet of altitude, and the ground was starting to get more detailed. The only problem was, my jacked arm was the one I needed to deploy my chute. My pilot chute was located on the back of my right leg. With my right arm dislocated, the only way to deploy my chute was to reach it with my left arm, and the chute seemed to be just out of reach. It was like a complex physics problem: *"I'm traveling about 160 miles per hour, one-armed, unable to deploy, and I have no idea if the guy I jumped with is directly above me. Hmm . . ."* There was only one route out. I started reaching for my pilot chute, trying to snatch the release while still holding my bad arm to my chest. It was comic book style: *"Can't . . . reach . . . pilot chute . . . must . . . deploy. . . ."* I finally snagged it and popped my canopy and thankfully didn't collide with Joe as I rapidly decelerated. *"Ahh, cool. Now I'll get my arm back in,"* was my first thought. Steering with dual toggles, applying the brakes, and landing using only one arm is pretty squirrelly. As I floated downward, trying to grunt and *umph* my arm back into socket, it was clear I'd have to initiate Plan B: half-brake all the way in. My last thought before impact was *Ah, God. This is gonna hurt*...

I hit the ground with a puff of dust and slid into home plate. My chute gathered and ruffled around me as I just lay there on my back, looking up at the sky and breathing hard. Fuck. One of the jumpmasters finally came over and asked, "What's the problem, chief?" I open my eyes and replied, "Hey, could you put my arm back in for me?"

Jump Off a Bridge

I continued nourishing my skydiving habit, soaking up live-and-learn lessons on the fly. I found myself frequently in conversation with my friend John Vincent. John is an undersea welder and Jedi Master of B.A.S.E. jumping. He has thousands of skydives and more than five hundred B.A.S.E. jumps under his belt. He's pulled off some burly ones like leaping off the Twin Towers, the Brooklyn Bridge, the Superdome, and more—and gotten away clean. Since most U.S. structures are private property, you not only need the skills to avoid being killed, but the stealth and willpower to trespass while making jumps. John wasn't so lucky when he suction-cupped his way up the St. Louis Arch in the dead of the night and leaped off at first light. The footage aired on the news and a federal arrest warrant was issued; he turned himself in and got locked up for ninety days, a criminal. But to me he's a guy who lets his passion take over, and I think this common link is what made us friends. John and I began scheming B.A.S.E. jumps, concocting super big stunts that I knew if we were to attempt, either one of us could wind up dead.

I was immediately attracted to the idea of B.A.S.E. jumping because of the similarities between B.A.S.E. and bikes. When you ride, you start to see things differently. You tap into a new part of your consciousness. You don't see a rail to grab onto when you walk up a set of stairs—you see what you could do with your bike on it. You count how many steps there are, and determine if it's steel or aluminum (because 4130 chrome-moly bike pegs slide faster on steel surfaces). You check it for obstructions, do a visual sweep for security guards or surveillance cameras, and then make a mental note of the rail location. If you ride it once, you never forget how to find it. Think of Manhattan, and imagine how many handrails there probably are there. I guarantee the local riders can take you to every single rail that's not a bust. B.A.S.E. jumping is the same way. On tour, I'd look at buildings, antennas, spans, and earth (B.A.S.E.) in every city to scope out good exit points and whether there was a decent landing space. I began to see the world in a totally different way, what psychologists call a paradigm shift. I liked it.

When I was in Shanghai, the only thing I could think of was what they would do to me if I jumped off the Orient Pearl TV Tower (1,535 feet). The population there seemed pretty mellow, but the military/state/cops struck me as a serious bunch, not to mention the fact that my Chinese language/negotiating skills are terrible. So I kept my size twelves planted on the sidewalk for that trip. Whenever I go to Japan, I salivate over the Tokyo Tower (1,026 feet). In Kuala Lumpur, the Petronas Towers (1,483 feet) get my mind whirling, and of course the desire to throw myself off the Eiffel Tower (986 feet) is a thought I always entertain when in Paris.

B.A.S.E. jumping is just about as gnarly as it gets. There only are four ways you leave the scene of jumps: in a getaway vehicle, the back of a police car, a life flight helicopter, or the coroner's van. There are no injuries in this activity, no do-overs. It takes pure concentration and you have to know everything that could go wrong and be able to instinctively, reflexively do the right thing the instant the shit goes down. The second it takes to *think* about what to do next is the difference between life and death. Veterans say B.A.S.E. jumping is the most rewarding thing they've ever done, and they advise nobody to ever follow their footsteps. Overcoming the risks, stepping up to the challenge, and experiencing the reward of controlling an out-of-control situation—where do I sign up?

I finally got a window of opportunity to B.A.S.E. jump in January of 1997. Actually, it was more like a peephole of opportunity. I was doing a vert demo at the Superdome in New Orleans, Louisiana—the same Cajun metropolis where John Vincent happens to reside. Immediately after the bike demo I was scheduled to make a trip to Colorado to see a shoulder specialist at the Steadman-Hawkins clinic. I needed to get my arm working again and knew I would be out of commission for a while after the surgeries. I was aching to do one last gnarly thing to hold me over during recovery time. The day after the demo we awoke with the chickens, five-thirty in the morning, and hot-wired an elevator. Our goal was to get to the top of a fifteen-hundred-foot-tall steel antenna on the edge of town. This structure transmitted Soft Rock Hits of the Seventies and other radio signals to the good folk of Louisiana. I was going to jump off it.

John generously loaned me his favorite chute. I was so driven to get this jump in that I actually talked my friend Bryan—who was completely terrified of heights—into helping pull off the caper. His role was to accompany me up the tower, not look down, and capture the moment on tape. The crucial three-chip digital video documentation was not so much for my glory reel—it was so I could study my technique and learn everything I could from my actions.

It was supercold, and we all had bed head and bad breath. The service elevator carried us up about a hundred feet and it froze. Try as we might, the thing wouldn't climb another foot. In retrospect this was probably a good omen. I was getting frustrated, excited, and desperate to get a jump in before I went under the knife again. My mind was so focused on jumping that there was no way I was backing down. I hadn't taken into consideration that John's rig was set up for B.O.B. (Bottom of Bag) deployment chute. My rotator cuff was so jacked up, and my shoulder was barely functional, so the reach and jerk technique needed for this type of deployment would have been extra hairy. My arm could have slipped out of its socket and I wouldn't have been able to get the chute open. I was being stupid, and even the best jumpers are smart and humble enough to back down on occasion. Thinking back on that moment, I feel fortunate the elevator denied us the opportunity to reach the exit point.

But John knew of a bridge. It was two hundred and seventy feet tall and spanned the Mississippi River, just across town. "*Hell,* yeah," I said. It was decided that for this short height I'd need to do a Hop-N-Pop, a technique in which you throw your pilot chute the second after your feet leave the ledge. I climbed up the concrete beast like an eager little tick, ready to suck on some life. The wind was gusting, and to add to the list of weather hazards, it started sleeting. I figured out the wind was going perpendicular to the river, which meant I didn't have to worry so much about being flung back into a bridge pillar or support buttress by a rogue blast of air. If anything, it was gonna blow me away from shore. I looked out over the surging brown waters of the Mississippi, with cold air filling my lungs. I had about eighty skydives in my logbook. I'd been practicing, I had my track down, had my on-heading openings down, landings down, everything. I knew if I waited for my upcoming surgeries to heal it would be four months. As I was up on the apex, psyching myself up and preparing to drop, a squad car was scoping out Bryan on the ground. Bridge, river, guy with video camera, and at seven thirty in the morning. What's wrong with this picture?

When you jump, it's like committing suicide but not dying. Even though you trust in your rig and your capabilities, it takes a moment of pure conscious decision to get your-self over the edge. You have to fly the Fuck It Flag and just . . . go. I leaped, got a brief taste of intense ground rush, and popped open. The wind made short work of me, and pulled me out over the water. I splashed down in the dirty, swiftly moving currents and went under. My winter clothes and a helmet were heavy, but the parachute was the real problem. A parachute works by creating lots of drag, even underwater. It was going to drown me if I didn't get it off, pronto. I felt guilty because it was John's, and not only expensive but, more important, it had a personal value that was irreplaceable. He'd done about five hundred hectic jumps with it, and it had never let him down. I swam for shore and crawled out soaked to the core and shivering. I ran, trying to beat the currents car-rying the parachute down river. There was a dock nearby where tugboats operated, accessible via a nearby building. The door was locked but shaky, so I gave it a few swift kicks. I whipped out two wet $20 bills and passed them off to Steve, who was on our ground crew. Through chattering teeth, I asked him to hire a tugboat captain for a res-cue mission to retrieve John's chute. I turned around to make my way back to John and Bryan, when I heard someone approaching from behind me.

"Son, what're you doin'? Are you stupid?" the voice of authority said to me as I sat in the back of the patrol car, cuffed. I was dripping bilge water everywhere, mildly hypothermic, had just replaced my surgery recovery time with a jail sentence, and I was worried about John's gear. "Yeah, I'm not arguing with you officer. I feel pretty damn stupid right now." The cop began running my name for a warrant check and noticed my Oklahoma driver's license. "Boy, what the hell are you doing down here in Louisiana?" Dejectedly and absentmindedly, I muttered that I was in town doing a bike show. The cop stopped and brightened up. A smile cracked under his moustache. "At the Superdome? Were you the one doing the flip?" The demo I'd done was indeed at a monster truck show in the Superdome. "Yeah! That was me all right!" I said, trying to sound chummy. The cop said his kids loved my show. In two minutes the entire situation was reversed—I was unarrested, and the city supervisors en route to press charges had been radioed and talked out of it. The cop gave me his card and told me to send a photo of the day's jump and advised me not to try it so damn early next time. Roger that, officer.

Jump Off a Mountain

When a human being falling at one hundred and sixty miles per hour collides with a jagged pile of granite, it's really bad. Your skeleton comes out of your body. All the organs, cavities, and sacs of fluid inside explode. Everything hard—bones, teeth, the spirit—shatters like glass. It has to be a terrible way to go, supereded by probably the purest, most alive, mind-blowing twenty-second ride possible.

John and I had been trying to find a way to combine bike riding with skydiving. We wanted to cook up a rush that would burn for months inside our hearts. He said he knew a place, a Norwegian cliff top B.A.S.E. jump hot spot called Kjerag. At thirty-two hundred feet tall, the exit point is higher than both the World Trade Center Twin Towers were, combined. And you could ride a bike right off the edge. Unforgettable, but also brutally unforgiving. A razor-sharp, diamond-hard shelf of rock extends from the cliff and creates a severe hazard about twelve seconds down. Jumpers have to use maximum caution and track far enough from the cliff face to clear this ledge. "I will figure out a way to get us there," I told John. I started making phone calls.

In late June of 1997 Kjerag attracted the attention of accomplished skydiver Stina-Ulla Ostberg. Stina had twenty-five hundred skydives to her credit, but Kjerag was unlike anything she had ever attempted. Sources say she failed to heed local experts' advice about the dangers of the shelf. At the twelve-second mark, Stina realized she wasn't going to clear the rocks and threw her pilot chute. Seven-tenths of a second later she impacted and was killed instantly.

I rolled into town eight days later. My shoe sponsor, Boks, was footing the bill, but John and I were on a simple mission: Get in, get off, get out. I brought Steve for support, and a camera crew of our friends Shon and Morgan to document. We stayed in the nearby village of Lysebotn, in a hostel. The most lavish expense on the trip was beer, which cost eight bucks apiece for cheap stuff. We were at the ends of the earth, down the fjords and up the mountain and in the middle of nowhere. But Lysebotn was infamous. B.A.S.E. jumpers from around the world were attracted to the cliff like moths to a flame. There was a community of jumpers who lived in the shadow of Kjerag, hiking up and hucking off as often as possible. The exit point was discovered and jumped for the first time in 1994 by Stein Edvardsen. He was one of the local masters and the go-to guy if you intended to jump. Because of the recent death of Stina and a series of other tragedies on the mountain, the Lysebotn locals were extra critical of who was jumping. They were assessing skill levels and strongly discouraging amateur attempts. They didn't want thrill-crazy tourists pillaging their playground and spilling blood on the rocks because of inexperience and stupidity. With John's help and B.A.S.E. jump street cred, I got the nod from Stein, who was a bit wary that this would be my second B.A.S.E. jump ever. I told him I was definitely an amateur jumper but ready to absorb any advice he had about successes and failures. I was humbled by what we were about to do, yet driven to do it. I wouldn't have traveled halfway around the world to Kjerag if I thought *maybe* I could make it. This was a stunt I'd spent seven years building up to; all the split-second life-death skydiving skills and tests would be put to use. Stein poured me a cup of tea and calmly said I'd need to listen to him carefully if I didn't want to die.

It took close to four hours to get to the top and earn our fun. We chugged along, swearing and joking, gasping for breath as the incline turned our legs to putty. Craggy boulders and rushing mountain creeks were crossed, the path put us through pockets of dirty summer snow and fields of mossy green lichen. With the Norwegian sun shining twenty hours a day, its rays bounced off the granite and made the ground sparkle like jewels.

We arrived at the peak and got a look over the rim; it took my breath away with its staggering beauty and sick vertical drop. Just seeing the bottom of the void felt powerful. Way down below, the icy waters of the fjord rippled with wind, and gray rocks the size of tract homes dotted the shoreline where the landing area lay waiting for us. It was less than a minute away via the Kjerag express route.

It never left my mind that a thing this gorgeous could also end my life, but my focus was needed elsewhere. I took a few moments to get into the mental state of 100 percent concentration on what I was about to do, my pulse racing and my mouth dry. Time to live. John and I exited together. Four seconds after my feet left the cliff I was doing one hundred miles an hour in a headlong dive bomb; my biggest concern was the critical factor of clearing the ledge. Because my rotator cuff on my

right shoulder was unpredictable, I was throwing my pilot chute left-handed for the first time ever. I was also wearing John's rig. Both of these factors increased the odds of a screwup, but I was in control and feeling great. My altitude awareness was sharp, and I held on for a few more seconds as I milked the ground rush of my life, then deployed my chute with about five hundred feet of air to spare. I made a landing as adrenaline charged my blood with electricity.

We hiked and jumped a second time that day. I asked John if I should attempt a double gainer off the exit point. "Sure, why not," he said, confident and casual.

The drop from the exit point gave me twelve seconds before I'd reached the jagged outcropping in the cliff face that had killed Stina, and it took a six-second lateral track away from the cliff wall to clear the outcropping. That gave me six seconds to complete two flips, six seconds to track away from the wall, and after I'd cleared the outcropping, I could drop another six seconds before having to open my chute. When calculating these details, I realized the numbers involved were 6–6–6. Weird.

I ran off the cliff and threw a backflip, getting an upside-down glimpse of the cliff wall blurring by just a few feet from my head. I could hear it whistling past, the spookiest sound in the world. John had jumped just a second behind me, wearing a helmet cam. I saw him above as I came around on the second flip. Then it was time to get my delta track in place, get out past the ledge, and pop the chute.

When I got to the bottom I told John I couldn't believe how scary that one had been. "Yeah, I'd never try that shit," said John, referring to my double gainer. It freaked me out a little to hear that, because there was one more thing I wanted to try on my last jump, and it would be gnarly.

The next morning I spooned oatmeal into my mouth and swallowed. Sometimes I'm afraid of myself. But fear can be good. It's the way my mind demands attention and concentration. A half an hour later we started our hike. My thoughts racing with each step, from what I'd need to do to survive the day, to *What am I doing here?* I had many friends tell me this was crazy. I hadn't even furnished Jaci with the full details—she didn't want to know. I knew the consequences if I failed, but I was at a crossroads in my life; I'd lost my mother, my body wasn't allowing me to thrive on my bike, and I wasn't interested in retiring to be a businessman, so where could I go? What was my purpose? I let spontaneity guide me, searching for an answer that changes every time I find it. Today was my day to live or die, to challenge my abilities against fate. Today was my day to ride a bicycle off a thirty-two-hundred-foot cliff in Norway and do a double backflip.

At the top of Kjerag it seemed especially pretty. Everything was in place, my head was clear and nerves were steeled as I prepared to toss my spirit off the mountain and into the air. Just as I had my thoughts collected and was ready to get it on, I realized the handlebars on my bike were totally loose. I patted my pocket for the Allen wrench and realized it was back at base camp. At first I was so pissed, but I tried to shut down my emotions so I wouldn't lose focus. "I'll get it," John volunteered and vanished over the rim. It happened so fast; it was funny. I had a few more hours to contemplate fate and take in the tranquility. I sat there next to my bike on top of the world, overwhelmed with awareness. Sometimes you've got to lose your direction to find your place, and I felt I had found it at that moment. I was at peace with myself, my past, and whatever was in my future. I took a nap on the edge of the cliff and waited for John. I had a dream I fell out of bed, and it woke me up.

The energy was in the air and it was time. My gear was perfect, the bike ready, and my head in tune with the task at hand. John uttered a brief B.A.S.E. jumper's prayer. Suddenly the radio came alive with a message that we'd have to wait a few minutes before we could jump; a mountain rescue team needed to make their weekly helicopter flight through the canyons just off Kjerag. We heard the approach of rotor blades echoing off the rocks and then saw the choppers. Talk about a heavy demonstration. Rather than freak me out, though, it just hardened my resolve.

The edge sloped down at a thirty-degree angle. I rolled down the rocks, and shot off the edge like a bottle rocket. I had speed to spare, but overcoming my momentum and nailing two consecutive backflips was going to be tricky. I had six seconds to play with, and six more seconds to track away from the ledge. I held the grips white-knuckle tight as I rotated through my first flip, feeling the rushing wind trying to steal my bike. I started my second rotation and maintained a hard arch to help coax it around. Never before had I felt so *in* the moment and experienced such a pure state of mind, body, and being. I was on superautopilot, not thinking about what I was doing but doing it exactly right.

I had gone over every detail of the jump mentally, had a countermeasure for every possible crisis. Except my stupid pant leg getting caught in the chain. I was flipped upside down, bombing toward earth at one hundred and fifty miles an hour with a bike stuck to me. I kicked both legs. Hard. The thirty-five-pound bicycle broke free and con-tinued its journey. I threw my arms back to track and straightened my legs, but was too stiff. I waffled out of control and forced myself to relax, let the wind flow with my body and carry me into a lateral track away from the shelf that was rapidly approaching.

I popped my chute and it opened with a violent jerk and in an instant it twisted around one hundred eighty degrees, sending me face first toward the cliff. Swooping toward the rock wall, I grabbed my risers on instinct, using both arms to pull with all my might to the right. If I'd followed skydiving protocol and grabbed the toggles and tried to steer, it would've been too late. My canopy snapped around toward the fjord and away from doom.

Suddenly I was on the ground, overwhelmed with emotion and just pure existence. I had never felt more alive. My heart was roaring. My soul was quaking with the power of what I had just done, something that was not supposed to be physically possible. At least, not without a parachute and a dream. I felt like I was living on extra credit, or I'd just earned an extra life.

I have always been jealous of people who can sit on the porch and watch a sunset and be content. No matter how hard I try, I can't be like that. To me, life-threatening situations seem like life at its best. Our small expedition left Norway the next day. I went to England for the Backyard Jam, then from there onto the World Championships in Holland. I spent the remainder of 1997 organizing and executing the first bike/skate tour in Malaysia. I put the parachutes in the closet all winter, waiting. Before the cliff jump, I promised myself if I lived through it I was going to close this chapter of my life and start a new one. But I just couldn't stop thinking of how to top it with something more intense. My rational side told me if I couldn't shake the feeling, I might not be around too long. I had developed a heightened tolerance for risk and continuously needed to make things even more dangerous to satisfy my spirit.

June 1998. Tony Hawk and I were doing a show for Charles and Jill Schultz in an ice arena in Santa Rosa, California. There was a box jump, and I decided to do a superman. My cranks flipped, I missed the pedal, and landed straight-legged on my right leg. Since my knee was weak, it buckled backward, and the leg completely folded with my foot coming up to meet the kneecap. My ACL (anterior cruciate ligament) and PCL (posterior cruciate ligament), which work together to keep the knee stable and the meniscus in place, were instantly blown out. As I continued to crash, my foot got caught between my rear peg and the ground, and my leg whipped around the other way and snapped back in the socket. It felt gross to see my leg bend backward. It was just ... wrong. I cried, not from physical pain but because I thought my riding days were over. For one year, I lost my knee and couldn't do anything with my leg, not even skydive. I was unable to pursue my passion and lacked any action. I was going crazy. During my downtime, I stepped back and examined my life and what kind of risks I was putting myself through.

I think this injury probably saved my life.

THE SOUND
OF THE
BONE DRILL

I've broken one wrist five times. The other wrist, three times. Between my ankles, I've had five breaks. I've snapped four fingers, my thumbs four times, my hand twice, busted my feet three times, and broken three toes. (You don't think a broken toe would hurt that much, but your entire body weight is on it.) I've busted my collarbones five times; snapped my pelvis, my fibula, and my elbow; and cracked three ribs and separated a couple from my sternum. (Breaking ribs off the sternum sucks—just about every movement you can think of is centered in your chest.) Then there's my head: one skull fracture, two broken jaws, two broken noses, a mouthful of teeth, and a partridge in a pear tree.

Every choice you make can be traced back to the instinctual need to seek pleasure, and avoid pain. These two forces are interconnected, different sides to the same coin. Since I started bike riding, I wanted more than anything to experience the highest highs. To get there, I was willing to accept the consequences. My medical records contain more than four hundred pages documenting my injuries. I've put myself in a coma, had over fifty knockouts and concussions, been sewn up with over two hundred stitches, dislocated my shoulder more than twenty times, broken about fifty bones, and had fourteen surgeries. I've torn ligaments, bruised tissue, severed arteries, spilled blood, and left hunks of my skin stuck to plywood, concrete, dirt, and bicycle components. I've had to endure not just physical pain, but the mental anguish of relearning how to walk, ride my bike, or even remember who I was. I've dealt with mountains of health insurance red tape and condescending doctors who took it upon themselves to lecture me before they treated my injuries, as if they needed to save me from myself.

Not everyone understands that I've asked for it, accepted it, and willingly volunteered. Not to sound sadistic, but I consider each of my injuries a tax I had to pay for learning what I could do on my bike. I wanted it all and wouldn't take any of it back if I could. Yes, I will be sore and broken when I'm older. I can feel it already, the aches and pains of a body that has been beyond and back. I've given up as much of myself as I could, because I love bike riding that much.

My insurance companies have always hated me, having paid hospital bills totaling more than a million dollars over the years. I've had to rely on surgery more than a dozen times to keep me going. You know it's getting serious when you start letting people take knives to your body to make you healthy.

Here are my patient notes.

#1: Collarbone Crush

November 1986. It was immediately following a Mountain Dew Trick Team show. I'd just learned 360 drop-ins and was uncorking them all day. We finished our demo, but I still wanted to ride. I took my chest protector off, figuring I'd just do easy stuff. I lined up parallel to the coping to do a simple hop drop-in, like Eddie Fiola used to do. I stalled in position for a second and went for it. For some reason my brain told my body to react as if I was doing a 360 drop-in. I fell straight to the cement and took the hit on my head and shoulder. My friend Page said it made a sound like a helmet being thrown off the ramp with nothing in it—a loud, hollow snap. That was my grand finale. I didn't just break my collarbone, I shattered it. I knocked myself unconscious, too. The show was right next door to a hospital, of all places, with two of the best surgeons in Oklahoma City on duty that day. In surgical terms, Dr. Grana and Dr. Yates performed a fourth-degree AC joint separation procedure, provided reconstruction of the coracoclavicular ligament, and did a partial removal of my left collarbone.

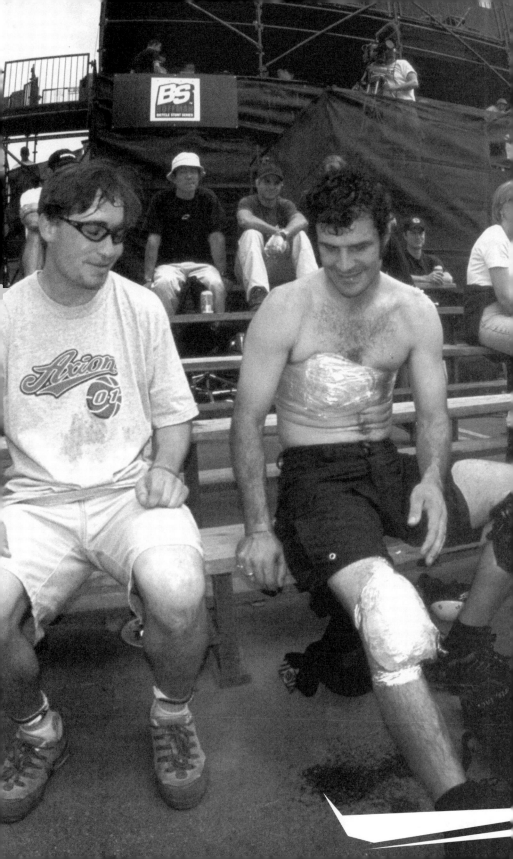

#2: Right Leg, Wrong Move

February 1988. The 540 is a trick that makes you earn it to learn it. The price is a lot of slams. I finally thought I had them just about dialed in and did one and looped out. My leg got caught behind me and I sat on it. There was a snapping sound and a blast wave of heat, pain, and nausea. Broken bones have a dull, throbby kind of ache to them. I got into Steve's car to go to the hospital. Every time he hit a bump my leg would sway between my knee and ankle. My body was in shock, and the pain began to subside. We started chuckling every time it swayed, and then started laughing harder about what the hell we were laughing at. Dark humor helps. The doctor I encountered in the ER had very little humor. My first question to him was, "How long before I can ride again?" He told me I would be lucky to walk without a limp and would never ride a bike again. "Okay, thanks . . . bye," was the next thing out of my mouth. I left that doctor as fast as I could, and my dad got me in to see Dr. Yates. Yates put in a titanium plate (the body rejects steel) and ten screws in my fibula to repair my right leg. I missed the first King of Vert in Paris because of this injury.

#3: Cartilage Carnage

April 1988. With a leg full of hardware, I followed the doctor's orders and waited patiently before I started riding again. Finally it healed, and I went to Kansas City to ride with Dennis and Rick. We celebrated with an all-night street session. I was careful not to thrash my leg too hard. The next day I woke up and my knee was swollen, supersized. It wouldn't move, either. I went home and got an MRI. The internal images revealed that I'd totally ripped both my medial and lateral meniscus in half when I'd broken my leg. The meniscus is a shock-

absorbing cartilage in the middle of your knee. When Dr. Yates had put the plate in, he'd never thought to check it for other damage, and I had no idea my knee was jacked. My street session with the Kansas City BMX Brigade had aggravated the meniscus more and more until it was wrecked. Dr. Yates sewed it back together from the inside. Arthoscopic meniscus repair is considered a less invasive surgical procedure than using the knife. Dr. Yates drilled pencil-sized holes and slid all the tools inside my knee, doing the operation using a tiny video camera. Tech.

#4: Ted Nugent Tumor Trauma

December 1990. I don't know how it happened, but a tumor grew in my right leg. I was diagnosed with Cat Scratch Fever, a shocking prognosis. My entire life, I thought Cat Scratch Fever was a just a cheesy fictitious disease, invented by the Motor City Madman, Ted Nugent. But it was real and residing in my groin. The viral infection caused a growth to form under my skin. It was about the size and shape of a bar of soap, and it hurt to do can-cans. I had to get the lump removed, and this was right after my mom had died of cancer, so I was sweating it. The growth turned out to be benign. The day after the surgery I went to Austin with Spike Jonze for a road trip. I had to ride with a drainage tube sticking out of my leg, leaking excess pus. I came up with a few tube variations on vert.

#5: Rotator Cuff Rip-Off

January 1991. I hadn't done a one-footed 540 in weeks, when I tried spinning one. I held back a little and did it low. I crashed and landed with my right arm fully extended to break my fall. The impact ripped my rotator cuff, the group of four muscles that lay over your shoulder socket, which keep your arm in place and help it rotate. Mine was wrecked.

The irony was I'd hurt myself because I was holding back, to avoid hurting myself. My whole arm stung with electrified hellfire, but it stayed in its socket and didn't feel like I'd broken anything. The day after the slam, I was scheduled to do some demos in Australia with Mark "Gator" Anthony, Brian Blyther, and Chris Miller. My shoulder ached superbad, but I iced it every night. From Australia I flew directly to the KOV contest at Thrasherland in Arizona. During the pro finals, I got a flat at the end of my second run. I borrowed the nearest bike I could find and dropped in. I had to literally hold on and hoped it responded to what I wanted it to do, which was a flip fakie. I almost pulled it, but the bike felt alien, and the seatpost was so low I had to stand up on the roll back. I bit off a little more than I could chew and paid for it with another slam. My rotator cuff tore some more. But I won the comp and the 1990 Pro of the Year title.

I got home from the Arizona contest and had to get the hardware (ten screws and a plate) removed from my leg because the bone had grown over it. I was still growing and it was going to affect the growth of my leg, so they had to go back in and chisel it out. The upside was, I would only have to take about a week or two off before I could ride again. I asked Dr. Yates if he could take a look at my shoulder during the operation because it had been aching. I woke up with a big puffy incision on my right arm and a shoulder immobilizer on it. Dr. Yates came in and said I had immensely torn my rotator cuff, and I was looking at a four-month recovery. Shit! I didn't expect that.

That one-footed 540 injury made me realize my pain tolerance was getting pretty strong, and even if I could handle the pain, it didn't mean something wasn't seriously wrong. It was also the gateway to serious rotator cuff problems, which plague me to this day. Every time I put my arm out when I slam, it tears my rotator cuff. All because I held back on that trick.

The incident convinced me to never try anything half-assed again.

#6: Arm Harm

October 1992. During the summer I took a bad slam on my elbow. I never got it checked and didn't know I'd chipped off part of the bone. The bone spur healed in the joint, and before long I couldn't bend my elbow enough to brush my teeth, brush my hair, or shave. I'm right-handed and had to learn all those tasks using my left arm. It sounds simple, but it's not. That was my mentality at the time—I'd modify my life around injuries, as long as it didn't inter-fere with my riding. I was getting accustomed to my unbendable elbow by the time I went to the Rider Cup in England, in October. A good day of riding came to a halt when I hung up doing a flair. I stiff-armed into the flatbottom with my right arm extended and hit my head on the top of my arm so hard I knocked myself out, ripping my rotator cuff again and worse. The slam put me in so much pain so fast that I knew I'd done something very bad to my body. It was a long, sore flight home. When I got back to the United States I immediately went to Dr. Yates for surgery. I asked him to check out my elbow while he was in my shoulder—two birds, one stone. I woke up with an immobilized elbow that hurt worst than my shoulder. It was a tough surgery. In the video of the arthroscopic portion of the surgery, a bunch of tools are stuck deep into my arm and Dr. Yates says, "I'll be filleting your elbow now." I didn't expect it, but it took a lot of therapy and time before my elbow would bend again.

It works fine now, and I'm back to shaving right-handed.

#7: Air to Spleen

April 1993. I talked about this earlier. The thing I've noticed about life after spleen is I catch colds quicker and have to take more antibiotics to fight the infections. Every time I sneeze, I have bike riding to thank.

#8: Supersplinter

August 1993. There's nothing like the feel of having stiff wood rammed into your ass. I'm talking, of course, about splinters. I was having a mellow session on the Ninja Ramp and the plywood surface was in tatters. I didn't really think too much about it. I started working on a few new tricks and crashed, sliding sideways down the tranny. On the way down, a piece of plywood peeled up and was driven through the right side of my butt. I got to the bottom and jumped up like my pants were on fire—a quick inspection revealed a wedge-shaped splinter with a tip thicker than a toothbrush. It had pierced my right cheek on one side, and come out the other. Deep. It was one of those laughing on the outside, crying on the inside moments. I got out a pair of vise grips, clamped onto the wood near the entry wound, took a deep breath, and pulled. It broke off inside. The tip was sticking out on the other side, so I pressed my luck and tried to pull the fat end through the exit hole. I broke off that end, too. By that time, the acute pain had subsided. I went back to riding.

We were holding a contest at the Hoffman Bikes compound in less than two weeks, and there was a lot of work to do fixing up the street park course. The day after my splinter, I was outside pounding nails with Steve, team manager Kim Boyle, and Jamie Mosberg, a cinematographer Airwalk had hired to shoot a promo with me riding my twenty-one-foot quarterpipe. Somehow, the subject of who had the hairiest ass came up. Jamie, whose nickname is Mouse, claimed he did and threw down the challenge. I started laughing that the first contest on the new Hoffman Bikes park was going to be a hairy ass contest. I dropped my pants and heard gasps. Mouse technically won, as we discovered his ass is carpeted in brown fur. But my bruised and inflamed splinter tipped the scales in my favor, and I was declared the champion. I hadn't told anyone about my splinter, and after the laughter died down, Steve and Kim began to get concerned. I was forced to go to the hospital and have it surgically removed. Mouse brought his camera and documented it and said he'd edit it to *General Hospital* music. The next day we shot the Airwalk promo, and I couldn't sit down.

#9: Shouldering the Pain

September 1993. We were holding a Bicycle Stunt comp at the Hoffman Bikes park over Labor Day weekend. My rotator cuff had been torn for a while, and I was scheduled to get surgery on it the Thursday before the comp. I told Dr. Yates we'd need to postpone the surgery so I could ride the contest. I was also intent on riding the twenty-one-foot quarterpipe, for the skeptics in attendance. I did a few airs more than twenty feet high, and on my last aerial my arm gave up the ghost. I totally ripped my rotator cuff off the humerus head. That is a very bad thing. Dr. Yates had his work cut out for him. His surgical notes start with a right shoulder diagnostic arthroscopy, followed by open repair of massive rotator cuff avulsion with bicipital tenodesis and subscapularis tendon. Translation? Yates told me my rotator cuff muscles were like a thin piece of fatiguing metal. They could snap anytime, and I didn't have

any control over it with my arm raised above my head. I could literally rip my arm off if I crashed bad enough. From that day forward, I had to use a shoulder brace with a string attaching the underside of my arm to my ribs, to keep my arm from extending too far up. I lost all movement and strength in my shoulder. After not having a haircut for six years, I shaved my head because I couldn't raise my arm high enough to brush the dreads out. My arm even dislocates in bed sometimes, and it won't go back in. Once I rolled over and my arm fell out of the socket. I had Jaci trying to yank it back in, but no go. Finally I had to call Steve at about 6:30 in the morning to help me get it back in. That's the sign of a true friend.

Despite the best medical treatment I could find, my arm has never healed.

#10: Weak in the Knees

July 1995. My meniscus tore in half again over the course of many slams. In the 1990s, street riding was the fastest-growing facet of bike riding, and there were many opportunities to see where the limits could be pushed even further. Riding was getting progressively more technical, and really burly. It sucked me in and I found myself riding more street and less vert. Street riding can be like therapy. I'd throw a Suicidal Tendencies tape in the Walkman and set out to unveil what the street had to offer. After a good session I'd come back relaxed and cured. It wasn't uncommon for people to jump off buildings, or if you messed up on a handrail, to tumble down long flights of concrete stairs at full speed. Whenever you crash riding street, your knees usually suffer the most because you try to abandon the bike and run out of the crash. During this era I tore my meniscus, my PCL, and a bunch of other cartilage in my knee. Sometimes the flapping meniscus would get caught up in between my femur and tibia and lock up my knee. Dr. Yates did another arthroscopic surgery on my right knee and Roto-rootered it out. He had to remove my meniscus. I had no shock-absorbing cartilage in the middle of my knee. Yum.

#11: Rotator Cuff Rebuild

March 1996. My shoulder injury put a limit on my riding. Dr. Yates said that there was nothing left to do; my shoulder was fucked. I think he was sick of spending hours putting it back together only to have me rip it right up again. Basically it had come to the point where I had to decide: If I chose to ride and challenge myself more, then I could lose my arm. I decided I wasn't done yet.

Yates suggested I see what the Steadman-Hawkins Clinic could do for me. It was located in Vail, Colorado, and I scheduled a stay, right after my first B.A.S.E. jump in New Orleans. Dr. Hawkins was the shoulder specialist and Dr. Steadman, the knee guy. They are a world-renowned surgery group and the team doctors for the Denver Broncos, Colorado Rockies, and the U.S. Ski Team. I flew into Denver and took a bus to Vail. This was my first solo mission to try and find a procedure that would get my body working again. My plan was to get Dr. Steadman to check out my knee and fix my PCL, which I'd torn a couple years earlier. At the same time I was there to have Dr. Hawkins double up the surgeries, with a rotator cuff overhaul. That way I could stack the recovery times together and be out for the least amount of time. However, after I arrived I found out the knee would take too long to recuperate, and I was scheduled to do the closing ceremonies of the Olympics. I decided to just get my shoulder fixed. I could still ride without a PCL, and live without one. During the surgery on my rotator cuff, I got a nerve block that made my arm completely numb. It was freaky to get a preview of what it would be like to totally lose arm function.

The surgery went well, and after it healed, my shoulder stayed in its socket better. But Dr. Hawkins didn't have much faith that it would perform well enough to withstand the rigors of riding.

#12: The Battle of Wounded Knee

When I wrecked my ACL and PCL at the Shultz Show in June of 1998, I knew what had happened held grave consequences for my riding. ACLs can probably be repaired a hundred times and still get decent results—their job is to keep your tibia and fibula from sliding up your femur and dislocating. PCLs are much harder to repair and can only be fixed two or three times before they're toast. I'd just wrecked both the ACL and PCL in one shot. I would have little to no chance of ever riding like I wanted to again and was looking at a lot of months of pain just to recover. I was twenty-six years old and had planned on building myself a twenty-six-foot ramp for a belated twenty-sixth birthday. My life had just completely changed. Bike riding, as I knew it, was over, and I would have to accept it.

I went home and Dr. Yates scheduled me for an operation. I had to wait for a cadaver ligament to be "available." Soon thereafter, I got the call that someone's Achilles was packed in ice, on its way to meet me. The surgery was a real challenge. Since I'd torn both my ACL and PCL, there wasn't any accurate way to ensure a tight, centered implementation of both ligaments. I wasn't encouraged that the outcome would be successful. But I had a very skilled master surgeon on my side, and the winds of fortune blowing my way the day of the operation. It took months, but my knee healed nicely with even tension from both the front and back ligaments.

The next time I got on my bike, I had to struggle to clear five feet of air. I was being mellow, trying to get acclimated to the feel of my bike moving underneath me. It was so foreign. It gave me a whole new respect for bikers. I couldn't believe how much I'd taken my skills for granted when I was at the top of my game. Now those skills were gone. I played around, sticking to lip tricks until my brakes slipped on a Canadian nosepick. I dropped to the bottom like a dot-com stock. When my leg hit the ramp, my lower leg sheared off and rode up my femur, completely tearing my ACL. I couldn't believe it. I wondered, *again*, if this was it for my days as a biker.

#13: The Synthetic Solution

February 1999. I decided I wasn't ready to give up yet. After crashing the Canadian pick and trashing my cadaver components, I became desperate for a way to fix my knee. I'd need another operation just to walk, so I figured I might as well research every alternative treatment done on ACL/PCL replacement. Thank God for the Internet. I found hope in the form of synthetic ligament replacement procedures. Just as quickly, I ran into a brick wall in the United States, because the FDA refused to sanction synthetics, citing that it wasn't a long-term option. By even giving me advice on how to get the procedure done elsewhere, a doctor practicing in the United States would put their medical license in jeopardy. It's funny how you think you own your body, yet the government really has control over us in so many ways. Dr. Yates knew the deal, though, and was very helpful in steering me in the right direction for plastic parts: France. Their top orthopedic doctors had been successfully doing ACL repair on rugby players using a thing called the LARS ligament. These guys were back on the field after only four weeks—my previous surgery took me out for six months.

I started sending faxes and E-mails to French doctors with unpronounceable names.

I narrowed it down to two options. I could go to France to have the surgery done, or go to the French province of Montreal, in Canada. I chose Canada for its socialized medicine. The prices were right, only about $5,000 for the entire operation. It ended up going down like a drug deal on *Miami Vice*. I had to go alone, and bring cash, and pay the doctor in my hotel room the day before. The downside was, they wanted me to be a human guinea pig. They were doing research on the operation and wanted to prove it could be done without extensive anesthetics, which are the most dangerous part of any surgery. By proving it was possible to do the surgery without anesthetics, they could promote it as a safe alternative to ACL reconstruction, increasing their odds of being sanctioned by the FDA.

The procedure called for them to open up my knee and drill a six-millimeter hole down the length of my femur. The drill bit was fifteen inches long. I would be fully conscious and have no pain medication for the surgery. In fact, I could watch close on three TV monitors in the room.

It was kind of like an interactive horror movie. My skin was numbed with a local anesthesia, and then the doctors brought out the drill. "We haven't figured out a way to numb the inside of the bone, so this will hurt," my doctor said to me. It hit bone and the room filled with a smell that, well, I don't think you ever want to get a whiff of your own bones smoking. The drill surged and grunted onward, the tiny motor straining as the pain began to increase. Then the tip broke though into the marrow. My heart rate was supposed to stay below eighty beats per minute, and it shot through the roof when

I felt the hot drill strike the soft marrow inside my femur. It was pain taken to a new level. On a scale from one to ten, the knobs turned to an eleven-kind of painful. It didn't help matters to actually see what bone marrow looks like; spongy red and yellowish pulp, like corned beef hash. I had to struggle and concentrate on my breathing to get my heart rate down, while squeezing the steel rails of the bed with my hands as tightly as I could. Every once in a while the nurse would lean over and say in broken Franglish, "You doing real well, Mot." This went on for the longest thirty minutes of my life. Once there were holes in my femur and tibia, the doctors threaded a poly-ester ligament through the bony tunnels. Basically, they put a ski rope where my ACL once was.

Afterward I was sewn up and I sat up on the table. There was an awkward pause as the doctor snapped off his latex gloves. I'd just had major surgery, without drugs. "Am I free to go?" I asked, my mind reeling and unsure of what to do. "Yep," said the doctor. We shook hands and I limped from the surgical table to go outside and flag down a cab.

I finally got a cab and crumpled into the backseat, marveling at the incredible strangeness of life. Ten minutes ago there were six hands shoving tools and titanium screws inside my knee, and suddenly I was in some dirty shoebox of a taxi, hustling back to my hotel. I kept thinking I was doing something wrong; there was very little postoperative pampering and nurturing going on. At the hotel, I fell in bed and flipped on the TV. I settled in for what would become a forty-eight hour pay-per-view marathon, starting with the buddy cop comedy *Rush Hour*, subtitled in French. Before long I had to use the bathroom and faced my first crisis; I couldn't walk and had no crutches. I got two chairs under my arms and used them to *slowly* crab across the room to the beckoning toilet. It was a painful, sluggish struggle.

On the third day I got in a cab to the airport, boarded my flight, and went home a new man, with a new knee, and a new lease on life.

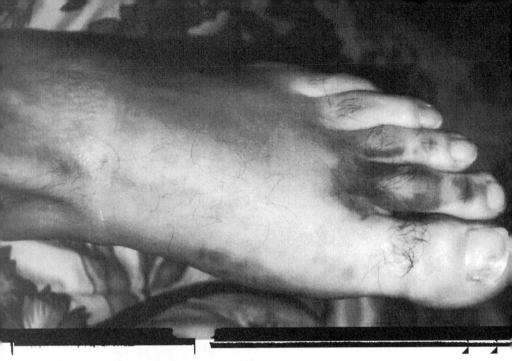

#14: Snapping the Ski Rope

May 1999. The LARS ligament healed up clean and quick, and I was back on my bike in a month. I rode and grew stronger, clearing my brain of business troubles by carving around on the halfpipe. Before long I was eyeing a line that had been calling me for over a year: a big transfer from the vert ramp to the street course. It was during a casual session at the Hoffman Bikes Christmas party, when I decided to give myself a present: the gap. I launched and pulled the highest backflip I could over it, and in my enthusiasm, overrotated. I was wearing a knee brace and still managed to dislocate my knee on impact. The synthetic ligament was ripped out of my femur, and I was back to square one. I didn't know what to do and felt totally defeated. It was another black day at Hoffman Bikes.

I sent a letter to the doctor in Canada who did the LARS surgery, and he said it would have been really hard to break the synthetic ligament; they were supposed to last at least five years. Dr. Yates did an exploratory surgery and found the ligament wasn't broken, I'd just yanked it out where it was anchored into my femur. He reattached it with a better procedure, implanting a little more titanium into my body. Two weeks later I had a fully functioning right knee again.

But I didn't hop back on my bike immediately. I'd just been through a frightening two years, plagued by knee problems, and I wanted to be mentally ready for what came next. I didn't want to rush out and push myself in a race to get back my chops. It was also a tough time to make this decision. The sport was bigger than it had ever been, and it was the most lucrative time to compete in the pro vert class. You could make $10,000 for a flawless two minutes on the ramp. I was staging events, running a company to pay back my debts, and watching everyone prosper.

I'd pushed the boundaries throughout my career and knew there were other things I still wanted to do on my bike. But I couldn't expect my body to keep up with my mind, without ending back up in the hospital. I wanted to go in a new direction entirely—one that was a challenge, but also without expectations. I took my brakes off, to rediscover my bike under the new terms I was dealt. I didn't know what was possible on a bike without brakes, and it was like a new sport. At one point I stripped my bike down to just the essentials: a frame, fork, bars, crankset, and wheels. Just to see what I could do with that. I was in my own world. I went back to the beginning, to the rewards that got me interested in the first place. Just riding. Not competing, not endorsing, nothing else but discovering what I could do with my bike and my body. I wasn't in a class anymore.

People ask me if all this trauma and suffering was worth it. I've invented over one hundred original ramp tricks. I can roll in and catch fifteen feet of air without pedaling. I've felt the rush of taking off my hands during 540s spun eleven feet out. I've jumped my bike off the edge of a thirty-two-hundred-foot cliff. I've shot up a ramp to see what the ground looks like from fifty feet above it and rode away from peril. I've ridden for crowds of screaming people, eighty thousand strong. And I've ridden by myself, where the only sound was my breath and my tires singing on plywood for hours on end, when there was no else left to ride with.

None of it would have ever happened if I thought the pain and suffering it would take to ride my bike and follow my heart wasn't worth it. If you want to experience life's pleasures, you have to be willing to take all the pain and failures.

I love what I do. No regrets.

TESTIMONIAL

PROVING IT

Once you know a trick is possible, it's a little bit easier. Nowadays you have foam pits and resi mats to help you take that next step, learning tricks on vert. Even if you don't have the foam, it's easier to learn it once you've seen it being done. Mat blazed the trail with the flip fakie. The flair. The endless different combo variations. He was the guy who took variations like tailwhips very high. I can think of a lot of instances where Mat was the one to do something big and gnarly. He took the slams for everybody else to learn a trick. He was the guy that found out what was possible.

—DENNIS MCCOY, PRO RIDER

can i have your

"CAN I HAVE YOUR AUTOGRAPH?"

Popularity is a trip. One that comes with a lot of extra baggage.

I grew up thinking bike riders were untouchable superhero-demigods. When I was twelve, my friends and I devoured every page of the BMX magazines (there were no videos in those days, and bikes were never on TV). We were under the spell of the twenty-inch bike industry-marketing machine—an industry that was small potatoes back then. To overcompensate for its limited size, the industry barraged its fan base with visual cues that pimped the dream. Pages were packed with action snapshots and advertisements. The images oozed with an undercurrent of success, fame, and glamour: hotshot pros throwing tabletops over top-end automobiles; sweaty gladiators brandishing giant cardboard victory checks, getting mobbed by hundreds of kids after winning a national event.

We didn't know it, but all of the factory-sponsored pros we idolized were regular

guys who rode bikes, just like us. Yeah, they were skilled at their craft, but outside the narrow world of BMX and freestyle, few knew who they were. The early promoters understood that the sport needed superstars, and using mostly smoke and mirrors, created the hype required to launch a whole category of bike riding. The recipe was simple: *more hype + more exposure + more kids into bikes = more money pumped into the industry.*

For about a decade that formula worked like a charm. Then the bike industry cannibalized itself and unceremoniously collapsed.

During the early 1990s, after the industry bottomed out, freestyle was left for dead. A handful of people—riders, mostly—picked up the pieces and continued pushing the sport onward. During the lean years, a new generation of rider-owned companies was born. At first, they all had the same thing in common: They were run by idiots (myself included). One of the more memorable early Hoffman Bikes ads was *Sex Sells*. Under that blazing headline was a full-page photo of me blasting an Indian air wearing nothing but shiny black latex Speedos and a shoulder brace. Not sure how many bikes that one sold. But the most we could hope to do was entertain ourselves, have fun, and create the products and events we needed to thrive. At one time it was possible to go to a bike event and literally know every single person there—riders and crowd—by their first name.

Like other indie manufacturers, Hoffman Bikes learned the business as we went along. We only really knew one thing:

We loved riding. What we lacked in financial firepower, we made up for in authenticity and passion. Nobody was there to get rich or famous, but there was a sense of shared vision fueling it all: Live to ride, ride to live. This seemed like a pretty good principle for a new foundation.

At the closing of the last BS contest of 1995, I got on the PA system and looked out at my friends in the crowd. I had a prediction I wanted to share. "This is the end of an era. Next year's contest series is the start of a new one, and stunt riding is going to be huge. Our sport is going to grow like crazy." ESPN2 had become part of the scene, like it or not, and bike stunt riding was primed to erupt for the second time in its short life. My biggest concern was how to maintain some control over the direction of the explosion. The steroid injection of mainstream media coverage had created a beast called "extreme sports," and there were now "extreme lifestyle products" that had little to do with skateboarding, bike riding, or snowboarding. Automakers, soda companies, and makers of snack foods and personal hygiene products were all looking to get (insert electric guitar whammy bar sound here) *extreme!*

For about five minutes, I was worried I'd be labeled a corporate sellout by a jury of my peers for joining forces with ESPN. The unwritten rule was you can't make money off your art. But I've never been much for rules. I *knew* I wasn't into bike riding for the money—if that were the case, I'd have bailed on the sport when it went broke back in 1990. With a new boom in our midst, the renaissance was happening with or without our input. I didn't want my integrity compromised when some bean counter with power started calling the shots. Bike riding is raw creative energy. For the rest of the world to understand it, and see it in the truest light, it needed a translator. That's one of the reasons why I learned to make bikes, run contests, organize demos, and create TV shows. What I do is too important to me to let someone else who doesn't know me interpret my life to the world. My philosophy is if you stay true to why you do what you do, then there's is a huge difference between selling out, and everybody else buying in.

Putting the "Core" in Corporate

At first, some riders were apprehensive about TV and corporate sponsors, because they didn't really understand what they were getting out of it. The irony was that the sport is a subculture created by free expression, and riding relies on one's ability to adapt to new surroundings. Outsider interest in the sport was definitely a new environment for most of us. I tried to use humor to shake up both the bike riders and the network a little. At the first BS/ESPN contest I put on, we designed the victory plaques to feature riders in corporate attire, and money swirling through the air. I bought suits for all my event staff. I gave everybody on the crew twenty dollars in singles and instructed them to randomly tip people, "just for showing up." By exaggerating their worst fears, I was able to get some of the hardcore bikers to loosen up and laugh. And I also wanted to make sure the network understood who we were, and what they were dealing with. That was the challenge I had taken on—mediating between two wildly different cultures that were popularizing action sports. Both sides had their own agendas, and each side could help the other, if they worked together. I knew the corporate side was guided by an entirely different set of principles. Often their viewpoint clashed with ours, but in their own stubborn ways, they could be a lot like us, too.

Not long after I started working with ESPN, I was running a contest that was off the hook—there were thousands of people in the stands, hundreds of bikers there, and the riding was great. Everybody seemed to be having a pretty good time. During the street event, one of my favorite riders, Jimmy Levan, saw a unique line nobody else had thought of—which consisted of a ramp transfer over a fence out of the contest area into the management area. As Jimmy was setting up for it, the X Games management freaked out. But Jimmy was used to dealing with people unable to understand his actions, and he jumped the fence anyway. He had to dodge the security and management guys who were totally in a tizzy over what he was trying to do when they realized, in terror, what he was setting up for. Jimmy launched the gap and cleared the fence, and the crowd went nuts. Instantly I was surrounded by flustered security and purple-faced management. Everybody was yelling at me, asking me why I wasn't disqualifying that rule-breaking bastard (sorry, Jimmy), saying things like, "that behavior is *not* tolerated." I had to chuckle, which made everybody even more pissed. The big wigs were blowing their collective stacks because insurance only covered riders *in* the fenced-off area, and if somebody had gotten hurt, the whole event, the whole series, the whole extreme world would be shut down. As this flagrant insurance infringement was explained to me, additional network people joined the fracas and added to the disarray. They didn't understanding how I could condone such an outrageous no-no in their world. I had to point out to them that Jimmy came from a different environment than theirs. They wanted to brand the guy an outlaw, but he'd done exactly what he would have if he were in his natural environment. The whole essence of street riding is to search out hard-to-find lines and create something out of nothing, to show others your unique approach to obstacles. "I understand your side of the story, that it wasn't kosher in this simulated environment," I said to the steaming promoters. "But this guy doesn't operate in the same boundaries as you do. His very goal is to show you ways *around* the boundaries." I also pointed out the mixed message they were sending us by freaking out over how bad it was, while their cameramen were setting up for the shot in the background.

I think both sides learned a bit about each other that day.

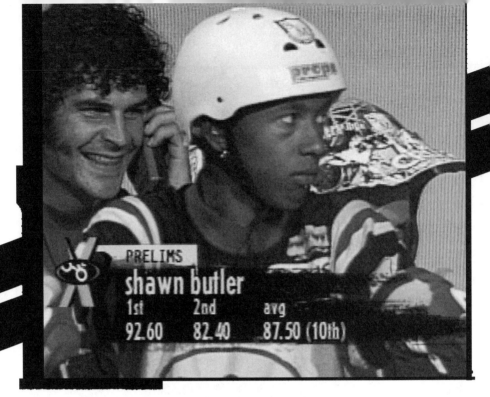

PRELIMS
shawn butler
1st	2nd	avg
92.60	82.40	87.50 (10th)

Taking Over the Satellites

Jimmy Levan wasn't the only rider to raise the hackles on the neck of authority during a televised event. I got in trouble once for treating the live TV feed from the X Games as my personal novelty item. It was in Rhode Island. We were broadcasting via satellite to twenty million people. I'd broken my foot practicing on the street course the day before and needed to take a one-day break if I was going to enter in vert. I rigged my shoe to work as a cast and helped Steve and the promotional team with running the event. I was spending the afternoon generally wandering the contest course tripping out on how insane bike riding had become but soon found a job to do: I was the starter for the dirt jumpers. I stood next to each competitor atop the starting concourse, and it was my job to give each guy their cues when to begin their run. While on the starting area, I noticed my head looming on the Jumbotron television. The camera guys were getting intro shots of the jumpers as they rolled in, and since the riders were looking at me to begin, I was in every shot. I Motorola-ed my wife. "Jaci, quick, turn on the TV." The camera stayed on me as I told Jaci about how the day was going, laughing about what we were doing. She was listening to my voice and watching me talk and wave to her on TV back in Oklahoma. "Your hair's messed up," she pointed out over the phone. I fixed it. We continued talking, smiling and waving, and had a nice chat thanks to the hijacked airtime. It wasn't until after the contest was over and they reviewed the tapes that the guys from the network saw what I was up to, but by then it was too late. Afterward, the network told me, ah, not to do that anymore, but they gave me a copy of the tape as a keepsake.

As the extreme coverage of the sport grew, the cultural shift kicked in. Alternative sports, action sports, extreme sports, hybrid sports . . . there were many names for what we did, and they were all becoming household terms. Soccer moms were putting bike racks on the minivans, and public ramp parks were getting as common as basketball courts. *USA Today* reported that skateboarding was more popular than Little League baseball. And bikes had the highest ratings during the X Games.

The bike industry sales swelled from the effects of millions of kids exposed to stunt riding. As a recruiting system, the contest coverage was working well. Kids would see the X Games on TV and entry-level bike sales would skyrocket in the weeks before and after the contests. And distribution shifted around, too. The mom-and-pop bike shops were still the source for the hardcore equipment, but sporting goods stores and big box bonanzas like Wal-Mart and Costco were selling hundreds of thousands of bikes with their "buy it low, stack it high, sell it cheap" tactics.

For established expert and pro caliber riders, there were a lot of new opportunities to plug into sponsorships. There were big(ger) bucks at stake and global exposure on TV, the Internet, video games, cereal boxes. You could feel it on the decks—what was once a space reserved for riders, and maybe the occasional brotographer, was now real estate that required a laminated pass to access. It was now a world of cameras, and postrun interviews, and in-depth analysis of things, like Dennis McCoy's fufanu reentry technique. It was so cool to see hard work and dedication paying off for the independent companies and riders who had dedicated their lives to a cause. It was also odd— several of the top riders bought houses with money earned off fingerbike sales.

One telling detail about the turning point from famine to feast could be observed by going out to eat with a table full of bikers. In 1993, the check would arrive at the end of the meal and everyone would root around in their wallets and half-heartedly chip in for the check; somehow the stack of cash would *always* be about twenty-five percent short of the bill. In 1997, the same situation usually resulted in the bill and tip being *over*paid by about thirty percent—everybody wanted to flaunt their success and make up for the days of being broke.

Another thing I noticed was a dramatic increase in the number of people approaching me for autographs. It seemed as if everywhere, from the grocery store to the airport bathroom, I'd hear my name spoken and turn to see a fan with a pen. For years, I'd ridden behind the disguise of a full-face helmet and lived a fairly anonymous life. I'd been on more than thirty magazine covers, and nobody on the street knew I existed. After a few times hosting TV shows, people suddenly knew who I was and wanted me to sign stuff. It was like fame created merit, instead of merit creating fame. I'd be asked by people who didn't know who I was to sign something for them, because they'd seen me signing an autograph for somebody else and instinctively *knew* I was somebody "famous" . . . *but who was I?*

It was weird. Cool, but weird.

Bikers were drawing unprecedented attention from a whole new fan base, many of whom didn't even ride or skate. A lot of this attention was the direct result of hype, and marketing. Those signs you'd see people holding up in the stands during the X Games that said "Miracle Boy," or "SPIN to WIN," or, "John Parker 3:16" were often made by ESPN2 interns, who then "placed" the signs in the crowd. The network reasoned this colorful spectator support would help create a fan culture and give the action a familiar, TV-friendly appearance to viewers. They used to do it all the time with stick and ball sports. As long as there were plenty of *active* participants in bicycle stunt riding, it didn't disturb me too much. What was hard to watch, though, was seeing the way a few riders became blinded by their own rising stars. TV had a way of converting natural charisma into a thing called an *image*. A few guys bit the hook and bought the hype and began to live up to the icon or nickname they had developed. I'd see dudes roll up to a session in flossed-out cars, boasting about bling-bling spending sprees that covered everything from jet skis to jewelry. It's hard to tell a friend who is skilled, successful, and enjoying themselves tremendously that they ought to slow down the frontin', because they could be one knee injury away from a heap of credit card and income tax debt. And on top of it all, the injury would render them unable to do what really matters: ride a bike for the sheer enjoyment of it.

The Bittersweet Flavor of Fame

Medicine has the power to cure and the potential to become poison if the dosage is too high. I saw the benefits of TV coverage—we had saved the sport from near extinction, and TV was definitely helping usher in a new era of prosperity. For this I was grateful. Amid all the new opportunities to ride, get paid, travel, and get coverage, the very thing that was growing our sport was also threatening to alter its history. The sport came from driveways, parking garages, and backyards. It was kind of freaky seeing it in the surreal space of prime-time television. For the first time, the sport had a season, because all the contests happened in a compact timeline building up to the Summer X Games. I don't want to snivel and moan about bringing a change I signed up for, but one thing I realized, in retrospect, was the sport was starting to develop a cycle of repetition. It was getting harder and harder for the voices from the underground to be heard or expressed, because they were overshadowed by the sport's success. I'd put on a contest. Television (ESPN) covered the competition. Kids, because they were rarely exposed to riders who don't compete, wanted to know more about the guys they'd see in the contest. So magazines understandably catered to their readership, by focusing on the "popular" riders. It seemed to be the same riders all the time because the choices were so limited. This, in turn, provided a shrinking perspective of our sport, making

it difficult for a rider who didn't become a part of the cycle to have an impact on the sport. Look at flatland riding—flatland is such a highly technical facet of bikes, it's hard to understand the nuances unless you do it. It didn't seem to get people fired up as easily as the lowest common denominator in excitement: big air and big crashes. So most of the coverage from contests ended up focused on dirt jumping, park riding, or vert (which, by the way, also gets shorted on magazine coverage). And the top flatland guys, all just as dedicated as any of us, made considerably less money for putting in just as much work.

Heat is how the entertainment industry calculates the popularity-to-dollars potential of people, places, and things that are *cool*. Pop culture icons are supposed to be "cool," which gives them "heat," and the hotter the heat, the cooler one is perceived to be. But stuff that's processed to be cool is usually lame. The *really* cool things are often not very popular, and in fact are considered lame by the mainstream—which is what makes the things cool in the first place. But if something is lame enough to stand out, it attracts other people with similar aesthetics, and a culture begins to form. Then this lame (but actually cool) thing that is underground heats up as more people discover it. Punk rock and action sports used to be considered lame, which was cool. Then they got cool, which is kind of lame. But I guess that's cool.

Being a pro bike rider has still got to be one of the best jobs on the planet. But, like the saying goes, pimpin' ain't easy.

THE COMEBACK KID

As the middle 1990s stretched toward Y2K, my riding ebbed and flowed through spurts of progress. Airtime was cut into by injuries, surgeries, recovery periods, and workload-related drama. I'd taken on a lot of responsibilities; keeping the bike company going full tilt, promoting Sprocket Jockeys shows, and running the BS event series and a TV production schedule put me under steady pressure. I was juggling and struggling to stay on top of it all and still keep focused on why I was spread so thin: I love being a bike rider.

One of the best perks about an occupation in action sports is travel. There's a magic, invincible feeling being a stranger in a strange land, riding with friends who all rule. Walking into an arena in a country where you don't even speak the native tongue, and hearing ten thousand kids screaming the universal language of stoked . . . and above the din, recognizing your name being chanted. It gives you chills, makes you feel alive and young. You want to try hard to be the invincible guy they think you are.

From the start of my career, I racked up enough frequent flyer miles to get a free ticket to Jupiter. The irony: For the longest time, the only thing I'd see on most trips was the hotel and the halfpipe. If I was lucky I'd get a chance to street ride. Jaci convinced me to start making the effort when traveling to visit a museum or two and to embrace foreign culture as a truly unique aspect of my job.

When I was offered the opportunity to bring the first western riders into Malaysia for a bike stunt tour, I didn't leap at it right away. Sitting in my office in Oklahoma, reading an E-mail talking about something called the Golden Dreams tour, I was a little skeptical. I didn't even know exactly where Malaysia was on the map. The Golden Dreams guys asked me to assemble the very best riders in the world—often a sign of people who had no idea of the price tag for such a request. It sounded iffy, and I figured the promoter would recoil when they realized the costs associated with importing ten bikers and three skaters. I spat out a number off the top of my head: A twenty, followed by three zeroes, per rider, for seven shows. But the golden dream turned out to be real—a few weeks later our posse arrived in Kuala Lumpur, greeted by a wall of insane air pollution and superfriendly short people. Our first demo was in a stadium, so we went over to the check out the ramps they'd built us and found an incredible disaster—twenty-foot transitions cut down to ten feet tall—not the ideal big air devices we'd need. I got out the pen and a few sheets of paper and started scrawling. I handed it to the lead builder, who spoke little English, and asked him to see what was possible in twenty-four hours. I have no idea how many laborers they roped in, but we came back the next day and there was a street course and a vert ramp built to spec. We'd arrived thinking we could show up, strap on our gear, and get down. The Golden Dreams promoter pulled me aside before our first show and asked how our choreography was going to work with the DJ they had spinning our music. Uhm, choreography . . . *right*. I told him to hold that thought, while I called my crew of riders over for a quick huddle. In fifteen minutes we'd worked out a pretty tight show that went off without a hitch. This format was repeated for our shows throughout the remaining cities on the tour; we also got downtime to hang on the beach, eating omelets, getting sunburns, and acting like fools.

In Zurich, Switzerland, I helped put on an event called The Freestyle.ch. This trip marked my introduction to photo radar traffic cameras. Our host, Reni, was driving me and few riders around and I spotted the traffic surveillance cams hovering over intersections. "What the heck are those things?" I asked. When I found out they were there to take pictures of drivers, I was amazed and wanted to see one in action. Before the end of the day we'd done a "photo session" around the city, running red lights on purpose and hanging out of the car, posing in the intersections, or crashing through with faces pressed up against the windshield. It was fun, but I never considered what would happen to our poor host three weeks later when the barrage of tickets arrived in the mail—she lost her license for a year. Sorry, Reni.

The Tabron Rule

Sometimes, you fuck the rules. And occasionally, the rules fuck you.

We were running a BS contests in Portland, Oregon. Simon Tabron had come over from England and was giving the pro vert class a reason to believe he was going to win the contest—Simon was going to town and, as usual, looking smooth as glass. Then came the 900 attempt. Simon took a bad spill and got knocked out. The danger in getting knocked out comes when you start repeating the process. I've seen bike riders tempt fate (and done it myself) many times—after a bad slam they hop back on their bike and try to pull the trick before it puts them down for the day. Which is what Simon did when he came around. Mounting his bike, it was clear that Simon wanted to try another 9. As the organizer, everybody began telling me not to let Simon ride anymore. But I couldn't make up a rule midway through a contest, a decision that could cost Simon $4,000. That would have to be his choice. I told Simon he probably shouldn't be riding because of the KO, but I was leaving it up to him. He dropped in and crashed another 900, got up, and tried it one more time. He pulled it.

Immediately thereafter, all the pros were notified of the Tabron rule: If a rider got knocked out and had trouble recognizing what was happening around them after a slam, they were done for the day.

At the next X Games, Kevin Robinson crashed a no-handed 5 that left him on his back in the flatbottom, in an eyelid-fluttering slack-jawed daze. It was scary. Suddenly his eyes popped open, and his mouth started jabbering a mile a minute, "Mat, Mat, I can do this. Let me do this." He'd been out for a minute, and the Tabron rule was in effect. I sighed. "Kevin, I hate to do this to you, but . . . I'm gonna call the Tabron rule on you." He was bummed. But at least I knew he'd still have his marbles at the end of the day.

A week later there was a demo disguised as a pro contest in Japan. The pro class of Kevin, Dave Mirra, and I were about to drop in and ride. Suddenly the arena went into a blackout. We were up on the decks wondering what happened when the house lights blazed to life, and in the flatbottom of the ramp there was a full squad of Japanese schoolgirls in Western cheerleader outfits. The PA system began crunching out X's version of "Wild Thing." The cheerleaders bopped around, shaking pom-poms. Up on the deck, all the pros exchanged confused, amused, "Did you know about this?" looks with each other. After a couple minutes of foreplay, the ramp was cleared, the Japanese fans had been thoroughly stoked up, and we were ready to get busy. I dropped in, and during one of my runs I went for a rocket barspin, back to a barspin, to a late no-footer. The thing about Japanese crowds is they all come strapped with the latest technology. In this case, everyone had a point and shoot camera with compact flash. In midair, with my handlebars spinning and my feet on the back pegs, thousands of camera flashes lit up the arena in a crazy strobe effect. My chrome handlebars flared and stuttered through a spin. As I reached for my grips, I thought I got them, and then . . .

There was an Asian man grinning at me through the view out the front of my helmet . . . *Hey, why was I wearing a helmet? Why was there a bike next to me? How did I get in front of four thousand Japanese people, and why are they all clapping at me?* In one ear, a medic was asking me questions in Japanese. *Huh?* Someone who spoke English nudged the medic out of the way and began asking me what my name was, over and over. At the same time, another English speaker popped up on the other side of me, saying, *Mat, Mat, Mat, How are you Mat?* I was still baffled how I got there, what happened, what my connection was to these people, and why I just woke up on the bottom of a bike ramp. They said I was out for three minutes, but I had no recollection of any of it. Then, without warning, *snap.* My memory flooded back all at once, and I was a little shocked—it never went from totally blank to good as new, but hell, I wasn't even hurt. I had energy, and my balance was fine. I'd only crashed on my fifth wall. I could still finish my run. I went for my bike. Kevin Robinson tapped me on the shoulder. "Mat, I hate to do it to you, but I'm gonna call the Tabron rule on you." Damn!

I ended up winning $2000 anyway, and they paid me in cash. After the contest, I accidentally left the entire wad of bills sitting in a restaurant and didn't realize it until the next day. I called back and asked if they'd, uh, found a big stack of cash lying around. The manager had been expecting my call. I got her a gift certificate to her favorite sushi bar as thanks.

A Different World

I can't pick out and describe my best run of all time. In contests, I don't plan out what I'm going to do; I just drop in and go, and let the run happen. When it's over, I'm already forgetting what I did as I clear my head for my next run. I can say for certain that my best run ever was not in a contest. At a comp, the window in which you're judged is two one-minute runs during the course of a whole weekend—sometimes the skills flow effortlessly; other times it seems like the whole world is against you.

For a long time, I won most of the contests I'd entered. It was rewarding in some ways, but then again, winning all the time is boring. You lose your motivation, because you don't get pushed enough. You realize you can never get better than winning. That's why I loved losing. It inspired me to push myself harder and progress.

As the X Games era exposed the sport to millions of kids, and the equipment and riding facilities got better, I watched a new breed of pros come into the sport, trickling up from the amateur ranks. Raised on resi mats and foam pits, their precision skills were a product of the solid ramps and superfacilities like Woodward BMX Camp in Pennsylvania. The new guys were smooth, their runs usually planned and tight. And for the first time in my life, I didn't care if I could test myself against the best riders in the sport. All I wanted was to ride again, on my own terms. My biggest competition became my health.

The Emperor's New Clothes

Even though Steve and I were in charge of running the biggest contest series in the sport, it felt like the scene was getting jacked around quite a bit. The BS contests of the early 1990s had been absorbed by ESPN and become the gateway to the X Games, and everything in the sport was focused on that once a year event. The X Games were centered around television, which had permeated our culture and become a huge force in the sport. To their credit, the ESPN crew had evolved into a great group of guys who were dedicated to the sport and respected the riders as equals to any athletes on the network. Another upside was the prize money was getting pretty big, but the bottom line was, the contests were a zoo: fans, crowds, parking, passes, photographers, interviews—the last thing on your mind at a contest was actually riding.

Steve came up with the idea to hold a biker-run, biker-produced, biker-officiated series like back in the days before TV. We worked out a deal with Ron Semiao to create a structure that benefited everybody: We would still hold comps that would provide a buildup to the X Games, but the new contest series was centered around riders, not TV. When we came up with the name BS series in 1992, we'd joked about how funny it would be if the contests ever got on television. After we realized it was possible to get strait-laced sportscasters talking about BS on TV, it became our Holy Grail to think of a way to elevate the level of televised profanity. I proposed calling our new contests the Crazy Fuckin' Bikers Series. Soon after, I worked out the deal to produce the TV for the contests and knew there was no way we could get away with the word *fuckin'* on ESPN. The title was abbreviated to CFB, and we vowed that if anybody from the network ever asked, we'd tell them the F-word in the initials stood for *freakin'*. But strangely, nobody ever asked. The first day of our first CFB comp in Merritt Island, Florida, I got a call from Ron. He'd heard a rumor. "Mat, I just want to let you know, we have rules. Rule number one is, you're never allowed to use the word *freakin'* on ESPN networks. Rule number two is, you're never allowed to use the word *freakin'* on ESPN networks. And rule number three: Always obey rules one and two. . . ." I'd already written and recorded the theme song for the show. All around me at the contest were banners blaring the words *Crazy Freakin' Bikers*. "Hmmm, Ron. I think it may be too late."

We rode in it, hosted it, judged it, documented it, and after it was done, made a TV show about it. Rather than show the top three riders' runs in a blow-by-blow format, we tried a more relaxed coverage format. There was a lot of humor, and montages of the top riders' best tricks from the day, plus candid footage to give viewers a sense of a rider's character in addition to their strengths, style, and skills. Above all, the approach was very noninvasive. At the end of the contest, we'd have a session in the edit bay, then hand ESPN a tape and they could put it on the air. It was a way we, the riders, could translate our sport for the masses so people could see it through our eyes, instead of watching some random television producer's take on it. Luckily, the content proved to be more valuable than the controversial title, and every show of the series aired. The end of the year award for the CFB would be something special—the BS series awards had always been giant belts, like the ones awarded to prizefighters. Hoping to top the goofy glory somehow for year-end honors, we came up with the CFB Golden Straitjacket award.

In 2000 and heading into 2001, I had an opening in my career where I took nothing for granted. Riding had progressed so much. I wondered if I'd progressed with it. While I was out being injured, the sport had gotten *good*. Double tailwhips, 540 tailwhips, high flairs, 900s, and more were the stuff one needed to throw down to win a modern pro contest. I started to get back my tricks one by one, like flairs and double tailwhips, and I came up with a few new ones like peg grab 540s and no-hand, one-foot 540s. Without brakes, my lip trick abilities were limited, but if I could maintain my aerial bombing runs at high altitude, peppered with double and triple variations, maybe I had a shot.

When I started getting solid again, I gained a new respect and a stronger love for what I could do with my bike. I cherished the moment I was able to ride at pro caliber. 2001 was a year of celebration, full of the *I'm riding!* type of joy that interested me in the first place. I entered a few contests for fun, concentrating on flow, not a set routine with a preplanned array of tricks. By the end of the 2001 season, I'd won my eighth BS contest series belt, my tenth World Championship title, and the first CFB Golden Straitjacket award. I was stoked. I'd done what I wanted to do.

The Philly X Games in 2001 would be my last big-time contest. With a full pro class going for $63,350 in prize money, the competition was fierce. Jay Miron, Dave Mirra, Dennis McCoy, Jamie Bestwick, Simon Tabron, Kevin Robinson, and I scrapped it out. Dave won, Jay came in second, I got third. I was happy. I'd ridden my heart out, and I pulled a 900—the first one I'd made since 1994. But after over seventeen years of staying in the mix on the contest scene, I just decided to step back. I didn't make a big deal about it, but I mentioned to a few people that I wasn't planning on hitting the circuit to chase a title or riding in the X Games in 2002.

The sports media, especially the mainstream, didn't understand it at all when I said I was retiring from contests so I could have more time to ride. They couldn't figure out how I could be retired and still participate in the sport as a professional. They wanted to know how I could contribute if I didn't compete. I told the confused journalists the only contender you need in our sport is your personal limits, and I had a few projects up my sleeve to challenge those limits.

From Badass to Dad

My biggest prize in life is at home, waiting for me every day when I walk in the door. On December 19, 2000, Jaci and I had a baby, Giavanna Katherine Hoffman. Baby G was amazing, inspiring, and pure energy. Being new parents threw our schedules into chaos; five o'clock in the morning wakeup calls, feeding, playing, and the comforting needed to make a baby feel safe and loved. Gianna was definitely into lung power her first year, crying a lot. She progressed into crawling and quickly dominated our house, drooling on all the electronics and terrorizing the pets. I never thought I could top the feeling of riding vert. Now I have a tidy little package with a smile on her face and eyes that light up every time she sees me, and I truly know how good I have it. People would say, "When you have a baby, you'll mellow out." But Gianna inspired me to celebrate who I am even more. She added a love to my life that I didn't know was possible, and this came out when I got on my bike. With her as my fuel I didn't need to focus my goals around competition. She is my inspiration to ride and keep progressing.

I've experienced the intensity of driving myself—and a sport—for almost twenty years. Now I've got this beautiful little girl, who doesn't give a damn what I can do on a bike. I'm not a world champion, or a crazy freakin' biker. I'm just . . . Dad.

That's the only gold I need.

SETTING
THE RECORD
STRAIGHT

Ramps are not dangerous unto themselves. Confidence. Now that can be dangerous.

In 1994, I pulled a twenty-three-foot aerial out of a twenty-one-foot-tall quarter-pipe. It was the highest air ever done on a bicycle, and one of the most fantastic feelings I'd ever experienced riding vert. But I have an addictive personality. Even as I cleared my own world record, I knew it was possible to top thirty feet, given the right ramp and the proper speed. Injuries kept me from my elusive dream for seven years.

In 2001, I had the indoor park adjacent to the Hoffman Bikes warehouse updated with some new terrain. The featured attraction was a halfpipe with eleven-foot-tall transitions, capped with nearly two feet of vert. I could roll in from a platform twelve feet above the deck (twenty-five feet off the ground) and B-O-O-M, a fifteen-foot aerial on the first wall without breaking a sweat. It was the perfect place to play, and of course, I got injured very quickly. I knocked myself out pretty good on one occasion and wasted my knee on another. It took knee surgery and a new approach to my life before I was consistently floating fifteen-foot airs again. And that was when I steered down the path of no return: the desire for impossibly big airs was reignited. The more I thought about it, and what a cool stamp it would be on my career . . . *thirty feet!* . . . the more I wanted it.

When I lock into an idea that stokes me, I enter a state of mind I can only describe as *consumed*—I'm basically along for the ride and at the mercy of whatever project is on the table. That drive, combined with a love for looking down past my right shoulder and seeing the coping way below me, is what led me back into big transition territory.

Raising the Stakes

The first obstacle I faced was my family and friends. I'd always been blessed to have an inner circle of people who believed in me through good times and bad, who contributed to my success in a million different ways. Everybody should be as lucky as I am to be surrounded by such great people. But I started bringing up the term giant ramp and ran into a wall of resistance from everybody on this one. Jaci didn't want me to do it. Steve didn't want me to do it. Nobody wanted me even thinking about riding another big ramp. I'd always justified the unacceptable aspects of my lifestyle by calling my conviction an addiction: "I can't help it—this is the way I am, it's who I am, and what I have to do." *So, despite their best efforts to dissuade me, my family and friends gave in. I was beyond help.*

I knew exactly what they were afraid of—the same thing I was. I'd lost a spleen on previous high-air attempts. The force of impact from a fifty-foot crash could leave me broken beyond repair, or worse. But rather than be intimidated by the odds, I let the possible consequences dictate just how seriously I needed to approach my goal. I didn't want any excuses, and if I did get, as the saying goes, majorly fucked, I never wanted to look back and say, "I should have built a better ramp."

I called Tim Payne, a vertical engineer of serious reputation, and laid out the plan. Tim and his crew of Dave Ellis and Mike Cruz—Team Pain—arrived in Oklahoma City within a couple weeks. They brought the power tools of the trade and a sizable shopping list of materials. No more screwing around, nursing the project along for weeks and months, or standing on scaffolding in the middle of an ice storm trying to finish. I wanted this ramp to be flawless. Perfection came with $30,000 tag. The crew tore into the job like piranha, and my ramp went up in four days. When it was done, the structure stood twenty-four feet tall—twenty-two feet of transition with two feet of vert. Tim shook his head, shook my hand, and wished me luck. I cut him a check, and he was gone.

The final factor in the formula was momentum. I needed speed to get high: forty-five to fifty miles an hour at least. Early experiences with Steve's YZ 125 revealed his cycle wasn't cutting it. To get rolling that fast meant a motorcycle purchase, a bigger bike with a 250 engine, with the get-up-and-go to tow my 165-pound body and 35-pound bike. Forty-five hundred dollars later, we had a Yamaha YZ dirt bike. Steve, my tow pilot, needed convincing that I would not kill myself. I bartered with him, promising that if he towed me, just this one last time, I'd start wearing the seat belt in my car (a dangerous habit not to, I know...but...I just never could do it). Steve was aware that if he refused, I'd just get Page or one of the other guys to tow me. I was radiating confidence that I could pull it off, and so Steve reluctantly agreed.

The ramp was stationed on some unused acreage on my dad's property. There was a four-hundred-foot long plywood runway leading up the face. We made giant Mat Hoffman Pro BMX stickers, stuck them at the edges of the ramp, and painted a huge Hoffman Bikes skull logo in the center. At the peak of my airs, I had to aim for the paint,

which lined me up about eight inches away from the coping. That comfort zone gave me plenty of transition to land on but also ensured I didn't hang up if the wind pushed me back toward the deck. Landing too low or hanging up from a height of twenty-something feet over coping would have catastrophic results.

There was a mix of tension, concentration, and glee as I started warming up. The ramp was solid as a mountain, and the runway was reasonably smooth, with the exception of a small bump where water drainage had formed a contour in the ground. I had my approach timing worked around the topography and knew when to ready my body by the way the earth felt as it sped by underneath my wheels. When I passed a certain tree I'd throw the knotted nylon towrope, being careful not to run it over. Then I'd hit the tranny and go straight up. Instead of airs, it felt like I was doing kickturns or fufanus in the sky. There was very little arc, just an incredible rush of momentum shooting me off the coping, and a few seconds later I reached my peak and gravity stalled out. Then I had to figure out how to turn around and get down from almost five stories up.

I felt it right away. The first day I was hitting the twenty-five- to twenty-seven-foot range, higher than I'd ever gone before. There were a couple of airs that were absolutely beautiful—the perfect merger of flesh, steel, air, and wood. Despite the smooth form, I was just a couple feet short of the height I wanted. I could taste victory. I knew it was only a matter of time before I solved the puzzle of the perfect pump up the transition, and

a thirty-foot air would be mine. There were a few kinks to work out, like the speedometer on the motorcycle. It was registering a steady fifty miles per hour on approach, but sometimes it felt as slow as forty-eight, and on other runs it might have been up around sixty. It was one of those things I had to adjust to on the fly, using only my instincts.

The confidence I felt was blinding me to the dangers at hand, however. Riding big ramps required me to convert all my natural sense of caution into a sort of hyperawareness. I was so focused on what I had to do that I ignored the warning signs: a couple of sketchy landings where my arms almost gave out, another where I slid out on the way down the tranny and was sent skipping across the ground, leaving divots in the turf. I bounced to my feet and threw both arms up—to signal that I was okay—but it was close. I could feel everybody around me tighten up. There was another air when I missed my timing so badly that I just shot straight up, stalled, and began falling in sideways. I dropped a good six feet drifting in that position before I was able to coax my front end and point it into the ramp, using body English to finesse myself around. Old school riders may remember a ramp trick called the Jammin' Salmon—you used your bike like a fin and "swam" through the air. That's what I had to do to save that one. I played it back on the video camera and the height was almost there, though. Another couple feet and I'd top the pole. I could feel the thirty-footer in me, just waiting for everything to click . . .

Fade to Black

The second I left the coping I could tell I wasn't going to ride away from it. That was the worst part, being powerless to alter the situation as I shot straight up past the twenty-, twenty-two-, twenty-five-foot hash marks on the pole. Fifty feet and change above the ground. At that height, it's pretty insane to toss your bike and try to run out of it, so I held on, angled my bike to avoid hanging up, and came in crooked. I mentally braced myself to take the hit and landed way too hard. My arm, weakened after four rotator cuff surgeries, gave out and I nailed the ramp with a mighty spank. I don't know if it's a good thing, or a very bad thing, that I still don't remember much of that day. The impact erased those memories—and all my memories— from my hard drive. Later, I could barely bring myself to watch the crash on video. It was bad.

When I hit, even the best helmet in the world could only do so much to save my head. My helmets are made by Simpson and are, bar none, the best head protection you can get. They're the choice of pro stuntmen and NASCAR drivers and cost $450 and up. Mine was even custom-made, the ultimate armor with enhanced peripheral vision. As I piled into the ramp, my face shield exploded, and the jagged fragments tore my lip off. I was instantly knocked out, and as I plowed across the ground my body was dead limp. It took my friends and family about three minutes to revive me by screaming my name, afraid to move me for fear of spinal injuries. There were a lot of tears that day. An ambulance arrived and rushed me to the hospital, where I spent the day in and out of consciousness, and then another three days in a total fog, blacking out at random. Plastic surgeons put my face back together. A battery of brain scans and EEGs revealed more terrible news—my brain activity was all over the place, registering abnormal. My memory was wiped, and I was so dizzy I didn't regain my equilibrium for nearly three weeks. The doctors said there was nothing they could do except treat the symptoms and prescribed a huge bottle of pills that I was supposed take every day for the rest of my life. The medication was definitely not an improvement; instead of balancing my brainwaves, the pills doped me up to the point where all my senses were blunted. Riding was not an option.

In all my years on a bike, I'd learned to diagnose injuries and had developed an internal sense of what was necessary to recover. But a head injury like this was impossible for me to assess—I'd damaged my brain and was unable to use the very tools I needed to gauge the extent of how badly I was hurt. I kept forgetting things and had no memories of vast chunks of my life. Jaci would mention something—like a trip we'd taken to Japan. "I've been to *Japan?*" I'd ask, stunned. She'd have to fill me in on the trip, or show

me photos, and something would trigger a vague memory, and I'd be able to mentally reassemble my experiences. As the weeks passed, my physical scars and injuries began to gradually heal. But there was a lot of emotional damage, too.

The people around me were worried for me, but they were also kind of pissed. I'd come damn close to taking myself out—twice. While everybody wanted to see me break my old height record, they wanted it because they hoped it would put an end to my obsession with huge airs. I don't have a death wish; I have a life wish. I've always craved the experience of living at my potential—that has been the driving force behind every crazy thing I've ever done. The twenty-four-foot quarterpipe was part of that need, and for a long time I thought I'd never be able to top the feeling I got from fifty feet up. I was wrong.

One afternoon during my recovery, I was goofing around with our little girl, Gianna. She was only about four months old—since the day she was born she'd been basically a cooing, crying, gurgling little squishy thing wrapped in fuzzy clothes. But her senses were developing bit by bit, and that afternoon a change happened inside her, right in front of me. I made a face and a silly noise. Gianna looked back at me with a sparkle in her eyes, and for the first time ever I made her laugh. I did it again, and her reaction doubled—she cracked up, hysterically. This funny face game was repeated about five hundred times. It was so awesome. Her laughter and the look she gave me was the most precious substance. I think I changed during that moment, too. While my family and friends always had to accept me for who I was—a guy prone to high-risk activities—my daughter had never agreed to those terms. I brought her into this world, and I had a responsibility to be there for her. That feeling I got from her laughter was a high that overpowered even my love for pushing my own limits. It put a knot in my stomach to think I could've missed out on her first laugh. As I lay there with my nose pressed to Gianna's, everything clicked.

It was time to leave the big ramps alone and be satisfied with what I had: Twenty-six and a half feet, and a little person who could always count on me.

"You win," I said to Gianna.

"Bloo," she replied.

HOLLYWOOD

The first time I met Johnny Knoxville he was a skinny joker known as PJ Clapp. That's his real name. PJ was a writer/slacker who'd transplanted from Tennessee to Hollywood, eventually slipping into the commercial acting scene with his charming personality and jacked-up sense of humor. I think I'd seen him once or twice on TV before we actually met; he'd be holding a can of Coors beer looking stoked or eating Taco Bell nachos in a rowboat looking confused.

In 1996, PJ came to Oklahoma to do a commercial to promo the X Games. The theme of the commercial was PJ pretending to be a laser-guided supergroupie, driving around the country in a car and hitting up all the hot bike and skate spots on an odyssey to find athletes. He was going to sneak into the Hoffman Bikes warehouse and steal some T-shirts. The HB crew and I were supposed to chase PJ through a field and kick his ass.

We did.

The next time I saw the T-shirt PJ had snagged from the warehouse, it was a year or two later. PJ was wearing it while waving a gun around, a nickel-plated .38 snubnose revolver, as a shaky-handed videographer documented him in some remote location. It was the most gripping scene in the second *Big Brother* magazine video, *number two*, and PJ was about to "field-test" a Kevlar vest. He set up the scenario by suiting up with the vest, then tucked a slim stack of porno mags underneath the shirt, for extra armor. PJ scrawled a circular target on the shirt with a marker, then he stuck the gun in his ribs and pulled the trigger. The .38 slug could've easily gutted him, and PJ had no idea if his stunt would work until the moment of truth. The bullet blew a smoking hole through the cotton and left a deep dent in the Kevlar and a giant bruise on PJ's concave chest. But the vest did its job and saved his life, and the insane act topped a long list of totally unbelievable moments in action sports videos. It would later become the shot heard round Hollywood.

Fast-forward about a year: I was in LA for the E3 convention—an electronics and video game industry trade show. Kelly Slater, Shawn Palmer, Tony Hawk, and I had all signed deals with Activision. It felt pretty cool to be handpicked alongside such legends, and each of us had a video game coming out to represent our sports. Before the trade show, I was sitting around the hotel, bored. I gave PJ a call. "What have you been up to?" I asked. He cackled on the other end of the line. "We're coming over to show you," he said and hung up.

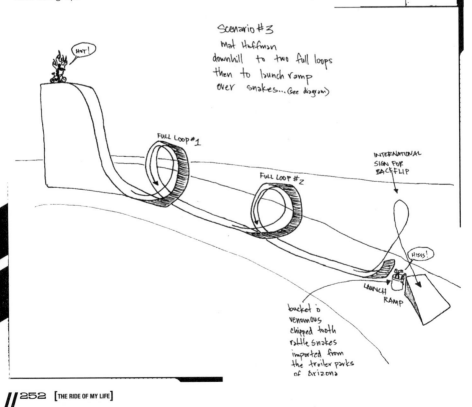

A second later he called back, to get my room number, then hung up again.

In the months that had transpired since the *Big Brother* video premiered, PJ and friends Jeff Tremaine (*Big Brother's* art director; old school readers of *Go: The Rider's Manual* may remember Jeff's name) and Spike Jonze (also a *Go* alumni) had been busy. When PJ and Jeff knocked on the door to my room that night, there were holding a VHS tape—the product of their labors. They were calling it *Jackass*. The tape was popped into the VCR, and the TV screen lit up with a barrage of home-brewed street skits involving fire, trampo-lines, weapons, self-induced animal attacks, clowns on stilts, bad driving, vomit, shit, midgets, pranks, and farting. It borrowed from the best of *Big Brother* magazine and skateboarder Bam Margera's infamous *CKY* underground pranks video. The *Jackass* run-and-gun digital video style was documentary/reality TV taken to a new level. It was, in a word, hilarious. It was also a little like watching a car crash—you wanted to turn away, but... couldn't. After the tape was finished, PJ and Jeff both had stupid, triumphant grins on their faces. They were going to try and sell it to a TV network but didn't know how or who quite yet. "That would be the best show on TV—*if* you could get it on TV," I said, still laughing. We decided to head downstairs to the hotel bar and have a beer. Or two.

The Sky Bar is the highlight of the minimalist-chic Mondrian Hotel. The bar, designed by Philippe Starck, is an open-air oasis overlooking the LA Basin from its million dollar Hollywood hills view. Popular with movie stars and musicians, artists and ad agency slicksters, the Mondrian is nice—but the kind of nice you pay out the ass for. It's "fourteen dollars for a drink" nice. I suppose it's because you're not buy-ing a cocktail, you're buying the view from the top. Jeff, PJ, and I stayed in the bar, jabbering about *Jackass* until two in the morning, when they closed. We were the last ones there, and a hotel security guard came over to our table and announced it was time for us to hit the door. As we were exiting the bar, PJ piped up in a loopy voice, "These guys need *water*." He'd stopped in his tracks and was pointing to the plants on the poolside patio. As we ambled past the thirty-gallon terra-cotta pots, PJ announced in a concerned tone, "My God, what are you people *thinking?*" He picked up the first of several plants and hurled it into the swimming pool with a mighty heave. It was so loud.

Ten minutes later, we were all in the lobby wearing handcuffs. PJ, who had jumped in the pool to save his plants, was dripping water all over the fancy wooden floor. We were being guarded by the hotel security. The hulking, silent one with his arms crossed was an ex-pro football player, three hundred pounds of beef wrapped in a black leather trench coat, capped off with a headset earpiece and a cowboy hat. The other guy, the chief of security, was a supershort, superpissed Australian who was determined to be the most commanding figure in the room. He was chewing us out loudly, doing his very, very best to intimidate us. The Aussie was absolutely furious, threatening each of us with a punishment worse than arrest or

death. We couldn't bear to look him, or one another, in the eyes because we were afraid we'd all start cracking up. This would have, of course, made the blunder from down under even more livid. He stopped in front of me, got up in my face, and growled, "You son of a bitch, if we were on the street I'd show you a new definition of pain. You don't even know the *meaning* of pain." The irony of his words did not escape me.

Behind him, even the police who'd entered the lobby were smiling at what a tool this guy was being. The outcome of the evening was ultimately successful: We got let go because I was a hotel guest, and PJ was now on some special list of people who were banned for life from the Sky Bar.

The *Jackass* demo tape was twenty minutes of nothing the TV industry execs had ever witnessed; a boiling hot gumbo of ridiculous humor and stunts. It became an instant sensation in TV network conference rooms and acquisition meetings, and within a couple months after the showdown at the Sky Bar, Spike, Jeff, and PJ had inked a deal with MTV. They got a modest budget and proceeded to make history.

Jackass debuted on MTV on Sunday, October 8, 2000, at nine o'clock at night. The response took the network by surprise, pulling in 2.4 million viewers, the highest ratings share for that timeslot in the network's twenty-year history. The next week, the entire time block was renamed *Jackass Sunday,* and ratings got even bigger. Within four months, every cool kid in the United States knew the name Johnny Knoxville. The risky mix of stunts and subversive humor were invented in the skate, bike, and snow worlds, and this humor was turned into a new kind of experimental, highly physical comedy by the *Jackass* crew. A few fans had taken their appreciation too far, ignoring the *"Hey. Stupid. Don't do this . . ."* disclaimers and numerous skull-encrusted warnings that ran before, during, and after each dangerous skit. Some jackass on the East Coast set himself on fire, trying to film his own *Jackass* stunt (the show doesn't accept submissions). In January 2001, just four months after debuting on national TV, Johnny made the cover of *Rolling Stone,* one of the entertainment industry's barometers of cool. The only other phenomenon in history to go from nowhere to *Rolling Stone* cover status that fast was in 1987, by a band called New Kids on the Block.

During the same time *Jackass* was on the air, MTV had another show that was strictly stunts, called *Senseless Acts of Video.* It didn't have the lovable stupidness and gross-out factor of *Jackass,* but *SAV* regularly featured guest daredevils. They'd been asking me to cook up something crazy. Although I was still turned off from MTV Sports' lack of tact the day I lost my spleen, I kept thinking about their offer to pick a stunt, any stunt.

For years, I'd wanted to try riding through a loop. Constructing an elaborate, sixteen-foot-tall wooden circle is one of those things, however, that has a really, really limited use. I never had the motivation or spare cash to justify building a loop for the thrill of doing it once. But *SAV* kept calling, so I began to view it as an opportunity to get a project done on MTV's dime. I told them I wanted to do the loop. The producers from *SAV* wanted something more glamorous and dangerous. I could do without the "glam-

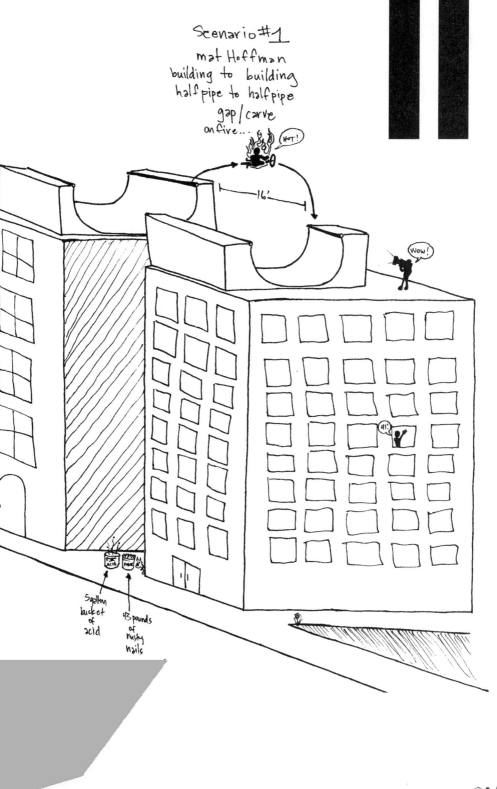

orous" but keyed in on the word *danger*. I began firing off E-mail proposals: I wanted to be lit on fire, go through a loop, then exit the loop and backflip a bucket of venomous rattlesnakes imported from various trailer parks in Arizona. They said no. They insisted on something sexy, serious, an extremely extreme stunt, and I wanted to just be goofy. I started to screw with them.

I propositioned a quarterpipe to quarterpipe canyon air, and in the gap between ramps I wanted a lava pit with fire-breathing piranhas. I'd have M-80s in my pockets. That idea got shot down. I volunteered to jump from one rooftop to another, twenty-five stories up, with a huge bucket of acid and rusty nails at the bottom. They didn't even reply to that E-mail.

The producers at *SAV* kept pressing for something *really* dramatic. I told them I'd do a backflip over a helicopter with the rotor blades spinning, and when I landed, I'd go through a loop. That was the dealmaker for me, the loop. They agreed to film the heli-stunt but kept procrastinating on a shoot date. My schedule filled up with other commitments, and they ended up getting the ever-confident Mike "Rooftop" Escamilla to jump the whirlybird; he pulled a clean backflip, but the loop was nowhere to be seen.

Not long afterward, Jeff Tremaine called and said it was high time I made my debut on *Jackass*. Before the words were even out of his mouth, I told him I wanted to get lit on fire and ride around a loop wearing a chicken suit. Because of the ongoing controversy with the East Coast kid who'd burned himself trying to out-*Jackass* Johnny Knoxville, the MTV standards and practices lawyers had declared anything having to do with heat, matches, lighters, flames, hot stoves, candles, or powerful flashlights was forbidden. But a looping chicken, that was perfect.

A few weeks later Tony Hawk and I arrived at the loop shoot in Florida. I thought it was going to be a cakewalk. I could envision exactly what I needed to do, how I would steer through the giant transitions and where I would pump out the backside. I called a physics expert to ask about the G forces going around a complete circle and found out that the forces of gravity were doubled every quarter of the transition. So, if I entered the loop and the first quarter was at two Gs, I'd be riding down the last transition with a force of sixteen Gs on my bike and body. That's the equivalent of me weighing thirty-two hundred pounds for a fraction of a second. I hoped my knees and arms could take it. The stunt started atop a long plywood roll-in, and after the loop the plywood runway led to a dock with a launch ramp into an ice-cold lake.

It took me twelve progressively more punishing attempts before I made it. I didn't have brakes on my bike, so when I finally survived a full circle, I had to purposely crash myself so I wouldn't get my bike all wet in the lake. True to the title of the show, I felt like a jackass. After I'd made it around the loop twice successfully without my costume, it was time for the money shot.

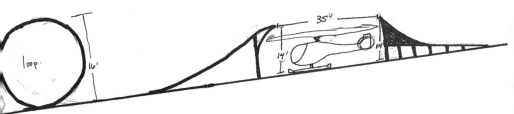

The secret of going through a loop on a bike wearing a chicken suit, in case you ever find yourself in that situation, is to do exactly the opposite of what you think you should do. Your brain tells you to go really fast. Wrong. The compression makes your knees collapse if you hit the loop with too much speed. You need to time it so you relax and go so slow it feels like you won't even stick when you're upside down. It's a lazy, carving corkscrew motion. A handful of brotographers and cameramen clustered around the loop, each yelling comically at the others to "Get the fuck out of the background, dick." Once they were all positioned, somebody yelled "Action," and I dropped in. With yellow feathers fluttering in the wind and Tony Hawk riding my tail, I shot through the loop. Tony tore down the roll-in next to the loop. I pulled a delayed no-handed backflip and flapped my wings off the launcher into the lake. Tony tucked and aired to aqua right behind me. I broke the surface and heard cheers and saw rescue lifeguard Chris Pontius aka "Bunny the Lifeguard," dressed as a seminaked bunny rabbit, swimming out to help me drag my bike through the mucky lagoon back to shore.

My *Jackass* experience delivered all I could hope for, and then some.

Got Mat?

The American Dairy Council is the organization behind the Got Milk? *ad campaign, and the celebrity-studded spin-off* Why Milk? *ads, featuring famous faces encrusted with a milk moustache. Van Halen, Michael Jordan, Tony Hawk, Jackie Chan, and other wholesome role models have helped immortalize the reasons why milk is awesome. One day my in-house publicist April Tippens got a call from the milk people, asking if I'd like to do a trick to help pimp the white stuff. I explained my sugar fetish to them, and they quickly countered with an offer for a chocolate milk ad. "Now you're talkin'," I said. Anybody who knows me knows I start out every day with a tall glass of chocolate milk . . . with four shots of espresso in it.*

Before the shoot, I had to hook up with the creative director and give my input about what I wanted to do. I suggested a backflip, during which I'd pretend I was pour-

ing milk into the glass at the peak. I pictured a nice, big box ramp—a quick transition, a flat platform on top, and nice mellow landing ramp angling down the backside. The milk could rest on the top of the platform and as I jumped over it I'd be positioned the right way to reach for the glass—totally upside down. I wanted to hit the ramp full speed and get twelve feet of air on my arch. To get the height needed to spin a flip that big, I'd need a ramp at least six feet tall. I carefully went over the details and suggested a couple of proficient park builders to create the structure—the venerable Nate Wessel and Dave Ellis. These guys ride what they build and make sure it's done tight, right, and certified for flight. The creative director assured me his crew had the carpentry covered. Having been part of a few commercial advertising photo shoots in the past, I mentioned it might be a super idea to let me check out a blueprint before they actually started pounding nails. A few days later a drawing arrived. It was their interpretation of what I'd described during the phone call: a two-foot-tall wedge ramp with no lip and no transition. It was like a wooden speedbump. There was a grind box down the side of the ramp, however, in case I wanted to blast that twelve-foot backflip and land it doing an icepick down the rail. Evidently these guys either really wanted me to earn my keep, or they had done their research for the ramp by playing my video game, which allows for fantasy tricks and unreal altitude. I got Dave Ellis on the phone, and he was imported to sort out the situation. A few days later I arrived on location, at an abandoned military base in Long Island, New York. There was a nice, steep five-and-a-half-foot-tall kicker with a twelve-foot deck and another twelve feet of landing ramp on the backside, waiting to greet me. *Hello, beautiful.*

Backflips are fundamentally dangerous because if something goes haywire, you're in a very vulnerable position to land directly on your head. Pulling them at twelve feet above the ramp is not something many people do every day. But I wanted this photo to look good and wanted it done "live" instead of posing it in a studio. I started putting my gear on, and they told me it wasn't going to work if I wore a helmet to promote the healthy benefits of good old milk. They thought I wanted to wear my helmet for looks—the reason I wear my helmet is because this shit is dangerous, and I need it. I agreed to ride without a brain bucket but pointed out the stupidity of the message we were sending—*drink milk for strong bones, and test their strength by landing on your skull.* I told them I couldn't do it unless there was a serious warning on the ad.

The stylist on site noted the rugged condition of my hairstyle—the result of cutting my own hair for years. In fact, I've only been to a real barber three times in my whole life. When I was younger, my mother cut my hair. Then I let it grow for about seven years but finally had to cut it off after I hurt my arm and couldn't manage it any more. Since that time I'd been trimming it myself. Apparently, this feat did not impress the stylists. A professional barber was dispatched. He shook his head in dismay, and took a whack at my 'do. With

01

02 03

07

08 09

clipping complete, I was ready for the final touch: my upper lip was spackled with a no-drip choco-marshmallow fluff, forming the moustache. It was windproof, wipeproof, and lickproof.

Just to clear the deck I had to crank full speed, and when I'd throw a flip it sent me flying upward twelve feet, upside down. We started shooting around ten in the morning, and by midafternoon we were still going. It had turned into a much more difficult day than I'd planned. The wind picked up and was gusting about thirty miles per hour. I had to keep guessing what the wind was going to do on my approach and laid out over fifty flips that day, all without a helmet. Every few flips, the moustache pit crew would inspect my 'stash for bugs or other inconsistencies. The wind got so bad I finally had the ramp turned around so I could approach it with the wind at my back. A gigantic, invisible hand boosted my speed, scooped me up the tranny, and sent me sailing—I cleared the entire landing ramp and just about crushed my wrists from the impact of dropping a flip to flat ground from twenty feet up.

The photographer wanted me to try a one-handed flip so they could superimpose the bottle of chocolate milk in my hand during the art direction process. Every time I tried a one-handed flip I couldn't maintain an even pull tension on the handlebars. I did a few, and each one I flew through the air with such stink butt style, leading the trick with my ass instead of my head. I didn't want my moment of milk ad stardom to be marred by stinky style. So we faked the one-handed part. I lay upside down atop of the platform and poured my milk into a glass. The wind actually helped, making it look more real by blowing the milk around as I poured it.

A few days after the shoot, I got to check out the photos and go over the composition and what the backdrop was going to be. From the angle it was shot, my flip looked about seventy-five percent lower than it actually was. But hey, the spilling milk looked perfect. As a lifelong chronic beverage spiller, that was nearly as important as a sky-high backflip. The art director suggested the ad layout feature me doing a flip through outer space, with the glass positioned on a nearby planet. I asked about flipping through New York City, grabbing for the glass over the Twin Towers of the World Trade Center. The ad was going to debut in national print, billboard, bus shelters, and on the Internet in August 2001 and be up for a while. I am so glad they declined to use my Twin Towers suggestion. We decided on the nondescript ramp edge, and blue sky as the backdrop. When it finally came out, I can remember standing in my brother Travis's coffee shop and picking up a copy of *USA Today*. On the back cover of the sports section there was a full page *Why Milk?* ad, sort of an end-of-the-year compilation featuring six of the top athletes in the world, including my shot and the *Why Milk?* ad starring Tony Hawk. People in the coffee shop crowded around, clapped me on the back, and congratulated me for being included among such superstars. They were so stoked for me. I felt like an idiot—I had no idea who any of the other athletes were on the page, except Tony.

I guess I just don't watch enough TV.

Extreme Guy #1

I've always secretly wished I'd been in RAD, *the first film focused on freestyle back in 1987. The opening credits of* RAD *were highly promising and featured straight documentation of a gaggle of pros hotdogging in the fog. That was the scene I wanted to be in. After the first two minutes of the film, the story line kicked in. The plot had so much cheese slathered on it, you didn't even want to admit you owned a bike, much less rode one. At one point in* RAD, *there's one pivotal "tender moment" in which flatland pro Martin Aparijo, in a bad wig and stunt doubling for a female character, rides a bike onto the dance floor of a nightclub. He attempts to seduce a guy (played by Olympic gymnast Bart Conner, also riding a bike indoors on the dance floor) by doing flatland freestyle. The routine is delicately lit with a rainbow of lights and choreographed to the rhythm of the 1983 synth hit "Send Me an Angel," by Australian haircut band Real Life. It's one of those moments that's just so bad, your entire body cringes when you're exposed to it—like radiation.*

The effects of *RAD* were so long lasting, it would be fifteen years before another flick with bikes hit the silver screen. And then, suddenly, there was a glut of bike footage being thrust into the spotlight. It started around 1999, when a crew from Imax contacted ESPN2 about making a documentary on action sports athletes. The Imax films are projected on screens five stories tall, so the "more-is-more" philosophy applies to the coverage. When Imax film crews showed up at a contest, some riders and skaters balked, because they were concerned they wouldn't be compensated. I got lucky and was interviewed off-site, so I got paid. But cash wasn't my top priority—I was more concerned about how cool it would be seeing the big ramp in such a big environment, and I let them take a few clips of me from the X Games and supplemented that with some footage of the airs I did on my twenty-four-foot-tall quarterpipe.

Around the same time the Imax film was being put together, another documentary, *Keep Your Eyes Open,* began production with director Tamra Davis at the helm. It featured segments on big-wave surfing, skateboarding, freestyle MX, snowboarding, and bike stunt riding. I was pretty psyched to have a segment in *Eyes Open,* alongside guys like skaters Eric Koston and Steve Berra, MX heavyweight Travis Pastrana, and snowboarding siblings Mike and Tina Basich. From the clips I've checked out so far, all the people featured in it seem amazing. It's the best film I've seen documenting our sports that wasn't made by bike riders, skaters, or snowboarders. There's also a couple of comic relief scenes with Spike and Tamra's husband, Beastie Boy Mike D, playing hard-assed security guards.

In 2001, Rob Cohen, a veteran director responsible for a fistful of action movies (including *Dragon: The Bruce Lee Story,* episodes of *Miami Vice,* and the breakout hit chronicling midnight drag racing culture, *The Fast and the Furious*) began preproduction on another film grounded in action sports. Rob got together with Samuel L. Jackson, and the star of *Fast/Furious,* Vin Diesel, to create *XXX.* Vin plays an action sports adrenaline junkie named Xavier, and he's eventually recruited by an elite intelligence agency to become a modern-day James Bond. I got hired for a few days as a technical adviser, to help Rob and Vin understand some of the nuances of the hardcore action sports lifestyle. The production was heavy on stunts, ranging from B.A.S.E jumps out of cars plummeting off bridges to insane motorcycle leaps. Vin and Rob and the crew were pretty nice and totally in their element in the hectic atmosphere of a Hollywood production. For me, it definitely felt strange telling a guy who was getting paid ten million dollars how to act like he was into the same stuff my friends and I have been doing all our lives (and earning a fraction of a fraction of that salary). Rob and I had a good vibe from one another, and he asked me if I'd make a cameo in the film. I told him yes and got a copy of the script to study up for the shoot day.

I played "Extreme Guy Number #1" and was required to eloquently exchange a line of dialogue with Xavier in the midst of a surprise party. Just moments later, the party would be raided by jack-booted commandos in ski masks, and Xavier was drugged and kidnapped. My line was something to the effect of, "Yo, that last stunt was sick, dude. Can I join you next time?" I was flown to California for an all-night shoot and on the set hooked up with a few friends who were also there to play bit parts as extras and make the scene in general. Rick Thorne was there, and so was Rooftop, Tony Hawk, and a couple other skaters. We were all part of the action sports party posse. Our job was to stand around and look extreme. During the night, Rob approached me and told me how psy-

ched he was that I'd made it and said he'd dedicated the automobile B.A.S.E. jump in the film to me.

The set was still buzzing from a near-tragedy the day before. Larry Linkogle of the Metal Mulisha MX contingent had been doing a big air jump for a scene, leaping his Yamaha across an eighty-five-foot gap. A camera crew had gone up in a helicopter to get the shot. During one of the jumps, the chopper pilot brought his bird in too close, and a spinning rotor blade struck Larry's helmet. The force ripped Larry off his bike in the air and sent him pile-driving into the dirt. Another fraction of an inch and the blade would have lopped off his head. Larry blew everybody's mind when he got up and walked away from the crash. The intensity of the occupational hazards of action sports athletes had not escaped the Hollywood folks.

When it was my turn for the spotlight, I got ready and stood in front of the cast and crew, opposite Vin as the camera captured our scene at the party. I was stiff. Between takes, standing off to the side, Samuel L. Jackson gave me pointers on how to loosen up and be a more natural version of myself. He's one of my favorite actors, and having him giving me advice on how to act like me—it was so surreal. It was awesome. I hoped Sam's tips would be enough to keep me off the cutting room floor.

We stayed up all night filming, and I had to jet back to Oklahoma City to do a show in a mall. It was the first show I'd done in my own hometown in ten years, and it was the Saturday before Christmas— peak shopping season frenzy. A week before the show, the local radio stations had been plugging the demo, and my friends were getting that ominous, gleeful, "this is gonna be nuts, Mat" tone in their voice. I hoped I wouldn't blow it by eating shit in front of a hometown, capacity crowd. I was operating in a haze of jet lag and sleeplessness from flying to Los Angeles and back in less than twenty-four hours.

I touched down at the Oklahoma City airport with just enough time to bolt to my car, speed across town, hop on my bike in front of a big crowd, and drop into a ramp I'd never ridden before. Dennis McCoy, Jimmy Walker, John Parker, and vert skater Mike Frazier were there to help me do the demo. I couldn't believe how insane the crowd was—more than four thousand people stood clustered shoulder to shoulder in the mall, totally blocking the stairs, hanging off the balcony, and shutting down the entrance to JCPenney. The crowd had been waiting for over an hour. I grabbed my pads and took a deep belt off a bottle of honey from the bear I keep handy for just such sleep-deprived occasions. I perked right up and dropped in. Flairs, 540s, tailwhips, superman seat grabs . . . we gave it up, and the crowd gave us lots of loud love in return. Afterward, the auto-graph session clogged up the mall for hours, and it didn't even seem to make a dent in the line of people waiting to get stuff signed.

I felt like, for lack of a better term, a movie star.

new day rising

NEW DAY RISING

Never in a million years would I have guessed the best way to promote the reality of my sport was to re-create it as a digitized world.

During the arcade boom of the early eighties, one video game touched on the fringes of BMX. The game was called Paper Boy, *and the plot was simple: pilot through the suburbs, picking off points for accurately pitching papers. Steering a pixilated bicycle across the video screen and dodging animated obstacles was remotely entertaining to me when I was fourteen, but* Paper Boy's *roster of tricks and amplitude—pulling wheelies and bunny hops—didn't stand the test of time.*

About fifteen years later, video games had made the leap from the mall arcades to in-home systems and portable units with mind-blowing graphics and game play that was leaps and bounds beyond anything offered by Atari or Colecovision. At the start of 2000, software companies approached me on three different occasions. Each wanted my help building a modern-era BMX-oriented video game. As I sat in these meetings listening to the spiel, I realized I didn't want to help make a game just because action sports were an easy sell. The money the gaming companies were throwing around was on an entirely different level than any payday that had ever been offered to a bike rider. I could have closed my eyes, signed a contract, and cashed a fat check—but what was at stake was more than an easy bucket of cash. I knew a lame game would ultimately do more damage than good in representing bike riding. If a signature video game was in the cards for me, I wanted a good reason to make it. I turned down the offers from the first two game companies because I didn't think they understood enough about my sport to competently re-create it.

Activision and I got together in the summer of 2000. The company was riding a wave of success that they'd created with *Tony Hawk's Pro Skater*. Tony and Activision had nailed the details in developing the first awesome action sports game. Skateboarding looked realistic, fantastic, and the gameplay was superfun. It was also selling like crack. *Pro Skater* launched and became an overnight hit, eventually triggering a whole series of Tony's games for Activision—at last count, they were on *Pro Skater 3*.

I noticed right away that Activision was a company passionate about their work. Shipping a finished game required an army of programmers and producers, all staying true to an artistic vision. With Tony's game, they'd merged the cleanest technology and smoothest interface with a sport they had to learn to understand and appreciate the nuances of. When Brian Bright and Will Kassoy of Activision said they wanted to get inside my head and create a Mat Hoffman signature game using an enhanced version of the *Pro Skater* engine, I knew it would rule. In the months we spent in development, Activision was the first large company I'd ever dealt with where things just clicked from the start. They wanted my input (while managing to keep my nuttiest suggestions in check), plus they brought their own ideas into the mix and made it work great. Together, we built a game I felt stoked to put my name on.

Mat Hoffman's Pro BMX was released in May 2001 and sold in the neighborhood of a million copies—I'd gone platinum. I rode in demos throughout the United States to promote *MHPBMX*, and at every event I met kids who told me the same thing: They dug the game so much that they bought a bike and were now riding. I got flooded with E-mail from gamers who wanted to know more about my sport—were all the tricks in the game real? (a lot of them, yes), and did I really bleed that much when I slammed? (unfortunately, sometimes yes).

Making It Without Faking It

With the success of the first game, Activision wanted to keep the wheels rolling with Mat Hoffman's Pro BMX2. They began building a new gaming engine. In the time that had passed since the creation of Pro BMX, my brain was twitching with ideas for a follow-up. I wanted the premise of the game to reflect the realities of a modern-day bike rider. I told my team at Activision the second game should be a tour around the United States—we'd ride real streets, parks, parking lots, and even an old school backyard ramp jam. As the technology guys in the Activision labs cooked up the new strings of code to bring my ideas to life, I got busy putting together the crew of riders we'd need. I wanted everything as true to life as possible, which meant we'd have to hit the road with the riders in the game, shredding every surface we ran across while documenting the entire fiasco.

I talked Jones Soda into providing us with two crucial touring tools: a bright yellow Jones-stocked motor home with flames on the sides; and their legendary driver, Sweet Pussy Frank. Frank is a veteran of numerous tours; I first encountered him on the Birdhouse/Hoffman Bikes Whoop Ass expedition back in 1999. Frank can drive like jehu. He's one of those guys who wears a headband at all times, sunglasses at midnight, and is happy as a puppy dog, even behind the wheel for thirty hours at a stretch. On the road, Frank's as smooth as glass when confronted with massive traffic jams, tiny parking stalls, and horn-honking hicks who think he is the devil. We piled nine of my favorite guys in the Jones rig—Kevin Robinson, Nate Wessel, Rick Thorne, Mike "Rooftop" Escamilla, Joe "Butcher" Kowalski, Cory "Nasty" Nastazio, Ruben Alcantara, Seth Kimbrough, and Simon Tabron. We hit the highway for three weeks with a few cameras, plenty of digital videocassettes, and a loose agenda to ride our asses off.

We'd call some parks the night before and ask for access to their facilities. This was translated to, "free demo with ten of the best guys in the sport." We were met by crushing mobs of kids demanding autographs, stickers, and whatever else they thought they could talk us out of. On other tour stops, Frank's rolling dormitory would creep in unnoticed, and we'd unload in stealth mode, slip into the park, and be flipping transitions before anybody knew what was going on. With a good portion of our tour squad consisting of top-notch street assassins, we left our peg marks upon urban architecture, too. And, since I had Captain's powers of navigation, I made sure we made a swing through Elkhart, Indiana, so I could take my team out for the best Italian food east of the Mississippi, at Dantini, my Aunt and Uncle Dandino's place. It felt satisfying to parade into a swank restaurant with a greasy cluster of troublemakers, get the Mafia booth in the back, and rack up a quadruple-digit dinner tab—then write it off as "game research."

There were a couple stops on our jaunt that I was especially stoked to get in on—a series of mellow backyard sessions. One of the best was in Austin, Texas, a backyard vert setup where Pat Miller and Kevin "The Gute" Gutierrez play. I almost took myself out doing superman airs wearing a makeshift cape I found on top of the deck, but the casual vibe of a ramp, a deck full of friends, and a few decent tunes is an environment I just can't resist. We stopped in Riverside, California, at Cory Nastazio's backyard, a dirt jump utopia infested with bunkers and berms. Nasty's track was given a whipping by local motherhuckers like Stephen Murray, a kid they called Whitesnake, and Brian Foster. Nasty was in true form, cracking shirtless double bar spin backflips one minute, and proudly serving up his mom's custom chili the next. The tour ended in San Diego on Bob Burnquist's insane capsule-bowled, multilayered, multileveled backyard ramp. It stood like a fortress. I knew just by looking at it, the session was going to be good. The setting sun put a clock on our riding time as Simon, Kevin, and I rode our bikes while Bob and Tony Hawk skated. The casual backyard appeal was merged with a tingling rush as we explored the transitions of probably the second-best ramp ever built. The highlights: Kevin floating no-handed corkscrews over the channel, and witnessing the electromagnetic speed lines of Bob on his board and a bike he had tucked away in his shed. The lowlights: Simon and I both managed to knock ourselves out in no time.

When the tour ended, hundreds of hours of footage were sifted through and organized into bite-sized nuggets. The Activision crew merged our documentation within the levels in the game; players would be able to unlock videos along their route and check out the real tour and personalities of the people living it. *Pro BMX2* has ninety-nine videos in all, which works out to about three and half hours of bonus video footage buried deep within.

Thirty, Going on Fifteen

In January of 2002, I turned thirty. For my birthday, Steve and Jaci threw me a surprise party. My friend Page's band, 20 Minute Crash, played at the Hoffman Bikes warehouse, and about two hundred friends from around the country made it to town to welcome me to "Old Man" status. The best gift I got was from Steve and the HB crew, a vintage Hutch Trick Star, which they'd assembled part by part from Ebay auctions. It was an exact replica of the bike I had before I got sponsored by Skyway (I got on the cover of The Daily Oklahoma *doing a one-handed visor grab air with that bike back in 1985). As the party progressed into the night and the levels of frolic got more brazen, my new old school Hutch was put through the paces of many long-forgotten flatland moves in a marathon midnight dork session.*

With no contest season to train for, I planned on taking life easy and enjoying a few quiet months at home, chilling, riding, and working. But life had other ideas in store for me.

March Madness

During the month of February, my calendar clogged up like a toilet. March was overflowing with places to be and things to do. The first stop was a week in Merritt Island, Florida, for the first CFB contest of the year. Between hosting and helping my team run the event, I squeezed in some ramp time. I rolled in and did a few lines, savoring how great life was. A couple walls later, I woke up in the flatbottom with a dull throb in my wrist. End of session. Since I was supposed to shoot a poster for Steve Budendeck for Ride BMX magazine the next day, I taped up and rested my wrist. Throughout the night I woke up to test my boo-boo and see if the pain was subsiding. It was stiff and puffy, so I suspected there could be something majorly wrong with me, but "broken wrist" wasn't in the schedule so I had to block it out. The next afternoon Steve set up his gear on the deck. With a taped and braced wrist, I let fly with a few runs of my newest trick: a stretched no-footer one-hander, while controlling the bike grabbing onto one front peg. I had a contest running on Hoffmanbikes.com to let my friends name it. Three hundred thousand votes later, cock block was the title of the new trick.

After Florida, I bounced home for a half a day, then was on a plane to New York to participate in a panel of experts for Street & Smith's Sports Business Journal. The conference was in the ritzy Waldorf Astoria Hotel. My copanel posse were representatives from all the traditional sports—hockey team owners, tennis coaches, football players. The media and the sports industry were invited to the conference to discuss the future of sports. I talked to a room full of people who had no idea who I was or what I did. I just sort of kept them guessing during my panel time. Immediately after the conference I was on a plane to London for a conference of a different nature.

My British friends Stu and Ian throw a legendary shinding called the Backyard Jam, which is part contest, part demo, part throw down, and all fun. The last jam they had was in 1997, and things got so out of hand that they had to take a five-year hiatus until they were ready to put on another one. I arrived in Heathrow and Stu told me the media had been hounding him to see if I minded doing a press day. The Euro Activision crew was there, so I figured I'd help do some game promo for MHPBMX2. I went to the Sony Playstation Skatepark, retaped my wrist, and jumped a box jump for a glamour shot in Esquire. I then pumped out about five interviews in a row for Time Out, Metro, and other mainstream British mags. By the end, I wanted to tape my mouth shut—I was sick of hearing myself talk. We finally wrapped and drove the remaining four hours to Telford, where the Backyard Jam was going down.

The ramp was small, maybe eleven feet tall, but it looked fun. I was aching to ride, and my wrist was killing me. It hadn't healed much since Florida. I geared up, taped up, and rolled in to do a show. Since I made up the trick in 1990, I'd wanted to break eight feet on a flair—put some distance under my upside-down head and the eight-foot mark on the height pole.

The Backyard ramp felt quick and juicy enough for such a feat, so I pumped hard off a no-hander into a flip and cranked it, landing smooth enough to pull a tailwhip on the next wall. It was a good session, and afterward I checked out my flair on video replay. I got my eight-foot flair wish. After the demo, I undid my wrist dressing and was in a world of hurt. My ability to block pain while riding was good, maybe too good.

England is a great place if you don't have insurance and need to see a doctor. It's free, fast, and they don't ask a lot of questions. I got my hand x-rayed and the film revealed cracks through my navicular bone. Damn—those little bastards are supposed to be hard to heal (wrists constantly bend and move, hence, are rather weak). I was sent to another room to get a cast. I asked the nurse who was wrapping my wrist in plaster to keep the cast thin around the webbing area of my thumb and to position my thumb in the shape of a grip so I could ride my bike. "You must be kidding," she said. "Yeah, you're right. I would never do that. Could we modify it this way anyway?" My UK teammate John Taylor was there with me, cracking up.

The next day I showed up at the jam with a new cast, but it needed forty-eight hours to dry and I only gave it about twelve. It started to get mushy right away. The day was rough. I slammed on a tailwhip and knocked myself out. When I came to, my vision was haywire—everything was really bright—I was in battle mode. This is a state of mind I fall into where I go bigger and try harder just to spite the odds. I'm aware when I get into this emotional state, but I can't change it. I shook the slam off and got back on deck. Landing a flair so smooth the day before got me thinking. I wanted to see if I could do a dream line of mine, which was link four of the five elements of vert—the 540 air, the 900 air, the tailwhip air, and the flair—together back to back. (Fakie tricks and lip tricks could be considered additional elements, but the four aerial elements listed, plus the standard 180 air, are the essentials.) With my vision bright and my mind tuning out everything else, I dropped in and did a no-hander, to an invert 540, to a flair, to a tailwhip, to a 540. I was psyched and satisfied. Then I started playing around and linking variations together. I threw a lookdown switch-hander and tried to squeeze in a no-footer in at the last instant, but I missed my pedal and sat on my rear tire on reentry. I was launched into the back of my seat, and it felt like I got gored through the stomach. I thought I was going to puke, so I went behind the ramp and lay down. I kept my fish and chips from making an unwanted appearance, and after a few minutes' recuperation, I grabbed my bike and went back up to the top of the ramp. The crowd had dissipated, but I didn't want to end my session on such a bad note. I dropped in and did a no-handed 540 into a tailwhip on the other side and called it a day. I went to my hotel and packed my bags, jumped in a van, and took another four-hour ride to the airport. I flew to Oklahoma to pick up my family and then jet to Brazil for the South American X Games.

Rotating in Rio

The Hoffman Sports Association put on the bike events at the South American X Games. The contest pavilion was called Flamingo Park and was right near the water with Sugarloaf Mountain as the backdrop. Steve, who usually acts as our commentator, isn't exactly fluent in Spanish, Portuguese, or improvisational forms of communication. We got a translator who couldn't speak English but could write it. Rather than provide a running commentary in his usual flowing style, Steve's dialogue was typed into a computer and he read it like cue cards as the South Americans did their runs. Because wooden ramp surfaces don't last long in the rain and tropical humidity, parks south of the equator tend to be made of concrete. The local riders were thrilled by the rare treat of riding a plywood ramp. I thought it was pretty funny to hear them complain that "all" they had to ride were concrete pools and bowls.

South Americans are very passionate about their sports. Personal space boundaries are nonexistent in the heat of the moment, and the fans there love to cheer in your face, hug, wave giant banners and flags, and do special dances to show their appreciation. The crowd was superhyper and overjoyed.

After the contest was finished, I did a demo with Bob Burnquist, who was born in Brazil. There, he's considered a national hero, on the same level as Michael Jordan during his heyday on the court. This was apparent as we entered the stadium under a full security escort, who parted the crowd like bulldozers. Bob and I took the ramp and gave it up for a good hour. One of Bob's friends, Fortunato de Paula, was skating in the demo too. I did a flair over Fortunato while he threw a frontside 540.

By the end of the session, the sun was setting and shadows were falling across the ramp. It was humid as hell, and I was sweating so bad I could barely hold onto my grips. My right wrist was glowing and throbbing. On the other side of the deck, I spotted a trio of bikers who'd helped us with the contest. I'd met them at least six years earlier, doing demos in South America. They were old school guys, and I was happily surprised to see them still into riding. As I sat panting and sweating, ready to conclude the session and sign some autographs, the three amigos pulled up their shirts and stood in line shoulder to shoulder. Each had a number painted to his chest: 9, 0, 0.

"Mat, don't even think about," Steve said. I'd ridden well, managed to stay unhurt (despite the busted wrist), and we were done with the demo. It was almost dark, and I'd only pulled one 900 in the past eight years—which was at my last contest in Philly a few months back. "I've never done a 9 on this side of the equator," I said wistfully, trying to dry my palms on my sweaty pant legs. "I wonder if I'd have to spin it the opposite way?" I cracked. "MAT . . ." said Steve in a concerned tone, but I'd already dropped in. The crowd was chanting as I hit the wall and flung into a mighty spin, hoping my weak wrist wouldn't tweak.

I pulled it. My first 900 after age thirty. I slowed to a stop, laid my bike in the flat-bottom, and saluted the crowd. The ramp was attacked by Brazilians going nuts, and for the next two hours I signed, and signed, and signed. The language barrier melted away and words weren't even necessary. It's good being loved for doing what you love.

Jacked by Jackass

Jeff Tremaine, PJ, and Spike got a deal to make Jackass *into a movie. "Come to Florida," was all the information they would provide me with. Two days after my demo in Rio, I got a flight out of Brazil to Orlando. I had no clue what was waiting in store for me. All I had was a hotel address. I checked in, and walking through the lobby into the elevators, just as the doors were closing I saw Tremaine. I held the doors for him as he tumbled in with a sense of urgency. Jeff was struggling to keep from dropping a fifty thousand dollar digital beta camera, while simultaneously trying to hold up the camera operator, who appeared to be in rough shape. His skin was pale and clammy, and he was breathing funny and moaning. He couldn't walk by himself, and I thought maybe he'd been bitten by a cobra, run over by a golf cart, or perhaps had fallen out of a tree. "This guy's been a vegan for seventeen years and he just accidentally ate pepperoni," said Jeff. "Can you hold this and, uh, start taping?" I grabbed the bulky beta cam and flipped it on. We made it to a room and the camera guy passed out. I was told to keep the camera on at all times.*

Through the lens I saw Mr. Johnny Knoxville holding his toes open as Ryan Dunn took paper and slid it across the webbing between Johnny's digits, causing juicy red paper cuts. Ryan gleefully and carefully did each toe, and then moved onto the soft spots between Johnny's fingers. I got a good focus as the tub was filled up with rubbing alcohol and Johnny submerged his hands and feet into the liquid. A piercing scream filled the air.

Welcome to *Jackass*.

Fat Mat the Acrobat

After some more blatant sadomasochism with the Jackasses, *we went off to the Vans Skatepark in Orlando. I say "skate" park because like a lot of riding facilities, Vans-Orlando is biased against bike riders, allowing for very limited use of the ramps (skateboarders and in-liners can enjoy transitions every day). Vans has done so much good stuff for action sports and has made a tidy profit over the years selling shoes to not just skaters, but bike riders, too. I corner Steve Van Doren (the "Van" in Vans) and ask the same question every time I see him—when you gonna let my people into your playgrounds? He never quite has an answer. But this time we had carte blanche access to the park because of our film crew status, and the fact that we were about to break out one of the legendary* Jackass *props. The fat suit.*

I'd been jonzin' to ride in the contraption since I saw Bam Margera busting out, in the first episode of *Jackass* on my home TV. The fat suit consists of multiple layers of bubble wrap swaddled around the wearer's body like a Saran Wrapped sandwich. Then supersized thrift store clothes are worn over the plastic rolls—the pants alone are big enough to use as a tent. Basically, you look like you weigh at least five hundred pounds. The fat suit is actually light, however. It's just incredibly bulky. My goal was to pull a flair in it. As the last of the padding was applied to my body, I was in the mood to throw down.

On the deck of the vert ramp, I looked at Tremaine for my cue. He asked me if I wanted to warm up first. "I don't know," I said as I started to roll in. At the same time, Jeff turned to the camera and said, "I just killed Mat Hoffman." I dove into the flatbottom like an oversized lawn dart. I hit my head, saw stars, blacked out, and gave myself a concussion. The worst part was waiting for me when I woke back up—I'd just rebroken whatever mending had started to take place in my wrist. I couldn't help but laugh at how stupid it was. I still wanted to do a flair, but I knew it was going to be a long, painful, yet funny night.

Take two. I taped my wrist and strapped on a wrist guard to remobilize it and waddled back to the top of the ramp. I didn't think I could take another slam that grueling. I had to figure out how to roll in while only able to move one wrist and my toes. I tried a peg stall and pulled it, but I didn't have the speed to do a flair. I went back up and was ready for another roll-in attempt. This time I lined up with the edge of the ramp. Unable to suck up my bike and body over the lip, I hopped both wheels off the deck at the same time and bunny-hopped onto the transition. I held on but was so stiff I lost all my speed. I worked on pumping high enough to throw a flair, and when I got my height I left the ramp, leaned back, and turned. The next thing I knew I was upside down, holding on, and coming in fast. I hit the flatbottom like a giant sack of garbage. I tried it again, coming closer, but no banana. The plastic bubble wrap was overheating my body, and I was aching and dizzy from my opening slam. I suggested we try the street course, which was another bad idea. I couldn't even pedal. I wanted a superman and a couple flips over the box jump, but each time I was sent tumbling across the concrete in a ball of chaos. "Let's save some for tomorrow" were the words I was waiting to hear from the crew. We left the park and went back to catch some rest.

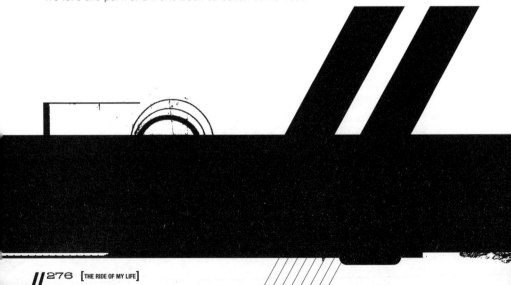

Wake-n-Scrape

I'd heard a rumor about some sort of wakeboard device they wanted to experiment with. They'd ordered a bike from HB and it had arrived, as I discovered when I got to the lakeside location on day two and found it being strapped to a wakeboard. It was one of the rare, collectable Evel Knievel signature models, serial number eighteen. It was going to be dragged through seaweed and muddy lake water for the next two days. The location was called the Pain Compound, and it was the same place we'd filmed the loop for TV. The description was fitting.

There was a fast-looking ski boat idling offshore as the crew made sure our costumes were looking tight—flannel shirts, headbands, and hairnets. The skit was titled "BMXican Wakeboarding." Ehren McGehey, Ryan Dunn, Chris Ponitius (aka Bunny the Lifeguard), and I were getting ready to take it on. Ehren was the first guinea pig. He set up, gave the boat driver the thumbs up, and instantly went down in a tangle of splayed limbs, bike parts, and spraying water.

I volunteered to be the next victim. The last time I'd water-skied was when I was ten years old, and I couldn't remember if I'd been good or was a water hazard. I'd never set foot on a wakeboard in my life. I got set up, gave the go signal, and was thrown into the water. It took awhile for the driver to circle around and return with the vessel, so I told him if I bailed, just take off and pull me around the lake until I figured it out. This method was applied until I unlocked the secret to balancing on a bike strapped to a wakeboard, hauling ass across a lake, dressed like a cholo. It was so fun. Chris and Ehren each took turns and got up, just as the sun went down. Across the lake I spotted what looked like a jump. Because of oncoming nightfall, investigation of the obstacle was postponed until the following morning.

The next day, I jumped into the water and got up right away. I was cruising the lake getting used to the balance, laying it back a few ways to represent some Vato style to match my outfit. I wanted to stand on the seat and bars and do a surfer, but it was too bumpy. I did a few Evel-style wheelies while standing on the seat, and tried to turn around to see if I could ride it backward. I went down. The contraption hooked my ankles and legs and gave them a good beating before I could clear my limbs. I got back up and decided we'd try the launch ramp. It was impossible to steer the bike, so I told the boat driver to position me toward the jump and carve a big turn, to whip me into it.

Water is hard at high speed. I came close to being knocked out, and I instantly understood why some wakeboarders wear helmets. I wanted to hit the jump and try a superman. My next attempt left a giant bruise on my ass, and on the follow-up I crashed on approach and got dragged over the jump. After a few more attempts, I was starting to lose faith. Every time I'd jump, the rope would go slack for a second, and when I landed it would yank my bike/wakeboard out of my hands. It was a bit nerve-racking as my ankles and legs got sucked into a tangle of metal and my skin was cheese gratered

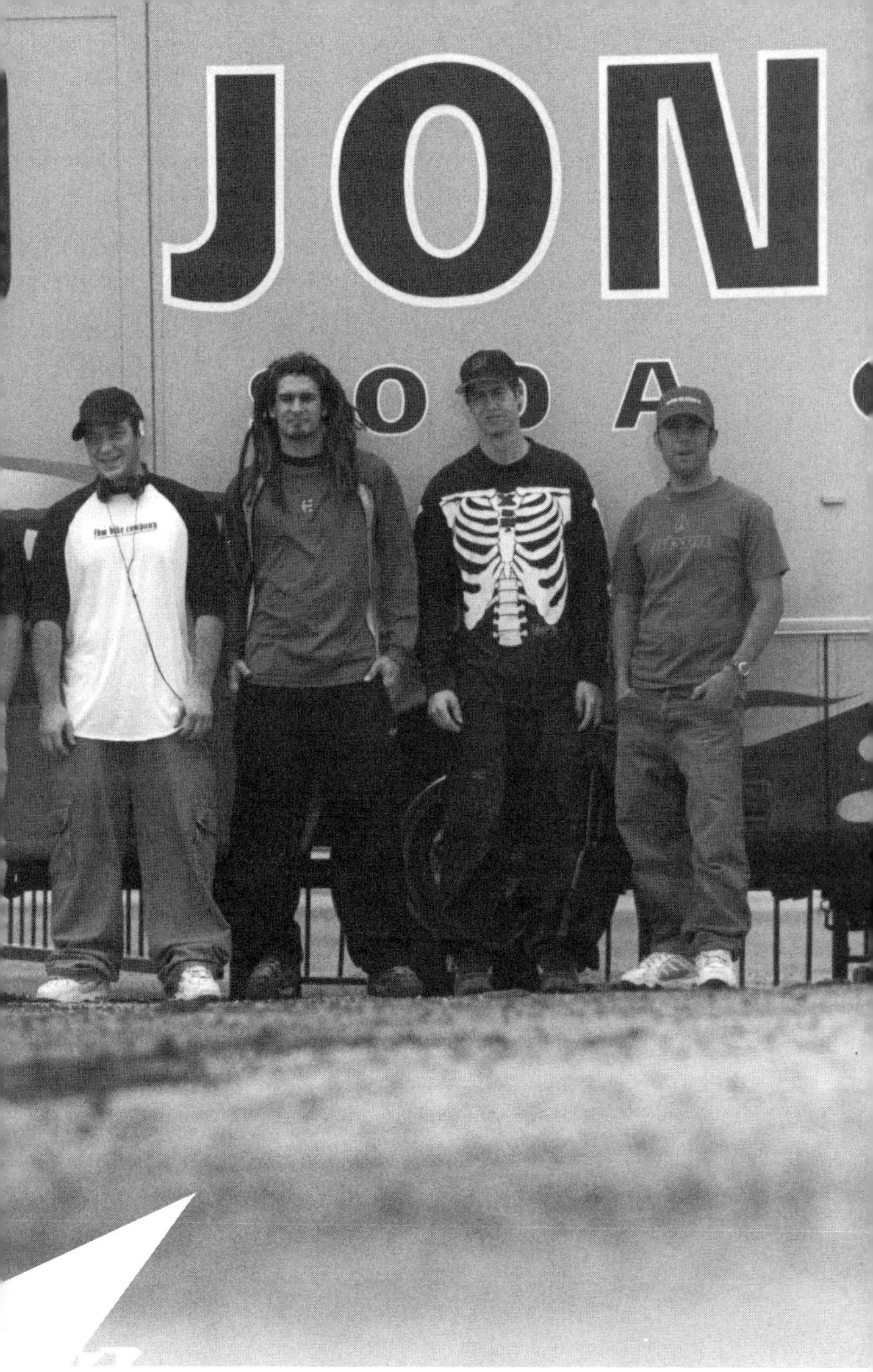
JON

by sharp pedals and axles. I couldn't see how bad the damage was, since I was submerged in a dirty lake. After each fall I wiggled my toes to make sure they were all still attached, before grabbing back onto my ski-boat-powered torture device. I kept up the jumps until finally I landed one. I tried to hang on and the grips were ripped off my bike. I did another without the grips and landed solid. Just as the triumphant *I did it!* entered my head, I fell over sideways and hydroplaned across the water at top speed, getting an unwanted enema. The bike was yanked out of my hands as I sank into the lake. I finally concluded it would be sheer luck to land a superman on a wakebike. And with a broken wrist, a throbbing skull, bleeding shins, and a bruised butt cheek, luck was a substance in short supply.

I dried off and we headed back to the Vans park for more fat suit follies. I still wanted that flair.

Jumbo-Sized Justice

By eleven that night I was exhausted. To wait and try riding another day would give the swelling from my numerous slams time to settle in, making any action even harder. I ran down a list in my head: I wanted to pull a 540, a tailwhip, and a flair on the vert ramp, a superman, and a flip over the box jump. I had my work cut out for me, but I was determined. I was in the fat suit, for Gods sake. It was a badge of honor, and I was ready to go down in the bubbles of glory. I figured out the secret of the fat suit: You have to enter the trick perfectly because you have no room to make any adjustments. It's "take off and hold on." I rolled in and spun a 540. I couldn't see the ramp over my massive gut, but I landed on my wheels. I hit so low it killed my wrist. I twisted my second 5 a little smoother and threw a tailwhip on the other wall. I couldn't lift my leg to whip my bike back under me, so it just spanked me on the side and sent me bowling down the tranny. The next air, I took my hands off and my handlebars disappeared in my belly, but I found my grips before I touched down. I was walking the razor's edge between "warming up" and "burning out" and it was time to see if I had the flair in me. I took off the lip and was sure I was going down, then I saw the ramp appear underneath me and I landed it. I still had some speed, so I threw a tailwhip on the other side, and I somehow got my bike back under my legs. Then my ass got sucked into the back tire and skidded me to a stop. I was happy like Santa Claus.

I turtled around the street course with Bam and got some bonus footage doing supermans, flips, 360s, and surfers, and at two in the morning, we called it a day.

I woke up with a whole new encyclopedia of injuries. I've slammed so many times riding that I can anticipate what I'm going to feel like the next day, but being dragged around a lake and hucking myself off ramps in a fat suit brought me to an elevated realm of morning agony. Day four's footage-gathering itinerary included the Jackasses' plans for making Ryan Dunn and me strap bungee cords to our waists. The concept was an in-flight tug-of-war. We were supposed to ride away from each other as fast as we could, time it so we hit each jump simultaneously, and see what happened. Like myself, Ryan had wrist troubles of his own, and his surgery scars were still pink. Together, we vetoed the tug-of-war.

Bam's imagination was fertile with diabolical ways to fuck people up, and he proposed a new activity, called the Scary-Go-Round. They found a playground-style merry-go-round and brought it to the Pain Compound. They wound a thick nylon rope around it and attached the other end to a truck.

The idea was to have the truck take off and jerk the rope, unfurling it and sending the Scary-Go-Round (and its passengers) into maximum rpms, like a hyperspastic top. The dangers of the whirling metal equipment, getting clotheslined by the thick rope, and the distance to which a human body could be flung were all hypothesized by the semiprofessional stunt squad. Nobody wanted to touch it. By default, Johnny Knoxville got the honors. I was trying hard to think of something—anything—to tell him to get him psyched up, but there was nothing to say. He was just going to have to take it. "Good luck," was all I could manage. After Johnny spun through a trial run and survived, battered and dizzy, it was time for a four-way cluster-fuck. Jason "Weeman" Acuna, Steve O, Ehren, and Johnny all mounted the equipment with nervous titters. The truck took off, the rope-activated contraption ripsawed to life and rapidly propeled the boys and sent them hurtling headlong through gravity's tornado. It was ugly.

Leaving the set for the airport, I could tell the *Jackass* crew was happy to be doing a movie, but it was also apparent they were relieved that soon they could take a break from beating the hell out of themselves. It'd been a long couple years for those guys. Masochism as a career isn't easy. I speak from experience.

Feeling Bizarre, Holding a Guitar

After a month of globe-trotting, it felt good to plant my Duffs back on Oklahoma dirt. I had a few days before another trip was scheduled, so I invested my time chilling with Jaci and Baby G, plowing into the mountain of mail on my desk, and, of course, I needed to pay a visit to the good Dr. Yates. During the recent demos and streak of self-destruction, my synthetic ACL had slipped, and there was an unsettling amount of slackness in my knee. Also on Yates's recommended service checklist; I needed to get three bones fused together in my wrist because I had completely torn my scapho-lunate ligament and broken my navicular, and my rotator cuff was ripe with a new rip. All totaled, about three months of postoperative recovery time. Wrapping up the exam, I told Dr. Yates I'd be back when I had the time to spare. There was one more suit I needed to try on.

The day after the diagnosis, I was on another plane to another destination: Southern California. My family, friends, and team joined me and we took up a row at the EXPN Sports and Music Awards show in the Universal Amphitheater. It was the second annual EXPN ceremony, already being touted as the Grammy awards of alternative sports (an oxymoron?). Attendees from the worlds of music and sport made the scene for an evening of entertainment, celebration, and recognition. It was cool mingling with musicians. I shocked Dave Navarro when I told him Jaci and I had danced to Jane's Addiction's "Summertime Rolls" at our wedding—eight years earlier. *"Eight* years? Man, I guess marriage doesn't always not work," was his reply.

Before the show, I was tipped off by Ron Semiao to make sure I sat on the end of an aisle, so I could quickly scramble to the stage to accept one of the crowning accomplishments of my career: an EXPN Lifetime Achievement Award. The only other person to ever get the award was Tony Hawk, the previous year. It was an honor, but also slightly bizarre watching the video summarizing my life while I sweated remembering what I wanted to say once I mounted the stage. Two hand-wringing minutes later, Johnny Knoxville presented the Lifetime Achievement Award to me, a Fender Telecaster guitar with a plaque built into the body. Standing in my new suit at the podium, holding an electric guitar, I looked out at the sea of faces. In a moment of clarity, I suddenly remembered I'd stood on the same spot on that stage when I was fifteen years old when I rode for Nancy Reagan on the Dan-Up Yogurt tour. That was the start of what would become my career—at the time, it hadn't dawned on me to think of bike riding as a way to make a living. It was just the way I wanted to live my life. I was a kid from nowhere, Oklahoma, who liked to catch air. Fifteen years and countless concussions, catastrophes, and a few victories later, and I still felt that way. Holding the guitar, I gave thanks to those who helped get me there. It took awhile, because the list was long.

What the Huck?

Two days after the EXPN awards, I reported for duty to Norton Air Force base on the smoggy outskirts of San Bernardino, a couple hours into the desert beyond LA. Stashed away in the bowels of an airplane hangar was a superstructure made of precious alloy metal and exotic wood—to call it merely a ramp would be an understatement. Cost? One point two million dollars. It was thirteen and a half feet tall and eighty feet wide with an eight-foot-wide channel tunneled through the middle. There was a roll-in towering thirty-five feet off the floor that shot riders down a sixty-five-degree angled runway (which was extra spooky without any brakes on my bike), through the tunnel in the halfpipe, and out the backside, over a distance launch ramp to clear a thirty-foot gap. To scrub speed after the roll-in launcher, there was a thirteen-and-a-half-foot-tall quarterpipe. Oh, and circling the entire ramp was an oval plywood section of simulated singletrack, with ten-foot-tall launch ramps aimed up the backsides of the halfpipe decks. Those were for the freestyle motorcross guys. It was gloriously huge, totally custom, and fully portable (once broken down, it filled eleven semi trucks).

The ramp was the best thing my tires had ever touched. It was perfect. Hard as concrete, lightning fast, stable, predictable. It was built like a Mercedes-Benz; every detail down to the tiniest screw was flawless. Tony Hawk was the one to blame. The ramp was his idea, and he'd funded the entire operation (apparently his Activision games are doing okay). The concept was to bring the ramp on the road as part of an action sports extravaganza and musical blowout. The top skaters, bike riders, and motocross jumpers would assault the ramp while bands played right next to the decks on a hydraulic-loaded stage. There was a mild amount of choreography, dangerously loud pyrotechnics, and at one point all eleven bikers and skaters were on the ramp at once—plus the FMX guys flying fifty feet overhead doing tweaked airs. It was a complete spectacle, but also respectable. The last time something like this had been attempted was the Swatch Impact tour, which seemed tiny in comparison.

We had two weeks of rehearsals to figure out the most insane and entertaining ways to merge our skills with the extraordinary ramp. A show was scheduled in Las Vegas at the Mandalay Bay events center—a sort of practice run for the real deal, which is a twenty-four city arena tour in the fall of 2002. If things went well in Vegas, it would ensure the success of the Tony Hawk Boom Boom Huckjam as a touring production and could change the way action sports are presented. If it flopped, it meant Tony spent a couple million dollars on the most expensive ramp session in history.

Aside from the dozens of roadies, production coordinators, and technicians, the success of Vegas rested on the shoulders of the talent pool. Social Distortion and The Offspring would provide sonic support from the stage. Tony, Andy MacDonald, Bucky

Lasek, Bob Burnquist, Lincoln Ueda, and Shawn White were the skating contingent. Dave Mirra, Dennis McCoy, John Parker, Kevin Robinson, and I represented bikes. On the motocross tip, Mike Cinqmars, Cary Hart, Dustin Miller, and old school supercross champ Mickey Dymond (subbing for the Clifford "The Flyin' Hawaiian" Adopante, who totaled himself in practice). Everybody had their own unique skills, and we were all focused on one job: Go huge.

Our group spent eleven hours a day inside the airplane hangar, tightening up the show routine, getting accustomed to the ramp, and figuring out our collective cues and timing. It was hairy—if one person was off by a second, it threw everybody into confusion and chaos. There were a couple collisions, and some very close calls. Most of the time, bikes have an advantage when riding with skaters because with a couple extra pumps, we can increase our altitude and air over them—but Lincoln Ueda made that impossible, because he was comfortably clocking twelve footers. He's like Sergie Ventura, Danny Way, or vintage Christian Hosoi— unstoppable. The skaters were also doing an insane freight-train-style run where they'd all drop in and work the ramp from end to end, practically touching boards the entire time. The FMX guys would circle the ramp like sharks, and gun it for the attack, throwing their machines high overhead two at a time and whipping off everything from handstands (Hart attack airs) to stretched bar hops, nothings, Indian airs, and more. It gave me chills just watching them skying directly above us on the ramps, like supersonic jets doing deck top flybys.

During our daily meetings we'd brainstorm our runs, and all the other riders and skaters decided Tony and I were going to end the show with a finale—side-by-side 9s. I've never tried to plan a 900 in a run. Ever. They either happen or they don't, depending on if I felt the spin inside me that moment. "Tony, are you consistent with 900s?" I asked him. He shrugged, gave a nervous chuckle, and rubbed a phantom hip pain, which let me know the same rules applied to a 900 on a skateboard—it's not a trick you can predict or control. You just throw. What were the odds we'd both pull them at the same time? Vegas was the perfect town to find out.

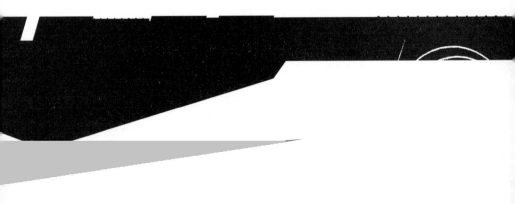

TOUR OBSERVATIONS

Mat and I have done a few demos together over the years. In that time, I have seen him dislocate his shoulder twice, get knocked out, dislocate his knee, break his wrist and hit a ramp harder than anyone in the history of our sports. In almost every instance, he managed to get up and ride the next day. I realized he was truly committed (aka crazy) when he tried to tape his broken wrist to his handlebars in order to finish out our 2001 Gigantic Skatepark Tour.

—TONY HAWK, PRO SKATEBOARDER

Boom Boom

Vegas is a city that's all about moving money around. It's a place to take risks, an oasis of entertainment for just about any taste. It's also the most extreme town in the USA—this was clear as I took a walk down the strip. Overhead, blaring billboards bombarded Sin City patrons with promises of loose slots, huge steaks, magic tigers, chattering dolphin shows, and the raunchy comedy of Mr. Jingles, the world's coarsest clown. Suddenly an animated rooftop sign lit up: TOMORROW NIGHT: TONY HAWK'S BOOM BOOM HUCKJAM. No turning back—we were part of the nonstop entertainment stream. There were eight thousand seats in the events center. Our goal was to fill the house, then rock it. If we could pull a grand slam in Vegas, it meant the HuckJam was certified for touring.

Our weeks of practice had paid off and the show was dialed—everything was tight, except for the last trick. We hadn't dared spend 9's in practice. I was already pushing the limits just to keep myself in the show. I'd separated a rib from my sternum taking a slam, and my wrist was worthless without gobs of tape. My body had totally exceeded the "ice, aloe, and TLC" treatment regimen prescribed by Tony's head trainer Barry Zaritzky, so I went to a local doctor and told him I needed anti-inflammatory medicine to bring the swelling down and loosen up my torso. With years of self-diagnosing my body, I knew just what I'd done and how to fix it. The emergency room doctor I saw was skeptical—he wanted a battery of tests to check everything from my heart rhythms to my bone structure. I pulled out a list of surgeries and injury descriptions, which Dr. Yates had written and showed it to the doc. "See, I do this all the time," I told him. He nodded, canceled the tests, and scribbled a prescription for the medication to put me back in the game.

Sitting at the blackjack table in our hotel casino a few hours later, I was still sore and needed to chill and get my mind to relax. A few rounds of cards would do the trick. The dealer began pestering the players at the table and picking on me in particular with snarky remarks every time I won—I was up $250 at a five-dollar table. The dealer's cracks were annoying, but who was I to disrupt my own winning streak by moving to another table? I stayed in a few more hands, until finally some lady at the end of the table began yelling at me. "Hey, Bucko!" she screamed. I tried ignoring her. "Bucko! Bucko! Look at me." It blew my concentration, and between this rude lady and the rude dealer I wasn't having much fun anymore. "Screw this, you guys are jerks. And, lady, quit calling me Bucko," I glared at her. She gave me a puzzled look. "I was talking to my friend standing right behind you, whose name happens to be Bucko," she spat back. I turned around and there was a Vegas bride in full gown, drinking a Budweiser. Mrs. Bucko, I presumed. It was time to get some sleep. Tomorrow would be a big day.

A DJ had primed the crowd on the ones and twos, filling in the air with beats and setting the mood for some fun. The arena faded to pitch black, and the buzz of the crowd turned to a roar. The house was filled with people anxious to see just what a HuckJam looked like. The lighting rig covered the entire ceiling ("more lights than Metallica's show" one veteran roadie told me). A huge curtain fell away revealing the ramp, cast in shadows. As the MC introduced each athlete a spotlight illuminated us, one by one. Then it was time to get it on. The BMX section was first, and all the lights flipped on to the opening drum kicks of "Paranoid" by Black Sabbath. Suddenly Kevin Robinson was upside down throwing a corkscrew over the huge channel. Dave Mirra sailed through the air spinning ridiculously high tailwhips, and airing both directions. Dennis cracked can-cans and 5s. John Parker gave up giant alley-ooping variations and looked smooth as grease. Then it was my turn. I pedaled across the deck and dove into the first wall with a ten-foot no-hander, spreading my wings and holding it stretched as the MC told the crowd the Condor was in the house. It felt great.

The HuckJam was divided into segments of BMX, skate, and FMX, then Social Distortion took the stage. During the band, we all rode in a jam format and watched the music from the best seat in the house—on the decks of the ramp. After Social D finished a twenty-minute set, the skaters and bikers did the gap jump down the giant roll-in, and then it was time for The Offspring to bring the noise. The whole time, the crowd was great—freaking out, standing up, and getting loud.

Finally, it was time for the finale. Time to put the Boom Boom into the room. Mike Ness from Social Distortion came back out with The Offspring and they ripped into a blazing cover of The Ramones' "Blitzkrieg Bop." As the opening riff kicked in and "Hey! Ho! Let's Go!" came out of the speakers, the energy in the building went into overdrive. Every single athlete was on the ramp at once—giant TNT bombs thundered to life, courtesy of the pyro expert, and shook the roof. Mike Cinqmars flew fifty feet overhead with his motorcycle completely kicked out sideways, and on the opposite side Cary Hart blasted past in a full Hart attack handstand. On the ramp, Dave was throwing eight-foot carving tailwhips over the channel with Bucky 540ing underneath, followed by Bob cleaning up with sizzling one-footed Smith grinds. The opposite wall was just as busy—I flaired next to Kevin as he pulled a flair, with Shawn and Tony spinning 360s and tailslides right behind us. It was three minutes of totally precise insanity. The whole arena was on their feet, shouting the chorus as one big voice, as we unleashed every trick we could.

Every trick, that is, but one. At the end of the mad jam, the song stopped and the crowd exploded with appreciation. We all took a bow, savoring the moment. The MC said there was one last bit to the show, and that Tony and I were the two originators of the hardest trick in the book. In seconds, eight thousand people were all chanting in unison, "Nine . . . nine . . . nine . . ." I looked over at Tony, who shrugged happily, but intensely. We dropped in and pumped a couple feeler airs until it was right. We both left the coping spinning and . . . came up with snake eyes. I touched down on my wheels and slid out into the opposite wall. Tony took a hard one to the tailbone.

But in the end it didn't matter. The show was amazing, and all the pressure about pulling one trick didn't seem to matter to the crowd. We'd just taken action sports to a new place, as individuals and as a group. The creative energy of music, art, and sport had been fused together and was powerful enough to fill a giant room.

It was long way from the days of sessioning a backyard ramp with a couple friends on the deck and a boom box blaring Black Flag.

Or was it?

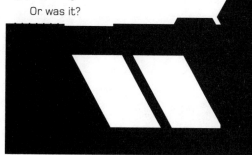

TRICK ROLODEX

The coolest thing about bike riding is that it's a sport that can be turned into an art. Fearlessness and balance will get you far, but creativity is king. Even when I'm not riding, my brain is at work trying to think up new ways to twist an aerial or throw my limbs.

I go through spurts of enjoying different tricks. Riding with good friends is a great way to learn new stuff. So is shooting photos, if you have a good relationship with a photographer you trust. They make you want to push your limits and ponder the question every bike rider asks themselves: What else can I do?

BARHOPS AND VARIATIONS

BARHOP
This was one of the last tricks I learned on my backyard halfpipe, and I debuted it on the Haro tour in 1988. I've never had them more dialed than the time I shot *Aggroman* and the *Ride On* with Eddie Roman. Size twelve feet make this especially hard for me. Barhops have been adapted by FMX riders to great success.

HAN SOLO
A one-handed barhop air. As you jump over the bars with your feet, you're controlling the bike with one hand, which is hard. You have to find a center of balance and stall, then steer and reenter while you get your legs back behind the handlebars.

SUPERHOP
This is a superman into a barhop. Your legs are at the furthest points they can possibly be on the bike—stretched behind you and then jabbed over your front tire. The only other person I've even seen try barhops in a long time is Leigh Ramsdell.

MISCELLANEOUS VARIATIONS

STUTTERING PIRATE
A can-can lookback to candybar. Your body has to be all the way in front of your bike with your back facing the ground to tweak the can-can lookback. Then you straighten out and throw a leg over the handlebars into a candybar and pull it back over the crossbar as you're headed straight down into the transition. If you don't make it, you're a dead sailor.

FIMINGUEZ
My version of hip-hop sampling. The two songs in this beat include a one-footer one-hander on the bottomside, in tribute to skatepark great Mike Dominguez, and when I throw the topside one-hander, bottomside one-footer it's a tribute to his greatest rival, Eddie Fiola. This is the only air I have named after other riders, both skatepark rulers.

INDIAN AIR
In 1987 there was a poster hanging in the Edmond Bike shop of Tony Hawk doing an Airwalk. It got me inspired to think of what else I could do with my legs during an air. I was stretching can-cans, and people were calling them Hoffmonian can-cans, so I decided to see if I could get my feet can-canned on opposite sides of the bike. This was one of the first tricks that put me on the map.

INDIAN BINGO
This is an Indian to topside no-footed can-can. You stretch from legs dangling below the bike, to legs flung upward on the opposite side. I'm constantly trying to find new balance points and stable places in different aerials, and see what I can build on them.

INDIAN AIR CLASSIC
I originally thought up the name for an Indian air before I did the trick, and it turned out to be a slightly different configuration than what I had in mind. I called this version, where I started doing them with my legs crossed, sitting Indian style, the Indian air classic. It was around the same time Coke changed their recipe and the name of their product.

OLD SPICE
Essentially a one-handed Indian air classic. This one has come and gone in my trick repertoire over the years. I redid it in the latest Hoffman Bikes video, *Testimony*.

SWINDLING INDIAN

The Indian air classic gets technical. I throw a no-footed air into an Indian, then back to a no-footer. My legs swing around from one side of the bike to back out again.

COUGH DROP

For years I did toadstool airs before I realized I didn't need my feet on the back pegs. Sometime in 1999, I took my feet off, grabbed the seat with one hand, and crossed up the bars with the other. I did it first try. I was sick that day, hence, the name.

PENDULUM AIR

One of the last tricks I learned on my original backyard halfpipe, circa 1987. A no-footed topside can-can to a no-footed bottomside can-can. Whenever I had piano lessons I had to watch the pendulum on the metronome go back and forth.

ROCKET QUEEN

Steve and I were riding the Ninja Ramp in 1989. I threw a lookback while standing with one foot on the seatpost. "Cool. What are you gonna call it?" asked Steve. I looked down at the deck and there was a Guns 'N Roses CD sitting there. "Rocket Queen" was the last song on the track listing and caught my eye.

BOTTLE ROCKET

A no-handed rocket air, one of the scarier variations I do. This is hard because with your feet on the back pegs, you have to lean forward to stabilize your bars when you take your hands off. I was shooting a photo session with Mark Losey in 1993 and was bored with the tricks in my library, so I thought this one up. When I asked Mark if I should try it, he wouldn't say yes or no, because he didn't want to be responsible if I crashed. I was also going for triple bar spins that day but could only pull two and a half.

SWITCH ROCKET

Once I got into the idea of combination airs, I would try every trick I knew and see what else I could throw in. This was the first rocket air variation I invented. I turn to the right and switch my right hand with my left.

WOBBLE ROCKET

This is a variation that feels sketchy. It's a rocket air with a one-handed X-up. When I cross the bars up, the gyroscopic effect makes my bike wobble, and since I'm only holding on with one hand it's hard to control.

SUPERGRAB

Nobody but a vert rider will know this, but this trick is probably the hardest variation I know. It's a superman seat grab X-up. I get locked way behind the bike with my bars twisted and am reentering the ramp that way, making corrections the whole time because the front wheel crossed up gives the bike a nice wobble. Very intimidating. On the crowd-appeal factor, this trick doesn't hold a candle to a big 540 or a tailwhip.

B2B

B2B is short for bumper-to-bumper. The trick is a superman to no-footed candybar—bringing me from the very back to the very front of the bike. This air feels awesome and uses the same rhythm as a superhop. The "B-to-B" in this one could also stand for Bob-to-Brian, since Bob Kohl invented the superman, and his riding partner Brian Dahl invented the candybar.

B2B PLUS

Takes the B2B to the next level by throwing a no-footed can-can in for extra credit. It breaks the air into three parts—the superman on the way up, the no-footed candybar at the peak, and the no-footed can-can on the way down. If you play *Mat Hoffman's Pro BMX2*, you can do these using the trick modifier.

LOOK FOOT

Lookdown to no-footer. Many times I accidentally tweaked lookdowns too far and had my feet come off. Then I thought I'd try untwisting the lookdown and throwing a no-footer on the way down. It worked, but it's a small window of opportunity to get my feet back on. I can also do these one-handed, which is harder because I can't snap in and out.

SWITCHBLADE

Kevin "The Gute" Gutierrez does switch-handed lookdowns on jumps. In 2000, we were riding vert at Patty's ramp in Austin, and I asked the Gute to do his switch lookdown as an air. He said he'd never done it on vert. I dropped in and tried it, and a couple of days after that session I did it at the first CFB. Losey took a photo of it, and I wound up on the cover of *Ride*.

NO-FOOTED SWITCHBLADE

Same as above, but throwing the no-footer on the way. Supertech trick. I constantly have people calling out flairs, tailwhips, 5s, and 9s. Maybe five times in my life have I heard requests from the crowd for tricks that are this technical.

SWITCH-HANDER

Nostalgia time. This is the first trick I ever made up, back in 1986. I went to pick up my bike off the ground and grabbed the opposite grip, then wondered if I could grab with my opposite hand in the air. I called it a can-hand. A vert rider from Texas named Jack Smith started doing it and called it a switch-hander. I changed the name because Jack's title sounded better.

SWING LEG

The first combo trick I ever learned, circa 1987. It involves finding the total rhythm of an air—I throw a no-footer on the way up, slip in no-footed can-can at the peak, and bring the legs back across the top tube for a no-footer on the way down.

NO-FOOTED ONE-HANDER TO SWING LEG

Throwing a hand and my feet off ups the difficulty of a regular swing leg. Once you've mastered the balance of an aerial, anything is possible. A lot of riders aren't interested in technical tricks on vert—and focus doing tech stuff on park courses or flatland. I think I overanalyze vert.

SWITCH SPIN

It was the spring of 1998, and I had a vert ramp set up outside. I was having a mellow session by myself and was getting bored with my variations, so I forced myself to come up with a new trick. I was tired, and kept chickening out, and the sun started to set. I told myself I could end the session by taking myself out, or learning this trick. I decided I didn't want to crash, and switched my hand, threw the bars, and caught them with my opposite hand. The same session I learned this doing a rocket air.

VIKING'S MUSTACHE

A no-footed switch-hander. The variation dates back to 1987, and you don't see this move very often anymore. It was tough to learn because the balance is very tough, like a mustached Viking.

UN-X-UP ONE-FOOTER

Another invention from the fertile Mountain Dew Trick Team era. I switch both hands (double switch-hander) and throw a foot off.

UN-X-UP CAN-CAN

Same thing as the above. Learned this one doing a demo at a sports car show.

NO-FOOTED UN-X-UP

In 1999, thirteen years after I learned the root air (the switch-hander), I came up with this one. I did it during a photo shoot and the trick wound up on a poster for my first game release in Holland. Stoked.

TOADSTOOL AIRS

In 1991, I made this up on Dennis McCoy's backyard ramp just before he held a little jam there. It's a one-footed rocket air grabbing the seat. No other pro does these, but they should. They're fun.

X-UP TOADSTOOL

Learned these the same day as the toadstool by crossing up the bars. The jam was good, and one of the last times Joe Johnson rode in an event.

TOMAHAWK

This is an old one, invented about 1987. It's sort of a backside, reversed Indian air. You do a superman, drop your leg around the back of the bike into a no-footed can-can. A lot of my tricks reflect the fact that Oklahoma is rich with Indian lore.

TOMAHAWK TO TOPSIDE NO-FOOTED CAN-CAN

My body swings the opposite direction as the bike is rotating and ends with a no-footed can-can topside. Freaky.

SEAT HAWK

I just learned this baby a year ago, working on lines for the *Testimony* video. I needed one more trick that would work as a superman so I could do an alley-oop on the big wall. The second time I ever pulled this trick—a tomahawk seat grab—is in the video.

BAR SPIN VARIATIONS

The bar spin debuted as a how-to in Freestylin' *magazine, featuring RL Osborn doing it as a kickturn on a bank behind Larry's Donuts shop in Torrance, California. Then Chris Moeller brought it to dirt jumping (at the time it was known as a bus driver). The first guy I saw do bar spins on ramps was Jeremy Alder, an East Coast local who rode with us at one of the Skyway shows in 1987.*

On vert, you don't really see your bars because you're looking at the coping, so you have to use "The Force" and feel where to put your hands based on the gyration in your bike. Camera flashes make it dangerous, and chrome-plated bars add even more danger in that situation. After my slam in Japan doing a bar spin, I stopped running chrome bars for good.

Variations of the bar spin I've invented include the following:

BAR SPIN TO NO-FOOTER

BAR SPIN TO X-UP

ROCKETED BAR SPIN

Also done to late no-footer.

ROCKETED BAR SPIN TO NO-FOOTED CAN-CAN

TOSSED SALAD

Bar spin to bar spin back.

ROCKET SALAD
Rocketed bar spin to bar spin back, also done to late no-footer.

CROSS DRESSER
Switch-handed bar spin, also done to late no-footer.

DOUBLE-CROSS DRESSER
Switch-handed bar spin to bar spin back, also done to late no-footer.

COSMONAUT
Switch-handed rocketed bar spin, also to late no-footer.

COSMO-TOSS
Switch-handed rocketed bar spin to bar spin back, also to late no-footer.

PIGS IN SPACE
Rocketed double bar spin, also to late no-footer.

TAILWHIP VARIATIONS
Brian Blyther invented the tailwhip as a ground trick in 1984. His friend Mike Dominguez took tailwhips to the sky as a flyout trick. By 1988, Joe Johnson had done the first tailwhip air. I really only have two decent tailwhip variations I've invented.

TAILWHIP TO NO-FOOTER
A tailwhip with a no-footer thrown in at the peak. I guess technically your feet are already off during a tailwhip.

BARHOP TAILWHIPS
The burliest tailwhip variation, besides a triple. I started doing these at the Shreveport fair in Louisiana, 1990. There were two people in the crowd during the first show of the day, so for personal amusement, we ran our demo backward. I did this as an example of an easy trick. Later I tried to shoot this trick with Spike Jonze and hung my heels up on the bars jumping back over and landed with my seat in my back. That was the last time I ever tried it.

CANDYBAR VARIATIONS
CANDYDANCE
A candybar into a can-can. If you want to extend your legs, you can't rush this trick or you clip your shoe pulling your leg back over the handlebars.

CANDY CAN
A candybar can-canned over the front tire. I learned this during a King of Vert contest in Flint, Michigan.

SAMMY DAVIS JR.
The man could do everything—play any instrument, sing, tell jokes, and dance. His biggest song was "Candyman." The trick I named after Sammy is a no-footed candybar to a no-footed can-can. I can also do them to late no-footers.

SAM-I-AM
A no-footed one-handed candybar, one of the more technical tricks I've invented. I had to fight like hell to get this trick as the cover shot of my new video game. It's not an in-your-face variation, but I've been doing it for fourteen years and it's stood the test of time. Somebody else has got to start doing Sam-I-Ams.

CANDIAN AIRS

A candybar Indian. This is a no-footed candybar with the bottom foot twisted around backside and pointing up, like an Indian air. Spike is the only person who ever shot this trick and made it look good. He used a fisheye lens.

ONE-HANDED CANDIAN

Taking it up a notch in difficulty by taking a hand off.

CANDYBAR LOOKBACK

I was lying on my back on the flatbottom holding the bike above me. My bike started falling over and I caught it with my leg as it fell into a candybar lookback position. Inspiration struck, and I learned it. Since about 1988 this trick has been one of my trademarks. I can also do this to late can-can on the way in.

NO-HANDED AIRS

No-handers are the first trick everybody learns on a bike, as in "Look ma, no hands!" Doing them in the air is a little more advanced. In 1985, Jeff Carrol debuted the no-handed air in a skatepark contest. Within a year it had become a defining trick for vert riders. If you were good, you knew how to do these. If you see me ride, you might notice I throw no-handers as one of my opening tricks during a run. Because my bike stays in the same balance point through the trick, what I'm really concentrating on is the feel of the ramp. Straight no-handers are a way for me to warm up, throw some style, and still feel safe while I get used to a new ramp. I hold my hands off as long as I can.

I've also added a few of my own twists to the no-handed air over the years.

NO-HANDED BODY JAR

Slap the back tire on the deck on reentry on accident, and you have a bad hang-up. Do it on purpose and it's called a body jar.

NO-HANDER TO NO-FOOTER

Probably the second combo I learned, after swing leg airs.

NO-HANDER TO NO-FOOTER ONE-HANDER

I was fifteen years old and doing a photo session with John Kerr for *BMX Plus!* on Mike Dominguez's backyard ramp. Mike came out and was casually riding with no gear and watching the session. I threw this trick, and he gave me some props. I blushed.

NO-HANDER TO NO-FOOTED CAN-CAN

NO-HANDER TO NO-FOOTED CANDYBAR

NO-HANDER TO NO-FOOTED CANDYBAR TO NO-FOOTED CAN-CAN

NO-HANDER TO LOOKDOWN

Kind of difficult because both tricks require upward momentum.

SLOT MACHINE

A no-hander into a one-handed lookdown. Jeff Carrol meets Joe Johnson.

NO-HANDED ONE-FOOTER

I learned this in a warehouse in Los Angeles practicing for the Dan-Up Yogurt tour with Dennis McCoy. After I pulled my first one clean, Dennis crashed, punctured his lung, and started puking blood.

NO-HANDED ONE-FOOTER TO CAN-CAN
The can-can comes on the way in.

CONAN O'BRIEN
A no-handed one-footer into a no-footed one-hander. When you do a no-hander one-footer, your cranks flip vertically so you have to do a half-crank flip as you put one hand on and take your feet off, which is fairly technical. This is one of those tricks I learned just to see if it was possible. It is.

NO-HANDER, HANDS BEHIND THE BACK
I did this first time on Ron Wilkerson's ramp. I had a Freddy Krueger doll zip-tied to my handlebars.

RIPSAW
No-handed air, grabbing both front pegs. I saw Dave Voelker doing this but touching his front tire. I tried it without gloves and thrashed my hands on my tire, so I found a less painful place I could grab.

RIPSAW TO NO-FOOTER
Requires a big ramp and high airs because it takes time to reach over and grab the pegs, then get back to the grips and throw the no-footer. I did it for the first time at the CFB in Merritt Island, Florida.

PEACOCK
The peacock was the first trick I ever pulled using a resi mat. I was at a CFB at camp Woodward in Pennsylvania, and I did it on my first try. I guess that's the point of the resi mat. I gives you confidence to take it to vert. I named the no-footed double peg grab a peacock because I had one as a kid.

HALF-COCK
A no-handed one-footed peg grab.

COCK BLOCK
I put up a contest at Hoffmanbikes.com and let my fans name this trick. Three hundred thousand people voted, and in less than a month, cock block was the name for this no-footed one-handed peg grab.

ROCK COCK
This is the hardest cock trick I know. It's one of the hardest vert tricks, period. You're stretched on the bike in the most awkward position, doing a rocket air and leaning all the way forward grabbing the front pegs. I was so psyched I learned this and debuted it at the 2001 X Games. Nobody even noticed what I was doing.

DISASTER VARIATIONS
Around 1988 skateboarding began to influence bike riding, and riders began doing a lot of lip tricks. The disaster is an aerial inspired by skateboarding. You hang up an air to the chainring and then dive into the ramp. The highest disaster I ever did was off a nine-foot air. I used to do them so often my neck started to hurt. My doctor said I had whiplash, so I took it out of my set. But not before I had invented these:

INVERT DISASTERS

NO-HANDED DISASTERS

NO-FOOTED DISASTERS

BARSPIN DISASTERS

FAKIE VARIATIONS

Another skate-inspired air. You blast over the coping but come in backward. Fakies have been around on bikes since Bob Haro first did them back in 1978. Every vert rider has a few fakie variations. My highest were over eight feet out, and I bent a lot of seatposts getting them wired. I finally had to stop doing fakies because every time you crash one you go straight to your wrists. My variations include:

NO-FOOTED CAN-CAN FAKIE

ONE-HANDED NO-FOOTED CAN-CAN FAKIE

NOTHING FAKIE

All limbs removed at the peak of the trick.

BARHOP FAKIE

Unveiled at the KOV finals the day I turned pro.

ROCKET FAKIE

CLARK KENT

Aka the superman fakie. This trick feels awesome.

LIP TRICKS

The early lip tricks on bikes were pretty clunky and didn't flow so well. As bikers started riding with skateboarders, lip tricks evolved in speed and fluidity. The first bike rider I saw doing skateboarding-style lip tricks was Craig Campbell. He did a double peg stall. Steve Swope took that idea and started doing grinds. I learned alley-oop double peg grinds. Suddenly, a door opened up. Here's what else I ushered through that door:

FEEBLE GRINDS

Front tire on the deck, back peg grinding.

ALLEY-OOP FEEBLE GRINDS

FEEBLE GRINDS TO FRONT PEG BONK

SMITH GRINDS

Back tire on the deck, front peg on the coping.

SMITH ALLEY-OOP 180 BAR SPIN GRIND

SMITH GRINDS TO ICEPICK SLAP

Learned this one two and a half years ago.

SMITH STALLS

ONE-FOOTED FRAME STAND SMITH STALL

ONE-FOOTED FRAME STAND SMITH GRIND

HOPSCOTCH GRIND

Feeble to Smith.

ICEPICKS

Back peg stalls, invented the same session Joe Johnson invented toothpicks. Rich Hansen, a rider from Minnesota, invented the icepick on ledges while street riding.

HANDRAIL DOUBLE PEG GRINDS
Adapted from street skating.

CLIFF-HANGER STALL
A stall with the grip and pedal connecting with the coping, done as a can-can with on hand holding the seat. I even went to a motorcycle shop and got an enduro bar-protector to see if I could grind this one.

BACK WHEEL COPING SLIDE
These look and feel smooth. I tweaked a couple so far I ended up learning downside icepicks.

DOWNSIDE ICEPICK
Clicking the downside back peg to the coping. A matter of learning to lean.

AIR TO ICEPICK SLAP

SEAT STAND GRIND

CANDYBAR FOOTPLANT
Racking my brain trying to come up with a new footplant trick back in 1988, I ended up here. Even though he can't do this trick, Dennis McCoy is never one to miss the chance to give me shit for doing what he calls circus tricks. I saw some guy do a candybar footplant during a run at the Soul Bowl recently and got so stoked. Take that, Dennis.

FRAME STAND NOSEPICK

FRONT PEG STAND NOSEPICK
A nosepick. With one foot on the inside front peg.

JACKKNIFE FRAME STAND NOSEPICK
I jab my right foot on the front tire, put my left foot on frame, kick it out, then hop into the tranny.

DECADE DROP-IN
In 1988, decades were the only impressive semiadvanced flatland trick I could do consistently. I took it to the deck of the ramp as a drop-in and perverted it for style points.

FLATLAND

The supercomplex battery of ground tricks in today's riding scene is confusing to even think about. But back when I was fifteen, I had a claim to fame as a ground rider. That move was the bar spin frame stand. In 1987 at the AFA finals in the Olympic Velodrome, Martin Aparijo and Dennis McCoy were tied for first place in pro flatland. There was a runoff, and Martin edged out McCoy by a slim margin. One trick Martin used in his routine—my bar spin frame stand.

ROTATING TRICKS

900
Only a handful of riders have ever pulled a 900. Simon Tabron keeps a journal of his 9 attempts. He's pulled maybe fifty his whole life. I went to the KOV contest in Canada in 1990 and I had a new 540 variation I thought I'd use as a finale to my pro run. I'd never tried a 900 before, and that day I pulled my first. It's a trick where you have to feel the rotation, because you're spinning so fast you can't see the coping.

NO-FOOTED 540
My new trick to show people at the Canadian KOV contest in 1990. It kind of got overshadowed by the 900.

NO-HANDED 540
I never get tired of this trick. I also like doing it alley-oop.

NO-HANDED 540 TO NO-FOOTER

NO-HANDED 540 TO CAN-CAN

NO-HANDED 540 TO NO-FOOTED CAN-CAN

NO-HANDED ONE-FOOTED 540

INVERTED 540

SWITCH-HANDED 540

JACKSON FIVE
A 540 while doing a double peg grab.

GRIZZLY ADAMS
An X-up 540.

FLIPS

FLIP FLYOUT DISMOUNT
I saw Tony Hawk doing front-flip flyout dismounts and learned them on my bike in 1990. It was a great trick to end a show with, until my knees got messed up.

FULL FLIP FLYOUT
I learned these right before the first BS contest in 1992. I could front-flip and land on the deck, on my bike. It's a trick that takes tons of energy, and at the BS contest I was sick and tired and couldn't pull it. Within a couple years, my rotator cuff got so bad I didn't have the ability to pull these any more. Another trick lost to injury.

FLIP FAKIE
Pulled in public in Paris, 1989. Spike shot it for the cover of *Go* magazine.

FLAIR
A flip with a twist. Flairs, tailwhips, and big 540s are probably the crowd favorites at any demo.

BACKFLIP LOOKBACK JUMPS

NO-HANDED BACKFLIP JUMPS
I crashed a no-handed backflip at the Charles Schultz show in Santa Rosa, California, and my bike got away and hit his grandson and broke his nose. I felt terrible.

BACKFLIP TAILWHIP JUMPS
Lots of spinning going on here. Learned these around 1993.

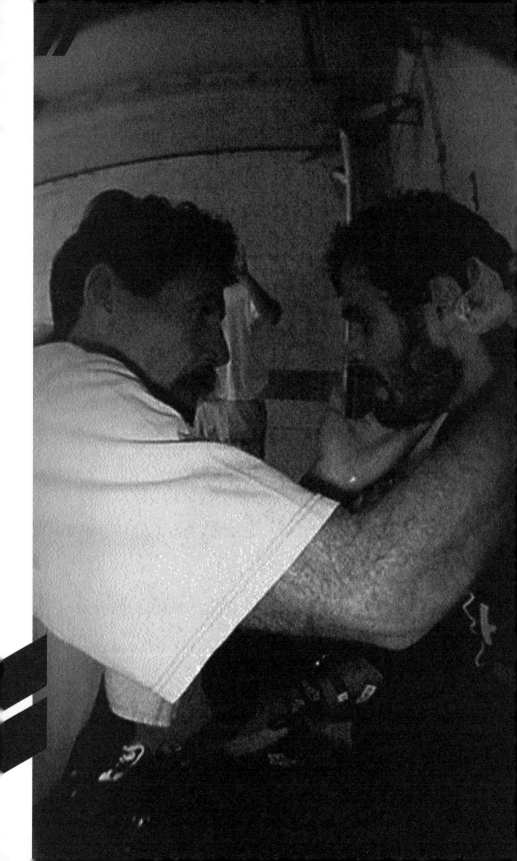

APPENDIX B

FOUR WAYS
FAME CHANGED
THE GAME

01 Bike Check

Checking your bike at the airport has long been a tradition pitting biker against airline. An airline-imposed surcharge on transporting bicycles allows carriers to gouge bike riders an extra $50 to $150 on top of the tickets, just for checking your bike as baggage. I'm talking about a bicycle broken down and packed neatly in a bike box. It's all the more ridiculous when you see people checking three or five giant suitcases or footlockers and not being charged for their bulky items. The wise way around it was to never admit you were transporting a bike. Creative excuses included calling it camping gear, trade show samples, and the ever-mysterious "exhibition equipment." The more prominent the X Games became, the less these excuses worked. The airline employees had learned to spot bike boxes. The last time the exhibition equipment line worked in my favor, it was beautiful. The airline counterperson was just starting to question me about what kind of *exhibition* equipment it was, when a stranger in line recognized me and approached. "Hey, Mat. Are you here to do an exhibition?" was the first thing out of his mouth. I got very chatty with the guy, keeping the word *bike* out of the conversation, and the airline employee gave up trying to figure out what I was exhibiting. Those days are long gone, now, though.

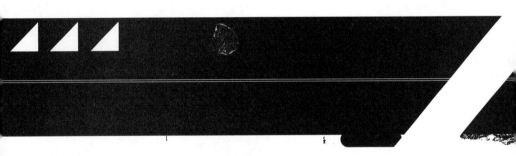

02 Groupies

When I started riding, the reality was, guys who rode pink and lime-green bikes were dorks. Even though the color palette has been toned down a few shades in recent years, bike riders are still dangerously dorky. Initially, the bike contest scene was 99.99 percent male, most of them teenagers with hormones boiling. It's too bad the sport didn't catch on with girls the way snowboarding (and to a lesser extent, skateboarding) did. But with very few exceptions, you'd be hard-pressed to even *find* a female face within a thousand yards of a halfpipe back in the old days. TV coverage attracted an avalanche of new fans—both guys and girls. I don't participate in the groupie scene, but today's eligible bachelors who've got the right image—usually helped greatly by a set of six-pack abs with a few tattoos, and the ability to pull backflips over the spine ramp—seem to enjoy endless nights of cheap, empty sex with "stripper class" bombshells anywhere they travel.

03 Stalkers

I am profoundly humbled by the fact that people are impressed enough by my bike skills to want to meet me or get an autograph. Sometimes it makes for some awkward situations. For a long time, it didn't matter if a top rider's address or even home phone number circulated freely in the bike community. It was very rare that fans got truly persistent enough to be, well, intrusive. Recently I've noticed more obsession has been creeping into the sport. Not long ago, I was getting into my car about 7 A.M. to go to the airport, and some lady's car was blocking my driveway. She hopped out when she saw me and ran up for an autograph. I don't know how long she'd been there. Overnight? I hadn't shaved or showered and had coffee breath—glamorous. Another time some guys from Portugal got my home phone number, and I would get these bizarre phone calls at 3 A.M., consisting of a mix of hip-hop slang in broken English and Portuguese. I had to change my number. The neighbors behind my house built a viewing platform over the fence so they could watch me while I chilled in my backyard. And I can't count the times that adults have just left their kids at the Hoffman Bikes offices to hang out for a few hours, like it's a drop-in teen rec center.

04 Insurance Claims

I can remember the good old days when I'd be on the phone with an insurance claims department and they'd think I was on some disability scam: "Let me get this straight," the operator would say. "Am I to understand you broke your *wrist* on the 4th, went in for a *concussion* on the 12th, needed *nine* stitches in your *foot* on the 23rd, and two days later you broke your *ribs*?" I had the fraud departments pretty suspicious of me for years. Eventually, they called me in and went over my occupation and hobbies. Needless to say, when they found out I rode vert, actively skydived, and was attempting to get a pilot's license . . . I got dropped, pronto. Now, with bike riders regularly on TV, the medical industry knows what bicycle stunt riding is and limits coverage accordingly. The key is to actually do enough work in the film industry to be eligible for SAG union insurance.

PHOTOGRAPH CAPTIONS AND CREDITS

All photographs courtesy of Mat Hoffman unless otherwise credited.

ii, 51, 260–261 I wanted to get lit on fire in the chicken suit, go through the loop then jump into the lake to extinguish myself. MTV wouldn't let me because some kid had lit himself on fire trying film his own Jackass stunt.

iv This was difficult to land because I couldn't see my landing through the smoke. Once I took off it was a blind jump and it became pretty intense. (Photograph courtesy of Brad McDonald)

v, 02 Geovanna Teresa Papa, AKA Joni Hoffman.

vi, vii, 32 Austin, Texas 1986. It was a demo for the Texas AFA—one of the first shows outside of the Edmond Bike Shop and Mountain Dew shows I was asked to ride in.

viii My dad's boyhood home. The only thing I remember about this house when we visited my grandparents were Raggedy Ann & Andy dolls. They kept me entertained on our visits.

02 What more can I say about this photo? My mom's skating! I'm so psyched I found this one.

03 Matthew Hoffman, looking suave and debonair.

04–05 When Jaci and I were married, I gave her the wedding ring my dad gave my mom in this photo.

07 Gina and Todd on top of their second home. Yeeeeha!

09 My first cast. I got it blue to match my bike.

09 I came home one day to find our house in flames. Some things just suck.

10 Dad surveys the damage from a catastrophic creek flooding. Dealing with disaster was a skill I learned early.

12 I grew up bouncing on trampolines. I loved gravity before I even knew what it was, and experimenting with ways I could play with it. I'm two years old in this shot.

17 *Mi familia* (left to right, top to bottom): my sister, Gina, Dad, Mom, my oldest brother, Todd, me, and my big brother, Travis.

18 I was involved on a recon patrol with my squad, searching for the enemy deep in the bush. Canteens were the only source of water.

22 This was my first half-pipe. The ramp was nine feet tall with twenty-two feet of flat bottom (primitive dimensions of the early days). Travis' bedroom was under the far deck. As soon as it stopped snowing I was out there scraping the snow off the ramp; I couldn't go a day without riding.

24 Travis and I after winning trophies racing. He raced BMX on his Skyway TA, I raced MX on my YZ 80. We both got second that day.

25 The Edmond Bike Shop team (left to right): Chad Dutton, Jeff Worth, Steve Worth, Josh Weller, Travis, Me, and Eric Gefeller.

26 The owner of the Edmond Bike Shop, Ron Dutton. He was the Godfather who sparked our imaginations by stocking his shop with treasure.

27 I won the tournament in my weight division, eighty-five pounds. My coach told my dad he thought I could win the state title if I stuck with it. That didn't make it much easier for Dad when I decided to stop and ride my bike full time. He still supported me, though.

29 My first contest. This was also the first time I rode a quarter-pipe that was over six feet tall. I could barely air out, but man, was I was excited to drop in on it. This was the day I realized how much there was to learn, and that I was just starting my journey.

31 The Mountain Dew team (left to right): Josh Weller, Me, Steve Swope, Keith Hopkis, and Travis.

36 When you're performing on tour day after day, you're so happy when rain gives you a day off. Here's Team Skyway rejoicing. (Photograph courtesy of Maurice Meyer)

38 I got into bikes straight from motorcycles, so a chest plate and full-face helmet were the norm for me. For a while, it tripped people out in the bike scene to such overprotection, but I put my gear to good use. I was also obsessed with stickers. (Photograph courtesy of Steve Giberson)

40 This was the first show I did with Kevin Jones. My goal that day was to clear the building.

42 This was the life. I got to pilot the plane between takeoff and landing, then go to a comp and ride. (Photograph courtesy of Steve Giberson)

44 I was fourteen and got a license to drive a scooter. I'd lay my bike across the seat and sit on top of it to get to the riding spots. Sometimes I'd just ride freestyle on my scooter, though. (Photograph courtesy of Steve Giberson)

46 The Dan-Up Team (left to right, top to bottom): Eddie Fiola Dennis McCoy, me, and Rick Moliterno.

47 I was fifteen years old doing airs with Eddie Fiola, "The King of the Skateparks," on the deck measuring my height. He was a superhero to me. It was very surreal. (Photograph courtesy of Steve Giberson)

50 This was my first show for Skyway. They flew me out to Redding California and I showed them how skilled I was by breaking my collarbone in practice.

52 Airing over Chris Miller at the Gold Coast in Australia. I tore my rotator cuff on a one footed 540 days before. Circa 1990.

54 Blowing out the candles on my sixteenth birthday cake at the AFA contest in Florida. My wish was to ride forever. (Photograph courtesy of Steve Giberson)

56 This was at Bercy Stadium in Paris, France, for the KOV. I had amnesia on this trip, so I can't tell you much about it.

59 Rocking it at Rockville BMX on the Haro Tour.

60 The building of the Secret Ninja ramp.

63 Just in case I forgot, the rest of the Haro wrote: "By Mat Hoffman" on the smashed bumper. Summer 1988.

64 Steve Swope and I at the Haro show in Tulsa, Oklahoma, 1988.

65 Rick Thorne arriving an AFA contest, welts on his head and all. He got beat down by some marines who didn't get his humor. (Photograph courtesy of Spike Jonze)

67 See if you can find anybody resembling me, Rick Thorne, Steve Swope, or Dennis McCoy. This was from the night of Dennis' bachelor party. Steve, Rick, and I chipped in to give Dennis and Paridy a three-foot-tall brass mermaid as a wedding gift. Last time I saw it, it was collecting dust in the McCoys' basement.

70 Manchester, England. This was the demo where I did the first flair. (Photograph courtesy of Mark Noble)

73 Part of the Swatch Impact Team (left to right): Brian Blyther, Mark "Gator" Rogowski, Kevin Staab, me, and Jimi Scott. (Photograph courtesy of Swatch, USA)

74 This was the first 900 I pulled in March, 1989 in Ontario, Canada. It was my second pro vert contest, and only the second time I attempted this trick. (Images courtesy of Eddie Roman)

79 The historic cover of *Go, The Rider's Manual*. This was the public debut of the flip fakie, shot by Spike Jonze in Paris.

80 Kevin Jones and I dressed up before the show at the Bercy Stadium in Paris, France.

84–85 This was the first flair I did. Announcer Kevin Martin jumped in the air and landed straight on his knees after I pulled it. He got more injured than I did. (Photograph courtesy of Mark Noble)

86 Open highway, big wheel of the Peterbuilt in my hand…life is good.

88 Rick Thorne and I dorkin' in Deer Creek. The Sprocket Jockeys were regulars at the Deer Creek fair in Indianapolis.

89–91 The original Sprocket Jockeys rig.

96–97 Redesigned with a fresh new paint job. I did a wall ride on it to christen it. (Photograph courtesy of Spike Jonze)

104, 107 The beautiful, the wonderful, the one and only Joni Hoffman. My mother.

110 A one-handed, no-footed candybar. This was at a 1992 BS comp at Stone Edge Skatepark in Daytona, Florida. (Photograph courtesy of Mark Losey)

114 Packing orders under the deck of the vert ramp. We were always crowded for space.

117 Hoffman Manufacturing. This is where the magic happens—the machine shop separated by a plastic wall. On the other side of the wall is the Secret Ninja ramp.

118 Adding the scores at BS comp in Oklahoma City.

120 My office, after I've cleaned it. (Photograph courtesy of Mark Losey)

125 Here's a little Hoffman Bikes humor to sell product to dealers. This was for a postcard we mailed to our dealers that said, "Everything must go, but the helmet." (Photograph courtesy of Adam Booth)

126 Candybar, at the Southsea Skatepark in England. (Photograph courtesy of Mark Noble)

129 Half the battle in airing the first twenty-one-foot ramp was getting to it via this sketchy runway.

131 This was the day we finished building the ramp. Steve and I rode to the top for the first time. It was spooky.

132 I cleared the Ninja Ramp height pole the first day. This was my victory air. I knew it was going to work.

137 I made the first Hoffman Bikes ad from this photo. I asked the Sprocket Jockeys to run out on the ramp to give it perspective. I had my sister shoot this with my mom's camera. Little did I know at the time it was published that I would get flack for this image. People thought it was fake.

140 This was the photo Mark Losey shot for the cover of *BMX Plus!* It was the third incarnation of giant ramp, and the first time I rode it after I lost my spleen on the half-pipe. (Photograph courtesy of Mark Losey)

146 Jaci in the ballet *Prey*. (Photograph courtesy of Keith Ball)

150 This handrail in Kerr Park in Oklahoma City was the first big rail I ever slid. If you go there now they have blocks riveted down it so you can't slide it. Damn surveillance cameras.

152–153 I used a Polaroid camera to photograph handrails before I slid them, and then laid the shot at the bottom of the stairs in case I got knocked out. Low-tech anti-amnesia devices.

155 The first time I dislocated my shoulder I was in Germany. I snuck out of the hospital to do a demo, and could barely ride. I had to because I needed the money. That day they rigged up a camera on a harness system so I could take this photo.

156 Jaci and I on our wedding day.

158 Evel Knievel hooked me up with a deal on one of his signature CMC Motorcycles. I'm on the way home from the dealers in this shot. They made less then fifty of these bikes. (Photograph courtesy of Paul DeJong—aka the Coach)

162 Doing a fakie on my Evel Knievel signature motorcycle.

164 One of the hundred flips I did at Venice Beach for the first X Games commercial.

168–169 Evel came through town in his RV and invited us to dinner. This was three days after I slammed on my twenty-four-foot tall ramp and beat my previous world record. I'm pretty worked in this photo.

172 Steve Swope airing over the tag Fugazi left on the Secret Ninja ramp when they visited in 1991.

175 Kevin Robinson, Chad Kagy, and me. I'd just given everybody on the Hoffman Bikes team new leather jackets.

177 HB in effect, circa 1993. Team rider Jay Miron; vice president Steve Swope; me; head engineer Chris Gack; TIG welders Shane and Paul Murray; and our do-everything guy, Mark Owen.

181 Jay "The Canadian Beast" Miron uses the front triangle of his prototype signature frame to open a beer for Chris Gack and Mark Owen. The bottle opener was designed into the rear of Jay's bike.

182 This was an intimidating jump. It was my first time B.A.S.E. jumping, and I landed in the Mississippi.

196–197 This was my fourth B.A.S.E. jump. There are no words to justify the intensity yet peaceful feeling these jumps create. It was beautiful.

202 I broke my ankle in the middle of the 1987 Skyway tour, and the van was vapor locked in a parking lot. So I had to entertain myself. Unfortunately, this photo illustrates how much time I've spent on crutches. (Photograph courtesy of Steve Giberson)

205 I hate ice! . . . but sometimes it works. (Photograph courtesy of Mark Losey)

206 This man is the reason I didn't have to retire at age fifteen. Thanks, Dr. Yates.

213 When I'm too injured to skydive or do anything physically active, my guitar is my passive therapy solution. (Photograph courtesy of GG)

214 I broke two metacarpals in my foot, so I had to rig a makeshift cast at the 1996 X Games.

To make my shoe stiff enough to ride with, I pounded a steel spike down the sole of my shoe and carved an insole out of masonite. It was a pretty interesting comp.

216 Doing a tailwhip during practice at the 2000 X Games. Media frenzy.

218 Clocking airs covered by nothing but Speedos and shoulder brace for an early Hoffman Bikes ad. The readership of *Ride* magazine were repulsed, and I found out the concept that "sex sells" doesn't work in the bicycle industry.

218 A postdemo autograph session at the Crossroads Mall in Oklahoma City. This was the first time I had done a show in my home town in ten years. The mob was so big, it was more dangerous signing than it was riding.

221 I was asked to put a team together for the closing ceremony of the 1996 Olympics. The ceremony was called Sport as Art. It was a great opportunity to put the best of the best together for a live audience of eighty thousand people, and a televised audience of tens of millions. It was a fun show. I did a no-handed 540 over Dave tailwhipping. None of the team was that stoked on the shirts they made us wear, though (left to right): Dennis McCoy, John Parker, Steve Swope, Dave Mirra, Taj Mahelich (obscured by Steve's "heavy metal" sign), Rick Thorne, and me.

222 As Jaci was watching me talk to her on live TV, she noticed there was a two-second delay. I told the ESPN techs they needed to get that fixed. They didn't find it humorous.

225 When we have a battle between the Gene Simmons action figure and mine, my daughter Gianna always picks the daddy figure.

226 I was young and I needed the money. (Photograph courtesy of Adam Booth)

228 This was right after I figured this trick out at Woodward at the CFB finals.

230 The 2000 World Championships, right after I won my tenth title. Simon Tabron, Kevin Robinson, and I got the top three spots.

233 2000 was an insane year. I never thought I'd make it back on top of a podium again after my knee injuries.

234 The best part about running the comps is you get to choose the prizes. The CFB Golden Straight Jacket Series award.

237 When a rider wins the BS Champion belt, the rules stipulate they have to wear the belt all night long, to whatever festivities take place. It makes for a comical evening at the finals.

238 This is the air that got me thinking I could double the height of this fifteen-foot air and clear thirty feet if I doubled the height of the ramp. (Photograph courtesy of Mark Losey)

240 So close to clearing the pole, but not quite...

241 Here she is. Tall, intimidating, unforgiving, and the thrill of a lifetime.

246–247 This little girl steals my heart. Baby G was born on December 19, 2000.

249 Dialing down the center.

250 Flipping for a 1997 X Games commercial directed by Samuel Bayer, the same man that directed Nirvana's "Smells Like Teen Spirit."

252, 254, 255, 257 These were the proposals I sent to the *MTV's Senseless Acts of Video* show. Hell yeah!

258, 265 The mustache was fake, the flip was real.

266 Yeah, we're both dorks. This was my thirtieth birthday.

271 The last contest I entered. X Games 2001.

274 Fans in Rio. Most fans don't understand the severity of their requests. If you commit to doing a 900 you also have to commit to the possibility of waking up on the flat bottom and brought to the hospital. These guys were bikers who knew what they were asking for, and would appreciate it, so I threw one for them. (Photograph courtesy of Bart DeJong)

278–279 Here's the infamous motley crew on the tour to make my second game.

288 Hoffman Manufacturing. A shoestring operating budget kept a steady supply of frames, forks, handlebars, and more flowing out the door. This batch is ready to get a paint job.

300 Barry Zaritzky is the trainer and medical guru on all the Tony Hawk tours. Barry's spent a lot of time over the years trying to fix me up after slams. (Photograph courtesy of Frank Barbara)

310 Matthew Hoffman selling medical equipment by the truckload. My dad could sell sand to an Arab.

ACKNOWLEDGMENTS

Lew: This wouldn't have happened without you. Thanks for pulling all the information out of me, adding your magic, and organizing and writing it in a way that best documents my life and our sport's history. You delivered so much more potential to this book than I ever imagined. You are amazing. You've been one of my heroes for the last twenty years. Thank you.

Jaci: For understanding passion and for letting me follow my heart no matter the risks and dangers. You're my inspiration. I love you.

Giavanna: For showing me how precious and beautiful life is, and for constantly testing how fast my reflexes are to save you.

Steve: For being such a warrior by my side through thick and thin. No matter how rough it got, I could always trust you'd be there ready to take on the world with me.

Dad: You made me who I am. Thanks for the determination and the will to try to make whatever I wanted happen.

Mom: For showing me how much you could love, and showing me the definition and direction of what life is and could be. You always told me I should write a book. Wow, I wrote one. This is because of you. We all wish you were here.

Ron Semiao: You're truly an entrepreneur with an amazing vision. Thank you for building that bridge between my backyard ramp and the living rooms of millions. You've offered many great opportunities for my friends and me. Thank you.

Evel Knievel: There's nothing that I can say that you haven't already said. You're Evel Fucking Knievel, man. Thank you.

Spike Jonze: I have never shot photos with someone that has had a better eye for bike riding. You're amazing at everything you do. Thanks for so many great memories and documenting so many great times. And thanks for giving me so many freakin' great photos to use in this book!

Mike Wanzer: Thanks for your faith in me and my companies.

Bob Haro: You're the originator of Bicycle Freestyle. Thanks from all of us.

It would be another book if I go into all the reasons for everyone who has inspired and supported me, so thanks to . . .

To my immediate family:
My brothers, Todd and Travis. My sister, Gina. To David Lindley, Luke Lindley, and Cameron Lindley. To all the Dandinos and Papas. To the "Sparrow" Keihl Hoffman; Blair; Jane Hoffman; Tom Rhude and the Rhude family; Don and Joyce Keel; Donnie and Jill Keel; Brett and Austin Keel; Doug Swope and last but definitely not least Martha Swope.

To my Hoffman Bikes family, past and present:
Mark Owen; Page Hussey; April Tippens; Bryan Baxter; Mark Udell; Jeff O Riley; Clarence Owen; Erick Petchprom; Mickey Esters; Mike Collins; Michael Castillo; Chris Collins; Annie Collins; Darrel Banks; Chad Kagy; Achim Kujawski; Davin Hallford; Kevin Robinson; Leif Valin; Seth Kimbrough; Mat Gipson; Day Smith; Mike Escamilla; Kevin Jones; Rick and Madonna Thorne; Chase Gouin; Dennis and Parady McCoy; Chad Harrington; Taj Mihelich; Ruben Alcantara; Eduardo Terreros; Brian Tunney; Paul Bailey; Simon and Pippa Tabron; Chris Breen; Paul Buchanan; Koji Kraft; Lawan Cunningham; Jim Petterson; Joe Kowalski; Pat Miller;; Daniel Randall; Sherry and Rollin Shu; Kris Gack; Chris Stauffer; Tom Stober; Jon Taylor; Art Thomason; Rob Sigaty; Scotty Yoquelet; and Jimmy Walker.

To friends not yet mentioned:
Jeff Phillips; Tony Hawk; Bob Burnquist; Steve Caballero; Eddie Roman; Maurice Meyer; Ron Haro;. Brian Blyther; Mike Dominguez; Stephan Prantle; Joe Johnson; Joe Rich; Leigh Ramsdell; Ron Wilkerson; Hal Brindley; Chris Moeller; Lee Reynolds; Chris Rye and Marco Massei; John Paul Rogers; Ronnie Bonner; Ruben Alcantara; Sandy Carson; Steve Buddendeck; Nate Wessel; Keith Treanor; Brian Foster; Danny Way; Mike Frazier; Neal Hendrix, Steve Ing; Terry Kim; Kevin Martin; Troy McMurray; John Parker; John Vinyard; Stewart Johnson; Jim Huff; Tina @ Trend; Jill Schultz; Charles Schultz; John Vincent; Roger Wells; Dr. Grana; Nick Adcock; Alan and Donna Vano; Robert Earl; Barry Zaritzky, Jack Weinert; Scott Hanley; Bernadette Hobson; Aileen Koprowski; Gary Morgenstern; Katie Moses; Suzanne Paige; Chris Stiepock; Susan McGowen and the entire CFB medical staff; Dr. Chow; all the parks who have hosted the CFB; Tom Archer; Esther VanHuystee; Bridgett Quinn; Kate Nelligan; Katie Moses, Joe Prisel; Drake Miller; Mark Rainha; Adam Streiby; Brain "Yellow" Gavigan; Keith Mackinnley; Jared Souney; Aaron Cooke; 20 Minute Crash; K Pop; Jerry Busher; Joey P; Ian MacKaye; Joe Lally; Brendan Canty; Guy Picciotto; Mike and Kim Dillon; Joey Zampella; Keith Mulligan; Mark Losey; Sean M Mulligan; Brad McDonald; Mark Noble; Mike Daily; Steve Giberson; John Ker; Andy Jenkins; Will Smith; Bart De Jong; Paul De Jong: Chris Hargrave; Adam Booth; Chris Hallman; Brian Bright; Will Kassoy; Ryh-Ming C. Poon; Rachel Silverstein; Brad Carraway; Deanna Natzke; Dave Stohl; Renee Iwaszkiewicz, Ian Kleinert, Brian Dubin, Skyway; Haro, Simpson; Jones Soda—Peter Van Stolk; Duffs Shoes—RP Bess; Skatelite Ramp surface; Paradise Parachute; Woodward—Gary and Ed; Adventure Travel—Sheryl Armstrong, Gary Ellis; Frank Barbara; Fred Bezark; Kim Boyle; Stuart Dawkins; Ian Morris; Rie Okamoto, Mike Devitt; Marge Peeler; Susan Urbach

For all the amazing ramps:
Tim Payne; Tim Kulas; Mike Cruz, Dave Ellis

For inspiring the world to be a Jackass:
Bam Margera, PJ Clapp, Ryan Dunn, Jeff Tremaine, Spike Jonze, and the rest of the *Jackass* posse.

And for having the ability to put me back together so many times, Dr. Carlan Yates